# Anita Page

## A Career Chronicle and Biography

Allan R. Ellenberger *and*
Robert Murdoch Paton

*Foreword by* Randal Malone

McFarland & Company, Inc., Publishers
*Jefferson, North Carolina*

LIBRARY OF CONGRESS CATALOGUING-IN-PUBLICATION DATA

Names: Ellenberger, Allan R., 1956– author. | Paton, Robert Murdoch, 1984– author. | Malone, Randal, writer of foreword.
Title: Anita Page : a career chronicle and biography / Allan R. Ellenberger and Robert Murdoch Paton ; foreword by Randal Malone.
Description: Jefferson, North Carolina : McFarland & Company, Inc., Publishers, 2021 | Includes bibliographical references, filmography, and index.
Identifiers: LCCN 2020052153 | ISBN 9781476676456 (paperback ; acid free paper) ∞ ISBN 9781476641072 (ebook)
Subjects: LCSH: Page, Anita, 1910-2008. | Motion picture actors and actresses—United States—Biography. | Motion pictures—United States—History—20th century.
Classification: LCC PN2287.P224 E45 2021 | DDC 791.4302/8092 [B]—dc23
LC record available at https://lccn.loc.gov/2020052153

BRITISH LIBRARY CATALOGUING DATA ARE AVAILABLE

ISBN (print) 978-1-4766-7645-6
ISBN (ebook) 978-1-4766-4107-2

© 2021 Allan R. Ellenberger and Robert Murdoch Paton. All rights reserved

*No part of this book may be reproduced or transmitted in any form or by any means, electronic or mechanical, including photocopying or recording, or by any information storage and retrieval system, without permission in writing from the publisher.*

On the cover: portrait of Anita Page by Clarence Sinclair Bull (MGM, 1930)

Printed in the United States of America

McFarland & Company, Inc., Publishers
Box 611, Jefferson, North Carolina 28640
www.mcfarlandpub.com

To the memory
of my beloved big sister
Sally Anne Paton,
an eternally beautiful and bright flame.
—*Robert Murdoch Paton*

# Table of Contents

Acknowledgments ix
Foreword by Randal Malone 1
Preface 3

Anita Page: "You Were Meant for Me" 7

## The Films

| | |
|---|---|
| *A Kiss for Cinderella* (1925) | 73 |
| *Love 'Em and Leave 'Em* (1926) | 75 |
| *Beach Nuts* (1927) | 76 |
| *Telling the World* (1928) | 78 |
| *While the City Sleeps* (1928) | 83 |
| *Our Dancing Daughters* (1928) | 86 |
| *The Flying Fleet* (1929) | 93 |
| *The Broadway Melody* (1929) | 98 |
| *Speedway* (1929) | 106 |
| *Our Modern Maidens* (1929) | 109 |
| *The Hollywood Revue of 1929* (1929) | 114 |
| *Navy Blues* (1929) | 118 |
| *Free and Easy* (1930) | 121 |
| *Caught Short* (1930) | 124 |
| *Our Blushing Brides* (1930) | 127 |
| *The Little Accident* (1930) | 130 |
| *War Nurse* (1930) | 134 |
| *Reducing* (1931) | 137 |

| | |
|---|---|
| *The Easiest Way* (1931) | 140 |
| *Gentleman's Fate* (1931) | 146 |
| *Sidewalks of New York* (1931) | 149 |
| *Under Eighteen* (1932) | 152 |
| *Are You Listening?* (1932) | 154 |
| *Night Court* (1932) | 157 |
| *Skyscraper Souls* (1932) | 161 |
| *Prosperity* (1932) | 164 |
| *Jungle Bride* (1933) | 166 |
| *The Big Cage* (1933) | 169 |
| *Soldiers of the Storm* (1933) | 172 |
| *I Have Lived* (1933) | 174 |
| *Hitch Hike to Heaven* (1936) | 176 |
| *The Runaway* (1961) | 178 |
| *Sunset After Dark* (1996) | 180 |
| Theater | 185 |
| Foreign Language Films | 191 |
| Shorts | 193 |
| Documentaries and Television | 195 |
| Video Films | 197 |
| *Chapter Notes* | 199 |
| *Bibliography* | 209 |
| *Index* | 211 |

# Acknowledgments

I am indebted to the late Anita Page who submitted to many hours of interviews, relating stories of her career and of the many people she knew, loved and worked with. Also, thanks to Page's daughters, the late Sandra House-Bhardwaj and Linda House-Sterne. In addition, a special thanks to actor Randal Malone, whose cooperation was invaluable.

Also, my thanks to Michael Ankerich, Jimmy Bangley, Milton Berle, June Caldwell, Mary Carlisle, Glenn Close, Ned Comstock, Douglas Fairbanks, Jr., Betty Garrett, Sam Gill, Eve Golden, Mark J. Gordon, Stella Grace, Sue Kane, Hugh Hefner, Frances H. Malone, Margaret O'Brien, Jonice Elizabeth Reed, Caesar Romero, Michael Schwibs, and Mel Tormé.

Thanks to the staffs of the following libraries and archives: Beverly Hills Public Library; Doheny Library, USC; Frances Howard Goldwyn Library, Hollywood; Glendale Public Library; Los Angeles Central Library; Louis B. Mayer Library of the AFI; Margaret Herrick Library, AMPAS; and UCLA Research Library.

And my sincere thanks and gratitude to my co-author, Robert Murdoch Paton, a huge fan and collector of Anita Page. It was a joy collaborating with him on his first book. Hopefully, we will see more from him in the future.

—Allan R. Ellenberger

First, I would like to say a heartfelt thank you to Randal Malone who graciously spent time with me in Hollywood and hosted my meeting with Anita in 2007, thus making my dream come true.

Sincere thanks to my mother Hilary, sister Jennifer, niece Iris and friends for their support while writing this book and for the many occasions that I've spoken at length on Anita Page and her story.

A special thank you to my dear friends Herbert Dobree, Richard Buller, and Antonio Picardi who for many years have given me encouragement and support while collecting, researching, and writing.

Thank you to my fellow cinephile Walter Guzzo for his help in selecting photos and our many conversations on Anita and the film industry during the Golden Era.

My thanks and appreciation to the British Film Institute Reuben Library in London for their help and guidance.

Thanks to the American Film Institute, *Archive.org* and CDNC (California Digital Newspaper Collection).

Last but not least, sincere thanks to my co-author Allan for being a wonderful friend, guide, and collaborator during this journey.

—Robert Murdoch Paton

# Foreword

*by* RANDAL MALONE

I first met Anita Page and her charming husband Admiral Herschel House some time ago through their daughters, Sandra and Linda. Over the years we became loving friends.

Anita would tell anecdotes of her film career and regale us with stories about Buster Keaton, Lon Chaney, and Clark Gable. An actor myself, I never tired of hearing about the Golden Age of Hollywood. Anita Page was one of the great beauties of the silver screen and lived during the historic time of the advent of sound—something we now take for granted.

Since the age of five, Anita longed to be an actress and, moreover, wanted to become a star. After taking classes with the famed John Robert Powers, Anita landed extra roles in such classic films as *A Kiss for Cinderella* and *Love 'Em and Leave 'Em*, which led to a starring role in the now lost film *Beach Nuts*.

After moving to Hollywood, she signed a long-term contract at the Tiffany of studios, Metro-Goldwyn-Mayer.

Throughout her career, Anita showed the raw gutsy nerve which kept the movie capital from devouring her. In later years, this lust for life helped her survive the death of her beloved husband and the stroke she suffered shortly after.

In all the years of our friendship, she never ceased to amaze me. She proved that she could rise to any occasion. She truly was an American original and there will never be another one like her; I loved her with all my heart.

I was thrilled to work with Anita the first time in *Sunset After Dark* and then on *Hollywood Mortuary*. After sixty years since being in front of a camera, Anita proved she had not lost it. She truly was magnificent. Afterward, she told me that I was her favorite leading man—after Ramón Novarro, of course.

When Anita left pictures in 1936, she more than fulfilled her desire to become a movie star. She immortalized an image of beauty and glamour in a golden era of Hollywood history.

*Actor Randal Malone appeared in such films as* Alien Force *and* Blood Legend *and had a stint on the popular MTV series* Singled Out. *A longtime friend of Anita Page and her daughters Sandra and Linda, he was Page's manager and caregiver in her last days.*

# Preface

In the 1950s, when Anita Page's name randomly came up in a conversation with screen goddess Ava Gardner, she exclaimed, "Anita Page! That beautiful blond girl? I adored her. Where is she?" When told that Anita had long since left the screen and was married to a naval officer, Gardner replied: "Lucky girl! I envy her! I wish that would happen to me."[1]

"The King," Clark Gable, compared Page, his former costar, to the gorgeous actress and future princess Grace Kelly. Talk show host Jack Paar referred to her as his "dream girl" to his late-night viewers. Italian dictator Benito Mussolini aggressively hounded the studios for a photograph of her, and Germany's Prince Ferdinand would not stop until she agreed to go out on a date with him.

Page, the object of desire for these men (and more), was a bright star in the Hollywood heavens for more than seven years, five of which were at the legendary Metro-Goldwyn-Mayer Studios, appearing in 21 films. With numerous public appearances, and friendships with many of Hollywood's most celebrated people, Page secured a legendary career in her own right.

Biographer Allan R. Ellenberger first met Anita Page in 1993 when he was researching his biography on Ramón Novarro, with whom Anita appeared in *The Flying Fleet*. She was one of Novarro's last living costars, so he was thrilled when she agreed to meet with him. Her husband had died two years earlier, so to keep busy she came out of retirement and appeared at film festivals and other functions.

At the time, she was living in a retirement center in Burbank. Her friend, actor Randal Malone, set up the interview. Anita was sweet and accommodating to his questions. She had suffered a stroke after her husband's death which slightly affected her short-term memory. Her long-term memory was still intact, but she would sometimes repeat a story. Other than a bit of frailness, that was the only noticeable evidence of her stroke.

Only once during the interview did she hesitate to relay a story about

Novarro. It was about his height. Evidently, Novarro was not a tall man—about 5'8"—so he would wear lifts in his shoes depending on the height of his costar. Novarro wanted Anita to be in his film, but the studio felt she was too tall and wanted to cast Josephine Dunn instead. Novarro told the executive: "I can always wear lifts in my shoes. Besides, I did a film with Joan Crawford and she's as tall as Miss Page."[2]

As we know, Anita was cast in the role, but she thought the story about his height might be embarrassing to the actor though it was many years after his death. Before telling the story, she asked that the tape recorder be turned off (her remembrance was used in the book).

From that evening on, Allan became friends with Anita and Malone, and over the ensuing years he was invited to their homes and events where Anita was appearing. When *Sunset Boulevard*, the Andrew Lloyd Webber musical, came to Century City's Shubert Theatre, the star, Glenn Close, invited Anita to attend. A living silent film actress meets a fictional silent film actress—what great publicity! Malone and his friend Michael Schwibs graciously asked Allan to attend. They had the best seats in the house—fourth row center—compliments of the theater management.

The play was breathtaking and the performances top rate. Afterward, they went backstage to personally meet Glenn Close, who portrayed Norma Desmond. Close was still in costume and in character when they arrived, and she spoke briefly with Anita. It was a wonderful experience and Close kindly signed programs.

On Anita's 83rd birthday (1993), Allan joined her family, acquaintances, and former costars at the St. James Hotel (today known as the Sunset Tower Hotel), situated on the renowned Sunset Strip. It was once the home of countless Hollywood stars and executives, including Anita's first husband, composer Nacio Herb Brown, who once lived in the penthouse.

The guest list that evening was a Hollywood Who's Who with Cesar Romero, Milton Berle, Hugh Hefner, Margaret O'Brien, Betty Garrett, and Mel Tormé, to name a few. They came to toast one of the last remaining silent film stars from the once-great studio, Metro-Goldwyn-Mayer.

The late Hugh Hefner, a silent film fan himself, recalled that Anita "fell down the stairs well," referring to her bravura performance in the hit *Our Dancing Daughters*, which put Anita on top. Hefner, who preserved old films, said: "Well, I think one of the things that are fascinating—because of the technology—things are being reproduced on laser and tape and there's a kind of rediscovery. I suspect as we move into the next millennium, this last century will be very special. It's really the dividing point in which the magic of an era has been captured and saved and I suspect as we move forward, the past is going to look better and better."[3]

Anita poses with actress Glenn Close after a performance of *Sunset Boulevard* in Close's dressing room at the Shubert Theatre in Century City, Los Angeles, California, in 1994. Close, who plays a fictional silent film star in the play, invited Anita, a real silent film star, to attend a performance (courtesy Michael Schwibs).

Betty Garrett, who costarred in *On the Town* and *My Sister Eileen*, recalled going to the movies as a child with her mother and said she "became a movie fan in those days."

"I saw Anita's films and adored her," Garrett recalled. "We're all longing for movies the way they used to be. I don't know what there was about them that was so intriguing—maybe it was because it was a new industry. It was so exciting to see a movie in those days. It was magic."[4]

Anita's oldest daughter, Sandra, said that evening: "Mother left the business for many, many years, but people didn't forget. She had a combination of sweetness and sensuality. It's what Marilyn [Monroe] had and it's what [Jean] Harlow had. It seems to be quite a good combination. She has all different ages of people that love her and remember her. It's been a complete resurgence, and she's so happy about it."[5]

Years later, in 2007, co-author Robert Murdoch Paton, a pre–Code film fan in his early 20s, flew to Los Angeles from England for his first visit to America. Here he met his favorite screen star—Anita Page, the radiant young lady of the 1920s and 1930s cinema whose dazzling beauty had at once caught his eye and his heart. Anita's close friend and costar Randal Malone had kindly arranged a meeting for Anita and Robert and introduced them. For Robert, Anita still owned the glamour and class from her days as a Hollywood movie queen. "She was such a sweet and charming lady that I shall cherish the memory always," Robert recalled.

For more than a decade after their meeting, Robert continued to collect memorabilia and research on Anita's career. When approached to co-author Anita's life and career, he was prepared. "I am thrilled to collaborate on this book with good friend Allan Ellenberger," Robert said. "I hope you'll [the reading audience] enjoy this fitting tribute to a glittering star."[6]

During the last years of her life, Anita had a popularity rebirth, making personal appearances at film festivals and answering fan mail from a new generation of fans. As former child actress Margaret O'Brien once said: "That's the wonderful thing about Hollywood. You can always come back!"[7]

# Anita Page
## *"You Were Meant for Me"*

"Before I was born, my mother used to borrow my little cousin Norma, and keep her, that is, when Norma's mother would part with her. Mother wanted a little girl, and she even had it all worked out that I was to have a short upper lip, blond curls and hazel eyes."[1]

On August 4, 1910, in Murray Hill, Flushing, Long Island, New York, Anita Evelyn Pomares arrived at her mother Maude's specifications. "Anita looked exactly like a doll when she was a baby," her mother said. "She weighed eight and one-half pounds when she was born. She was a healthy child and never suffered from anything except the measles."[2]

Anita was a second generation American, but her paternal grandfather, Marino Pomares, was Spanish-born. "Grandpa was a counsel from San Salvador many years ago. We even have our own family crest," she said proudly.[3]

Anita Evelyn Pomares age six months, 1911.

Anita's paternal grandmother's father, Manuel Muñoz y Castro, was from Caracas, Venezuela, and born around 1813. Muñoz arrived in New York on November 15, 1823, and as an adult he earned an appointment as consul at Havana, Cuba, where

Anita's grandmother Anna (née Ana) Muñoz Pomares was born. Later in his career, the elder Muñoz was minister from Venezuela at Washington during President Ulysses S. Grant's administration. Also in the family ancestry, Anita's great uncle, Enrique M. Muñoz, was for several years vice consul from Mexico under Consul General Navarro at New York.[4]

Anita's father, also Marino Pomares, was vice-president of Austin and Moore, a large New York electrical company. Her mother, Maude Evelyn Mullane, was named after her father's favorite horse. "Why couldn't that horse have been named Star," she joked.[5]

As Anita grew, her artistic talents developed, and she sketched family and friends. "Anita always had a great love for pictures, and she loved to draw," her mother said. Her parents first noticed Anita's talent when she was about four years old. She was at the dining room table with a pencil and paper, looking at the funny papers, when a visiting friend looked over her shoulder. "Why," she exclaimed, "the little child can draw! This drawing has life." Anita had copied the cartoon character "Happy Hooligan" from the paper. Later, when Mrs. Pomares understood that Anita wanted to be an actress, she hoped she would follow her artistic talents instead, but it was not meant to be.[6]

Anita did not attend public school until she was eight. "I wanted her to have a strong body," her mother explained. "I taught her to read and count at home. She loved outdoor games." Anita was athletic. She learned to swim when she was four years old at Sea Cliff, in Long Island, where her family spent the summers. Her father was an excellent swimmer and taught her.[7]

Anita at age 3 in 1913.

Growing up, her favorite actresses were Mary Pickford and Norma Talmadge. When she saw their names on theater marquees, "it was like magic." Despite her own dreams, she dutifully heeded her parents' wishes (in case an acting career was a bust) and enrolled in the commercial art program at Washington Irving High School.[8]

At the age of 12, Anita's face was stunning, but her thin and gangly body was undeveloped. One day, a friend at Washington Irving encouraged her to enter a local beauty contest sponsored by the Keith-Albee circuit. She was hesitant at first, but applied, though it was past the deadline. At the theater, with a handful of photographs, a tall matronly woman greeted the young beauty before her. "May I help you?" she asked. Timidly, Anita stammered that she was "hoping to get into the beauty contest, but I guess it's closed."

Studying Anita's features and cool cerulean eyes, the woman ushered her into the office, telling the young hopeful it was "okay, you can enter." The next week, Anita won second prize in the beauty contest.[9]

Anita complained to her parents about being an only child. She begged for a sibling until finally her mother announced there would be an addition to the family. She was overjoyed. "We prepared for him together," Anita recalled, "getting his little clothes and fixing his bassinet and talking over what we would do for him." On June 10, 1923, a brother, Marino Jr., was born. "I remember lying in bed that night gloating over it and saying, 'Now I'll never have to say, I'm the 'only child' again!'"[10]

Shortly after Marino's birth, the Pomares family planned to move to nearby Astoria where a new tract of large three-story houses was under construction. However, unfamiliar with the neighborhood, they wanted to make sure it was a proper place to raise children. They spoke with residents for their input, and at one house, an attractive, mature woman answered the door. Mrs. Pomares explained that they were thinking of moving there and asked her opinion of the neighborhood. "Oh, we like it," the woman replied.[11]

Unknown to Mrs. Pomares at the time, the woman she chose at random would play a part in Anita's acting career. She was Nellie Smith Bronson, the mother of actress Betty Bronson, who at the time was in Hollywood with her grandmother doing extra work, but would soon be the choice of author Sir James Barrie to play the titular role in the silent film version of his play *Peter Pan*; the role made Bronson a star.

That winter, Anita was sledding with the neighborhood children when she caught the eye of a good-looking boy; she timidly returned his flirtations. Sometime later, a girl asked to borrow her bicycle pump. She was the sister of the young man Anita flirted with and they invited her to their home. Anita agreed, especially if it meant meeting her admirer. Coincidentally, they were the Bronson children—11-year-old Eleanor and her brother, Arthur, who was 14; he became Anita's first boyfriend. But the romance was brief. Following Betty Bronson's success in *Peter Pan*, the Bronson family moved to Hollywood. Anita was heartbroken. "I missed them terribly," she recalled. "They were the only people there that I liked."[12]

Nevertheless, Betty Bronson's success rekindled Anita's acting bug. Determined, she pestered her parents to let her audition for parts. Coincidentally, Pomares' electrical company had rewired a stage at Paramount's Famous Players Studio in Astoria, so, hoping that a rejection would cure his daughter, he arranged for an interview. However, instead of discouraging her, the producer cast her as an extra in Rudolph Valentino's *Monsieur Beaucaire*.

More encouragement came when Anita met Betty Bronson, who was in New York to film *A Kiss for Cinderella* at Paramount. To her mother's dismay, Bronson offered Anita a bit part in her film as one of Cinderella's ladies in waiting. Anita begged her mother for the chance, but Mrs. Pomares had reservations. When Mrs. Bronson reassured her that she would be on the set to watch over her daughter, she gave her consent.

During filming of *A Kiss for Cinderella*, an assistant director was searching for a girl to do a bit in Louise Brooks' next film, *Love 'Em and Leave 'Em*. He saw Anita and knew she was the type to play a flirtatious French girl. When she had completed the scene, he offered some guidance: "You're only fifteen, but if you take dancing lessons and acting classes, and you come back in two years, you'll knock 'em cold!"[13]

Anita had the face but was awkward, so she joined the John Murray Anderson School for the Dramatic Arts founded by Anderson, a producer of *The Greenwich Village Follies*, and playwright Robert Milton. Choreographer Martha Graham was an instructor and took a liking to Anita. However, the acting class disappointed her. Graham allowed her students the freedom to be themselves, but the acting teacher did not allow uniqueness. Anita was wasting her time and told Anderson; she would leave his school. However, Anderson encouraged her that she was "one of the ones that might make it."[14]

Next, she enrolled at the John Robert Powers Modeling Agency. Anita's attractiveness and personality impressed Powers. His nickname for her was "my long-stemmed American beauty."

"Her mother brought her to my office as a little model," Powers recalled. "You can see that she was beautiful and full of personality. I'm always on the lookout for such models and she filled the bill ideally."[15]

Powers had founded his agency with his partner, Sir Herbert Beerbohm. They originated publishing photo catalogues and distributed them to ad agencies. His models, known as "The Powers Girls," included future actresses Barbara Stanwyck and Constance Bennett. That led to the Powers School offering training in grooming as well as modeling. Anita, however, had no interest in being a runway model, but Powers' classes could teach her how to carry herself.[16]

During her Powers education, Famous Players–Lasky announced an open call to "come and have a film test made." The studio received thousands of photographs, including Anita's; however, according to their experts, her "beauty did not register," so they rejected her. In a *Picture-Play* magazine article, "They Had Beauty, But—," they printed Anita's photograph and asked readers to "look at Anita Pomares, blue-eyed blonde, with naturally curly hair, and aged sixteen. Was Mary Pickford in the old Biograph days more lovely and trusting? The answer is, 'No!' and yet—"[17]

"Anita was not just an ordinary model," Powers said. "She acted so well that I got the idea of sending her over to a friend of mine who was directing a picture at Pathé Studios. I told my friend to give her a part, any kind of part."

Schoolgirl Anita posed for this portrait in New York and sent it to Famous Players-Lasky studio hoping for a screen test in 1926.

Powers', director friend, former actor Harold Forshay, liked Anita's work and offered her a contract on the spot. Anita was eager to sign and called Powers for advice. Knowing the business, he urged her not to sign unless they doubled their offer. Anita's stubbornness and insistence on signing angered Powers and he talked to her sharply until she listened to reason. However, she did sign—at twice the sum of her original offer. They changed her name to Anita Rivers.[18]

The producing company, Kenilworth Productions, had been in operation for more than six months at Fort Lee, New Jersey, and at Pathé's Park Avenue studios. *Variety* described Kenilworth's first film, *A Noisy Noise*, starring Willie Brown "of Boston," as a "very good two-reel comedy." Then there was *Beach Nuts*, a bathing beauty comedy short that Anita signed for with another discovery, Susan Hughes, a svelte, Kentucky-born, blonde-haired girl described as a bit patrician but without affectation.

A former Kenilworth employee called the short "bad." Finally, *The Spirit World* (the only feature), starring Wilfred Lytell (Bert's brother), was reportedly "pretty fair." *Variety* stated that Anita Rivers "appeared in all the pictures wearing curls."[19]

Though none of Kenilworth's films had a full release, Harold Forshay informed the company that their operations were moving to California. Anita's goal had been Hollywood, so if she were to be a success, her place was in the film capital. She had to convince her parents, but in the end, they had no choice—she had a contract.

Pomares had a friend who was the manager of New York's Cosmopolitan Theater. He knew a producer at a small Hollywood studio and gave Anita a letter of introduction in case her Kenilworth contract did not work out. Pomares would remain in New York and his wife (with their son Marino) would chaperone Anita and her *Beach Nuts* costar, Susan Hughes, to California at Kenilworth's expense.[20]

Wanting to be fair, Pomares gave his daughter a year to be successful in Hollywood: "I don't ask you to be a *star* in a year, but you must do well as an actress. Otherwise, I want you to come back and take art."

There were, however, cynics in the family who were not as supportive. Her aunt and godmother, Anita (for whom she was named), was a religious woman and not happy about her niece going to Hollywood. "Save your pennies," she warned, "you'll be coming back."[21]

Anita's grandmother, Ana Pomares, a devout Catholic who had her own church pew, was a strong believer that young girls should stay at home and not pursue a career. For that reason, the family kept the knowledge of Anita's career from her. "She would never have approved," Anita recalled. "When the newspapers ran a story about me in the beginning of my career, someone in the family would cut it out and tell grandmother that it had a recipe on it. They succeeded in keeping it from her until the day she died."[22]

## A White-Haired Stranger

On December 2, 1927, the Kenilworth company boarded the Santa Fe Chief for California. The train stopped in Chicago and everyone disembarked and taxied to the Drake Hotel. Later, as they were sitting in the lobby waiting to return to the train station, an older, white-haired man joined them, introducing himself as the company's production head and major financier.

At the train station, reporters surrounded them on the platform asking questions and taking photos of the gentleman. On the train, Mrs. Pomares panicked. "Do you know who that man is?" she nervously asked Anita. "We've got to get off this train right now!" Anita was shocked. She had no idea who the man was—his name meant nothing to her—but she knew if she got off the train, she would never make it to California.[23]

Anita questioned why this person was having such an effect on her mother. Finally, she told Anita about the infamous Harry Kendall Thaw. Had she known about Thaw's connection to the film company, they never would have signed the contract. Should Anita come to Hollywood under such ill-starred circumstances? Should they go back to New York? Nevertheless, they had no choice—she signed a contract and had to stay.

Thaw, whose reputation preceded him, was born in Pittsburgh of wealthy parents. When he was an adult, his mother spent millions defending him from sexual assault cases throughout the years. In the early part of the twentieth century, Thaw married Evelyn Nesbit, a young actress who was known as "the Girl in the Red Velvet Swing." Nesbit was a great beauty and a model sought after by New York's better artists such as illustrator Charles Dana Gibson (who idealized her as a "Gibson Girl") and photographer Gertrude Käsebier.

Before meeting Thaw, Nesbit was involved with the well-known New York architect Stanford White. White designed many New York landmarks such as St. Paul the Apostle Church, the Gould Memorial Library, and the triumphal arch at Washington Square. When White's relationship with Nesbit soured, Nesbit met and married Thaw, who was aware of her past association with the architect, and he developed a loathing for White.[24]

Thaw's relationship with Nesbit took a bizarre twist. He would, without warning, beat her with a dog whip and later beg for her forgiveness. Throughout his moments of jealousy and paranoia, Thaw was convinced that Nesbit and Stanford White were having an affair.

On June 25, 1906, Thaw arrived at Madison Square Garden, where White was attending the opening of the musical comedy *Mamzelle Champagne*. In full view of the rooftop garden audience, Thaw pulled out a revolver and discharged three bullets into White's brain, killing him instantly. After two trials and lengthy press coverage, jurors acquitted Thaw due to insanity.[25]

Thaw continued to attract publicity because of his sadistic activities. On various occasions, he was arrested for whipping young prostitutes. Once, he stalked a 19-year-old man and broke into his hotel room while he slept and beat him into unconsciousness. In 1917, Thaw was committed to the Pennsylvania State Hospital for the insane until his release in 1924. The next year, a woman whom he asked to marry him sued for breach of promise.

In 1927, Thaw embarked on the role of movie producer. That summer, the *New York Times* reported that a woman (Thaw's employee) at the Pathé Studios, where Anita would film *Beach Nuts*, slapped Thaw. The *Times* insinuated the entire incident was a stunt to publicize the company's comedy shorts; however, the producers released a statement denying the accusation[26]: "The public is asked to withhold judgement, pending the release of pictures now completed. I wish to assure all that competent critics have given complete endorsements to these pictures as to technique and artistic accomplishments."[27]

After the incident, Thaw left New York.

Anita was unaware of Thaw or his past, but Mrs. Pomares recognized him. Anita's chances for stardom were disappearing, so she tried to convince her mother to stay on the train, blurting out that if they returned to New York, people would believe that Thaw attacked her.

On the platform, reporters bombarded Thaw with questions. "Mr. Thaw, is it true you're gonna be makin' movies?" one reporter asked.

"Yes," Thaw replied, "we have been producing pictures in the East for about a year. We've made one or two good ones—they have been snapped up by United Artists."[28]

Seeing a chance for publicity, Harold Forshay brought Susan Hughes and Anita onto the platform. Thaw paused a moment to admire the two young hopefuls. "They're beautiful young ladies. You can't beat them. They screen well, too. We gave scores of them a tryout, but these are the best, the very pick."[29]

Anita returned to her compartment to calm her mother. "I'll tell you what," she told her, "we'll go down to the other end of the train and stay by ourselves, and we'll keep away from the rest." Mrs. Pomares agreed, and they were successful for the first two days.[30]

When their train arrived at San Bernardino, Thaw invited Hughes, Anita, and her mother to his compartment for breakfast and final instructions.

At Pasadena, photographers were waiting. Dressed in a modest gray business suit, Thaw was first on the platform, smiling pleasantly as reporters, photographers and the usual crowd at the station looked on. His manner was genial and cordial, and there was nothing to distinguish him as the Harry Thaw of infamy.

Mrs. Pomares did not want her daughter photographed with Thaw, so Anita suggested, "If they want pictures, let's put Susan next to Mr. Thaw." Unknown to them, Hughes was acquainted with Thaw and had appeared in public with him in the East; she did not care about his notoriety. "I'll stand next to Susan, and you and Marino stand next to me," Anita agreed.

Her plan backfired. The following day, the Los Angeles newspapers cropped Mrs. Pomares and Marino from the photos. "The papers kept on taking pictures of him with Miss Hughes and me," Anita recalled. "Mother

(From left) Susan Hughes, Harry K. Thaw and Anita arrive in Los Angeles, December 1927.

would try to get into the pictures and then afterward they would cut her out of them. It looked as if Miss Hughes and I had come out here with him alone."[31]

When a reporter asked Thaw his impression of the City of Angels, he replied, "What terrible liquor!" Then they asked about the two young ladies with him. "If anybody wants these girls for anything in pictures, the girls will stay out here," he explained. "Otherwise we will return east in about six weeks."[32]

Anita told reporters that it was "great to be in Hollywood, but Mr. Thaw says we can't have any boyfriends or go to any parties." When asked about her experiences, she added that she "won a beauty contest or two" and "played a part in one of the comedies Mr. Thaw has made."[33]

Anita liked Thaw despite his notorious past, but thought he was a strange yet funny man. "Mr. Thaw has the most wonderful memory," she later told *Photoplay*. "He can remember the littlest things that happened a long time ago—things about pictures. But it is so hard to follow him. He keeps changing the subject all the time. It really takes a very smart person to know what Mr. Thaw is talking about!"[34]

Afterward, the Thaw company motored to the Ambassador Hotel, where Anita and her mother had a bungalow.

Thaw had $200,000 to invest in filmmaking, but not surprisingly, he could not find a Hollywood producer that was interested. Thaw had assumed that the moguls would be anxious to welcome him and his two protégés, but there was no excitement, and publicity was scarce in the dailies.

Then he met with producer E.M. Asher, known to his friends as Eph. Thaw pitched him his ideas and added he would compromise on making a film comparable to Asher's *The Cohens and Kelleys*. Asher was not interested and told Thaw that he was under contract at First National.

Finally, because of the negative publicity, the Kenilworth producers no longer wanted Thaw's name connected to their films and asked that he take a lower profile. Thaw was livid. He said if they did not want to use his name, he would not make their pictures. He cut off his financing and Kenilworth ceased productions.[35]

"Well—finally they said they were going back East," Anita recalled. "They had decided not to make pictures right away. It seemed they could not release them or something. And he would not do anything unless they used his name."[36]

Anita was reluctant to return to New York; she convinced her mother to stay in Hollywood and try her luck. Mrs. Pomares hired an attorney and found that Anita's contract was never binding. Her costar, Susan Hughes, returned to New York, telling Anita that acting's "not for me."[37]

Harry Thaw never made another film. He died in Miami in 1947 at the age of 76. Evelyn Nesbit's career declined after the Stanford White shooting and she was condemned to repeat the story over the years, saying, "Stanny White was killed, but my fate was worse. I lived." Nesbit died in a Santa Monica nursing home in 1967 at the age of 82.[38]

## *On Her Own*

Now that Thaw and company had left Los Angeles, Mrs. Pomares rented an apartment in Hollywood at 7566 ½ De Longpre Avenue. With the Thaw fiasco behind her—or so she thought—Anita had headshots taken by photographer Edwin Bower Hesser, whose reputation collaborating with women trying to break into films was well known. He chose attractive subjects and charged three times the rate of other photographers.

With her photos and the letter of introduction from her father's friend, Anita called on the producer at the small Hollywood studio. Though he admired Anita's beauty, the producer did not feel she was suitable for the films he made, but he gave her his card and told her if she was unsuccessful elsewhere, he would train her. Anita thanked him and left.

Meanwhile, Betty Bronson invited Anita to dinner at her mother's Beverly Hills home on New Year's Day. Also attending was Harvey Pugh, Bronson's friend from Paramount's information department and the studio's postmaster. Pugh wanted to branch out and manage new talent. At the Bronson home, he saw Anita's framed photo and asked about the beautiful blonde-haired girl and wanted to meet her.[39]

On New Year's Day, 1928, Pugh gave Anita his card. However, she assumed that he was not interested. That evening, Anita recounted their meeting to her mother.

Anita posed for Edwin Bower Hesser in December 1927, a few months prior to signing with MGM.

"Are you going to call?" Mrs. Pomares asked.

"I don't think he was interested, Mother," Anita replied.

"Anita, dear," her mother added, "that's not the way to get into the movies."

The following morning, the phone rang. "Where are you?" a voice on the other end asked. Anita recognized it was Harvey Pugh.

"You mean you really wanted to see me?"

"Of course. I don't give my card to anyone unless I want to see them. Now you be at the front gate of Paramount at 9 o'clock tomorrow morning. And bring the picture."

The next morning, Anita met Pugh at Paramount's front gate. There, he introduced her to a casting director. "Show him the picture," Pugh told her. He looked at the photo and decided to make a test. He told her to go to wardrobe, ask for an Evelyn Brent dress and go to make-up. Anita was tested and went home to wait for their call.

Three days later, after watching Anita's test, Pugh met director Malcolm St. Clair on the back lot. Paramount had loaned St. Clair to MGM to direct *Beau Broadway* starring Lew Cody and he was having trouble casting the second lead. "I'm so tired," he told Pugh. "I'm not testing any more girls. I'm going to the movies."

"Do me a favor, Mal," Pugh asked. "Take a look at a screen test for me.

If after two minutes, you don't like what you see, you can leave and go to the movies."

St. Clair reluctantly agreed and watched Anita's test with Pugh. When Anita came on the screen, St. Clair reportedly jumped up in true Hollywood fashion and cried, "There! That's the girl I want for my film!" Whether it happened that way or not, St. Clair was impressed with Anita's look and wanted to talk with her.

In the meantime, Anita was a "nervous wreck" waiting for the results of her Paramount test, telling her mother, "I've got to get out of this apartment. Let's go for a bus ride." Mrs. Pomares gathered Marino and they rode around Hollywood the entire morning on the top of a double-decker bus. When they returned to the apartment that afternoon, the phone was ringing.

"Hello," Anita said.

"Hello, this is Mal St. Clair speaking," a voice replied. "Who is this?"

Anita was aware of Malcolm St. Clair from Betty Bronson and knew that he was an important director at Paramount. However, she did not believe that he was speaking to her at that moment, but assumed it was a friend playing a practical joke, so she decided to play along.

"Oh, hello, Mal," she answered. "This is Mary Pickford."

"Excuse me," St. Clair said.

"Oh no, I'm sorry. I made a mistake. This is Gloria Swanson."

By now, St. Clair was confused and questioned Pugh. Anita heard Pugh's voice and realized that it *was* St. Clair. Pugh took the phone. "Yes, Anita, that's Malcolm St. Clair. He'd like you to do another test at Metro. I'll explain it to you later. Let's do it next Wednesday."[40]

Before concluding the call, St. Clair told her that she reminded him of Esther Ralston. To Anita, it was an honor that such an important director as Malcolm St. Clair was interested in her. He told her to go to MGM in Culver City the following Tuesday to gather her wardrobe for a screen test the following day. However, during the weekend, Anita caught a cold but was not concerned.

## *Metro-Goldwyn-Mayer*

On Tuesday, Anita had a puffy face and red nose when she arrived at the MGM gate. The guard asked her name. "Anita Pomares," she replied. After the Harry Thaw incident, she decided it was best to drop Rivers and use her real name. "I'm here to pick up some wardrobe for a test tomorrow." Looking at his clipboard, the guard said, "Oh, you're here to see Sam Wood."

"Sam Wood?" she said. "No, you've made a mistake. I'm here to pick up wardrobe for a test tomorrow." The guard insisted, however, that her appointment was with Sam Wood.

"Well, who's Sam Wood?" she asked.

Suddenly, a man grabbed her arm and led her along a row of offices. "I'll take you." Her escort, producer Paul Bern, led her to the office of an attractive man with slightly graying hair. The man, director Sam Wood, saw Anita, picked up the phone and told the operator, "Get me Bill Haines." Anita was speechless and in shock. Within minutes, Wood had William Haines on the phone.

"Bill," he said, "I want you to come out to the studio and test with a girl today." Anita was horrified. He could not have meant her. She was in no condition to do a screen test that day. "I hope you're not talking about me," she protested. "I don't want to do a test today. I want to go home." Bern sensed Anita's anguish and took her outside. "Look, Miss Pomares, everything is going to be just fine." She appreciated his kindness, but St. Clair scheduled her test for the next day and she did not want to do it in her condition.[41]

Meanwhile, Haines had objected to making the test because he was going horseback riding, but Wood convinced him, and he agreed to stop at the studio on his way to the stables. Bern took Anita to the make-up department to fix her hair and cover her red nose.

Within an hour, Haines arrived in his riding clothes. "I took one look at him and decided I had to do it," Anita recalled, "red nose and all. It was the easiest test I ever had to do." A year earlier, Anita saw Haines in *Brown of Harvard* and developed her first teenage crush. She could not believe she was going to do a screen test with him. "Well, if I never do anything else, at least I made a screen test with William Haines," she reasoned.[42]

While waiting to hear from MGM, Anita met with Jesse Lasky, production executive at Paramount who told her that he was considering signing her. Encouraged, Anita waited to hear from both studios. After what seemed like an eternity, she received a telephone call. "This is MGM," a man said. "Would you please come out to the studio? We'd like to talk to you." Anita did not have faith in the quality of her test and assumed they wanted her to buy it from them.

At MGM's executive office, she waited in an outer office for 30 minutes. Finally, John Lancaster, a large but nice-looking man who was the studio's head casting director, greeted her. "Well, Anita, how would you like to sign a contract with us?" Gaining her composure, she agreed that she was interested, but hesitated. With great trepidation she said, "I'll sign on one condition." Lancaster waited for her to continue. "I must be put on the screen right away." She reasoned that Hollywood studios signed girls every day for bit parts that lasted for years. She could not take that chance. Lancaster smiled and said, "Don't worry about that. Your first role will either be the female lead opposite Bill Haines, or you'll do the Lew Cody picture with St. Clair."[43]

Unable to withhold her excitement, Anita called her father that evening, not realizing it was past midnight in New York. Pomares was pleased but insisted on three clauses to her contract. First, the studio could not send her on a date without a chaperone, unless that escort was a family friend or well known to the family. Second, she could not go on location and stay overnight without one of her parents. Third, no photography in a state of undress. Pomares told his daughter: "Now, I've been able to support you and your mother well for a number of years and I can do it again, but as long as you're in this business you're going to make a go of it."[44]

A Paramount executive heard about her MGM contract and phoned her the next day. "Is it true you're going to sign with Metro?" he asked. Anita admitted that it was true. "But we gave you your first chance," he said. "We'll send you a contract."

"It would have to be as good as Metro's," she told him, hoping they could not match it.

"If we offer you a contract that is just as good as Metro's, will you sign with us?"

Anita was in a dilemma; the executive had played on her sense of fair play. Though she wanted to sign with MGM, she wanted to be impartial and agreed to sign with Paramount if their offer was similar. To her relief, their contract offered less money and did not promise to put her on the screen at once. "I accepted the Metro offer because it was a guarantee of immediate work," she insisted.[45]

Because Anita was 17, her mother represented her in court. The next day, their attorney, several studio officials and her agent, Harvey Pugh, met at the downtown courthouse to sign her MGM contract. While they waited, their attorney—who knew about Paramount's counteroffer—told Anita, "Don't sign with either studio."

"What?" Anita cried, in shock.

"With both studios wanting you, I'll get you a better offer."

Finally, Anita began to cry from the stress. She told the attorney about her desire to work at MGM, so he eased off and the contract was signed. The deal included a guarantee that if she "clicked with the public," MGM would raise her salary. What the studio meant was not explained in her contract.[46]

## Being Anita Page

The first thing the studio addressed was her name. Pomares did not have "star" marquee value, so after deliberations, they settled on Page. "That sounded all right to me, I liked Page," Anita recalled, "but then they wanted to call me *Ann* Page. Oh no, I told them. I am not an Ann—I'm an Anita. Well, we fought that one out and they won, so I became Ann Page."[47]

Right away, the studio sent out a press release announcing their new aspiring young actress: "MGM believes they have a new screen find in the person of Ann Page, a 17-year-old who has signed a contract as a featured player with that company."[48]

**Portrait by Ruth Harriet Louise (MGM, 1928).**

Thankfully for Anita, the name Ann Page was short-lived. The wife of actor-director David Kirkland had already chosen the stage name Anne Page, so when she read MGM's announcement, she appealed to the newly formed Motion Picture Academy to stop Anita Pomares from using the name Ann Page. The Academy intervened and the studio adopted Anita Page as her name.[49]

## The Ghost of Harry Thaw

True to their promise, Irving Thalberg assigned Anita to William Haines' film *Telling the World*, directed by Sam Wood. However, a few days before filming began, producer Bernie Hyman told Anita, "I think they're going to let you go."

"What for?" she asked.

"I don't know. I fought for you, but they won't tell me why. If I were you, I'd go to the front office and find out right away."[50]

Anita was shocked. First, she had two studios competing for her services, and now she may have none.

Furious, she stormed the administration building demanding to see Louis B. Mayer or Irving Thalberg. Knowing why she was there, both men agreed to see her. Mayer came right to the point and questioned her relationship with Harry Thaw. He obviously was concerned about her box-office draw if the public found out. Anita lost her temper and began to rant. She cried. She screamed. It did not bother her that she was shouting at the two men who could make or break her career. "How dare you," she yelled. "To let me go when another studio wanted me." Anita paced up and down Mayer's office flinging her arms. "I was ordering Mayer around like some office boy," she later recalled. Both Mayer and Thalberg were speechless.

"My father is one of the biggest electrical men in New York City," she shouted. "Call him. He'll sue you and your studio for everything it's worth." In effect, she was convincing them how well she could act by weeping over Mayer's best mahogany desk and begging them not to release her. When she finished, Mayer turned to Thalberg and asked, "What do you think?"

"Oh, give the kid a chance," Thalberg replied. Anita was forever grateful to the "Boy Wonder" for his vote of confidence.[51]

However, that was not the end of it. Mayer sent Anita to Katherine Albert, the studio's director of publicity. Albert was a one-time actress who would later work for *The Los Angeles Daily News* and *Photoplay* and write numerous film and television scripts in the 1950s and 1960s. For now, she managed publicity for the studio. It was her job to "wring the truth out" of Anita and decide whether the Thaw mess would affect her career. After all, there were young girls wrecked by scandal before—whether true or false.[52]

That afternoon, Albert put Anita through a session that would have made any "first-class third-degree department proud." Albert threatened her, maligned her, got her mad and appealed to her sympathies. They wore her down, but her story held up. Albert believed it was through chance and ignorance that Anita had a connection to Harry Thaw. At the same time, other members of the publicity department were working on her mother. "The story stuck. It was all true," Albert said.

Still, what were they to do? They called a conference. Some were in favor of keeping Thaw's name out of it but others did not, for fear the newspapers would dig up the story and put their own interpretation on Anita's secret. Albert decided that for "once in our lives to come clean and tell everything there was to tell."[53]

They gave the story to *Photoplay*, one of the more popular fan magazines of the day. In the article "Anita Rivers Becomes Anita Page" by Helen Walker, Anita explained to readers how Kenilworth signed her, and she had appeared in their films before knowing that Thaw was the company's benefactor and financier. She feigned knowledge of Thaw's past, claiming she "didn't understand yet, just what he is famous for." She knew only what her mother told her, that he was "mixed up in a shooting scrape a long time ago—wasn't he?"⁵⁴

Past acquaintances came to her defense. The press interviewed John Robert Powers about Anita's association with the financier, since he was the one who indirectly sent her to Thaw's workplace. "I would not," Powers replied, "talk about the Thaw angle if it wasn't a case of straightening out something that has been a detriment to Anita. Not until the contract was signed did Anita and her mother learn of Harry K. Thaw's association with the venture. Then it was too late to do anything about it."⁵⁵

In any event, it was a good strategy. The public accepted Anita's version of her entrance into films without any noticeable repercussions.

## William Haines: "Nothin' could be sweeta' than to be with my Anita..."

Anita had had a crush on her first costar, William Haines, since she was 15. "I thought he had the most gorgeous teeth I've ever seen," Anita recalled. "He came in wearing riding clothes and we took the test. I was facing the camera and had my arms around his neck. It was the easiest test I have ever made."⁵⁶

During filming of *Telling the World*, Anita and William Haines became good friends. He introduced Anita to other stars and members of the crew and helped with her make-up, experimenting with different tones.

They dated, despite the fact that Haines was a homo-

**Anita with William Haines in *Telling the World* (MGM, 1928) (courtesy Joseph Yranski).**

sexual. Although Haines was good box-office, Mayer disliked him and pressured him to find a girlfriend to protect his squeaky-clean image. Unlike Ramón Novarro, who was also gay, Haines was open about his sexuality in Hollywood circles—a brave move, considering the times.[57]

Haines flirted with Anita. Every morning when she arrived on the stage, Haines broke out in song with "Nothin' could be sweeta' than to be with my Anita in the morning!" Every time, Anita would laugh and shake her head and admonish the actor, "Bill, I am not your Anita." On the set of *Navy Blues*, director Edward Sedgwick (Clarence Brown would replace him) joined in on the joke and asked Anita, "Why don't you marry him?" Of course, Anita was oblivious to what was truly happening—or at least pretended to be.[58]

On the set of their final film, *Are You Listening?*, Anita and Haines were standing near the stage door waiting for a scene to be set, and their conversation turned to the color of their eyes. Anita commented that Haines had "brown" eyes, but he interrupted her. "Anita, you mean you've worked with me on four pictures and you don't know what color my eyes are?"

"Well, they're brown, aren't they?"

"No," Haines said, howling with laughter. "They're gray." Spontaneously, Haines took her in his arms and kissed her. Anita was shocked. "I mean he *really* kissed me," she remembered. "I thought *wow*! I was in a daze." On all their films, when he kissed her, her feeling was that he held back. However, this kiss was different—it seemed real.[59]

While still in his embrace, Haines whispered in her ear, "Will you marry me?" Anita was speechless. At that moment, director Harry Beaumont called them to the set to shoot the scene which gave her time to gather her thoughts. While she was fond of Haines, she was not in love—so she turned down his offer.[60]

However, Louis B. Mayer heard about the marriage proposal and called Anita into his office. "Is it true that Bill Haines asked you to marry him?" Mayer asked.

"Yes, that's right, but I told him I couldn't," Anita replied.

"Good, because I would have forbidden it."

"What? Look, L.B., no one tells me who I can marry and who I can't."

"But don't you know what he is?"

"I know what they say, but I don't believe it and furthermore I don't care," she said as she stormed out of Mayer's office. As for William Haines, whenever asked if he was ever in love, he would reply, "I'm crazy about Anita Page, but she just thinks I'm crazy!"[61]

The following year, police arrested Haines at a YMCA after he picked up a sailor at downtown's Pershing Square. Mayer gave Haines an ultimatum to get married but finally released the actor from his contract. Haines

Anita reads a fan letter on-set of *Telling the World*, accompanied by director Sam Wood (left), mother Maude and William Haines (MGM, 1928).

had the last laugh. He opened an interior decorating business with the help of friends Joan Crawford, Carole Lombard, and others, and he became an enormous success.

## *Joan Crawford: A Real Dancing Daughter*

On the set of *Telling the World*, director Sam Wood spread the word that everyone should come by to meet "the most beautiful girl in the world." Joan Crawford accepted that invitation and was introduced to Anita by William Haines. Reportedly, Crawford was taken by Anita's beauty and developed a "crush," asking her out on several dates. "If she did, I would be interested to know," Anita told author Michael Ankerich. "So it may have been true in the beginning that she wanted to know me for that reason." When asked if Crawford made any sexual advances towards her, Anita emphatically denied those rumors. "Heavens no, not me!"⁶²

However, their relationship suffered when, during the making of *Our Dancing Daughters*, Crawford warned Anita to be careful not to injure

Johnny Mack Brown in a scene where she pummels the actor. Anita suspected Crawford's "advice" was meant to influence her performance.

Anita's mother's dislike of Crawford stemmed from her finding or seeing something in Crawford's bathroom. It is not clear what Mrs. Pomares saw but, in any event, Anita insisted that she would never tell anyone what it was—and she never did. "I will not betray my mother," she swore. Whatever it was, it was shocking enough that Anita was forbidden to be alone with Crawford or go to her house again.⁶³

With Joan Crawford (left) in *Our Modern Maidens* (MGM, 1929).

As for *Our Dancing Daughters*, Anita believed that it was *her* picture and she had strong opinions that anyone could have done what Crawford did in the film. "I'm not only thinking of when she did the Charleston on top of that table," Anita claimed. "I'm thinking of any acting she did. She would just pat somebody on the back, or she'd look a little sad. She did not seem to be able, in my opinion, to hold an emotional moment."⁶⁴

Over the years, Anita's view of Crawford softened. In the early 1960s, a fan sent Crawford a photograph of her and Anita from *Our Dancing Daughters* and asked for an autograph. "Could you have Anita Page sign it also?" the fan asked.

"I don't know where she is, but I'll find out," Crawford wrote back. Though it had been 30 years since they had seen each other, Crawford made the effort to track Anita to San Diego. "Glad I found you," Crawford wrote and asked her to sign the photo—which she did.

"That's how devoted she was to her fans," Anita said.

Although Joan Crawford was not Anita's favorite actress, she had strong feelings about *Mommie Dearest*, the exposé written by her daughter Christina: "That girl would have had a terrible life if it weren't for Joan. Joan was a little hard to have a good relationship with, her career was it. But you can't blame her—she was fighting for her life and her career."[65]

## Ramón Novarro: "Oh, the chaperones, the chaperones"

While filming *The Flying Fleet*, Anita and costar Ramón Novarro became friends and often dated, but every time had a chaperone. Years later, friends of Anita met Novarro and mentioned her. "Oh, the chaperones, the chaperones," he laughingly remembered.

Every day, Novarro greeted Anita by kissing her forehead. During breaks, she sat on his lap and he would tell her, "Oh, Anita, you're such a flirt!" In one scene, the script called for them to kiss three times, but they continued long after director George Hill called, "Cut!" Costar Ralph Graves teased Novarro and told him, "Why don't you marry the girl?" Mrs. Graves took Anita aside once and told her, "I think Ramón likes you."

Unknown to Anita, or to many at the studio, Novarro was under pressure from Louis B. Mayer to get married. Novarro was a homosexual, known only to friends and to Mayer, who got the Latin star out of a few scrapes.

Novarro genuinely liked Anita, and to him, it was possible she might help him change. On the final day of production,

Anita poses with a puppet of Ramón Novarro made by the Yale Puppeteers in imitation of Novarro as he appeared in *The Pagan* (MGM, 1929).

they were filming a scene with no dialogue. As the cameras turned, Novarro whispered to her, "I want you to answer me as though you really mean it." Anita was puzzled as Novarro took her in his arms and said, "I love you. Will you marry me?" At first, she thought he was joking.

"Oh, I might on an off Thursday," she replied, laughing.

Novarro did not laugh. She saw the disappointment in his eyes as he replied, "Well, thank you very much." When the scene was completed, Novarro left the studio and never mentioned the proposal again. Anita regretted that she did not apologize for hurting him. She liked Novarro, but her career was important, and she was not ready to marry. For days, there was a strain on their friendship. But eventually, everything returned to normal and they continued to see each other.

Once at a party, an attractive young girl came to their table and flirted with Novarro, monopolizing his time. Anita could not get a word into the conversation and was annoyed because Novarro ignored her. On the ride home, Anita gave Novarro the silent treatment until he pleaded, "Anita, would you say something?" She remained silent, but thought to herself, "You don't need me to talk to you. You've had that little chatterbox all night to do it."[66]

One of their last times together was at Marion Davies' Santa Monica beach house. By now, Novarro was drinking heavily (alcohol became a controlling factor in his life). Though intoxicated, he asked Anita to dance. Clumsily, they staggered across the dance floor, and at one point they almost fell. "Ramón, what are you doing?" she cried, pulling herself away from him.

When Anita read about Novarro's murder in 1968, she was shocked. "I just couldn't believe it. He was very sweet and kind to me. I was so crushed when he was killed."[67]

Ramón Novarro was Anita's most-liked costar. "I worked with many attractive men at Metro including Clark Gable, but Ramón was my favorite. He was so good to me that I hope he knew I appreciated it."[68]

## *Papa Knows Best*

In the film *Telling the World*, Anita's honey-blonde hair photographed dark in the long shots, so it was touched up—meaning it was dyed to an almost platinum blonde. "The first time my father saw me he almost collapsed," Anita recalled. "In those days bleached hair looked bleached. It was horrid."

"What will my friends think?" her father protested. The next day, Pomares ran into publicist Howard Strickling, who told him that MGM was giving Anita a great build-up, which inflated his ego.[69]

The Pomares family, Father Marino, little brother Marino Jr., mother Maude and Anita, September 1929.

Since childhood, Anita's parents held considerable influence over their daughter. During her early career, they knew of her whereabouts at any given time. In Hollywood, it became a running joke that if you dated Anita, you also dated her parents. Marquis Busby, a *Photoplay* reporter, wrote, "Hollywood is thoroughly familiar with the fact that whither Anita goes, her father or mother goes too. The original Ruth and Naomi. In one of the

**(From left) John Gilbert, Anita, and Ralph Forbes in a screen test for *Masks of the Devil* (MGM, 1928). The role went to Swedish newcomer Eva Von Berne.**

least conventional cities in the world, Anita is chaperoned like a Spanish señorita."⁷⁰

Though stage mothers have been infamous in Hollywood, Anita never held any ill will against her parents for being so overprotective. Quite the opposite, she welcomed their input because, in her opinion, "they were only doing it for her own good. Both my father and mother were wonderful parents. I feel they gave me an excellent upbringing with strong values, good morals and, of course, my faith in God."⁷¹

Most days, Mrs. Pomares was at the studio, but she stayed in Anita's dressing room, never venturing onto the set. "We were good friends," Anita said. "She told me once that her mother had helped her so much that she liked to pass that help on to me if she could."⁷²

Likewise, Anita's father was involved by managing her finances and showing concern for her health. "If Anita's call at the studio is for nine in the morning, then she has to get up at six, which means that she must be in bed by nine o'clock," Pomares told a reporter.⁷³

Despite her strict curfew, Anita had a social life, albeit not a wild one, mostly going to the Biltmore or the Grove. "I've been only once to

**Anita sketches her *Hollywood Revue* costar Conrad Nagel at MGM, 1929.**

the Brown Derby," she recalled, "and a couple of times to the Montmartre. We joined the Embassy Club, too. Sometimes we like to go to the Blossom Room at the Roosevelt. I think Marino [her brother] likes the pastries there."[74]

After the release of *Our Dancing Daughters*, Anita's popularity rose. Prince Louis Ferdinand, the second son of Germany's former crown prince, was smitten with her. During his 1929 visit to Hollywood, he officially asked that Anita be his escort to the Los Angeles premiere of the Universal musical *Show Boat*. When Mayer found out, knowing how overprotective Anita's parents were, he told the prince's representatives, "Please, we can get you anyone else. Anyone but Anita Page." However, Prince Ferdinand was firm: "I don't want anyone else."

Pomares was concerned about the prince's recent well-publicized affair and breakup with the French beauty Lili Damita, and he was cautious that a scandal might develop with his daughter. However, after some persuading from Mayer, Pomares agreed—with one stipulation. "We will allow it," he told Mayer. "Provided the Prince comes to our house and we meet him."[75]

On the night of the premiere, May 6, 1929, Prince Ferdinand arrived at Anita's home to get the once-over from her parents. An hour later, the prince was escorting Anita to the *Show Boat* premiere at the downtown Biltmore Theatre, but the night had its mishaps. "I was wearing a Spanish shawl," Anita recalled, "when Stepin Fetchit happened to be walking, slowly, in front of me and my fringe caught on one of his buttons. There stood the Prince and all his entourage, waiting for me, and here I was entangled with Stepin Fetchit."[76]

The next day, Louella Parsons, recalling how rarely Anita attends public functions, wrote: "Anita Page finally got out—but it took a Prince to do it." Later, Parsons gazed across the audience, and several rows back spied Anita's parents, there to be sure their daughter arrived home properly chaperoned. "Anita will never be queen now," Parsons added, which was fine with Anita; she was not interested in being queen or wife—nor was she ready for love.[77]

"I hope I don't fall in love for several years," she said at the time, "because I want to do something in pictures first. I suppose, however, it will depend on fate. My goal is to be in films five years and then marry. I believe in one marriage that will last as long as both people live, so I think it has to be founded on something besides good looks and being elusive."

About children, Anita said, "I've always been crazy about babies. Every girl wants children and I think it's important to a happy marriage to have them. I'd like two or three, anyway. I've noticed that people who can't seem to meet on any other ground can usually get together over the welfare of their children."[78]

The days of her parents watching her every move and intervening in every date ended when Anita turned 21 years old. On that day, August 4, 1931, the Pomares entertained a group of Anita's family and show business friends with dinner and a huge birthday cake at the Hollywood Roosevelt Hotel.

Actor Robert Young escorted Anita, who wore a frilly pink dress, to the party. Actress Marion Shilling, who was there, recalled that Young

**Anita on the MGM backlot with actress Dorothy Jordan (left), 1930.**

seemed nervous. "He stood on the dance floor, rigid, while Anita danced around the floor like a wild cat."[79]

Also attending that evening were Clark Gable, Jean Harlow, William Haines, Lili Damita, William Powell, Carl Laemmle, Jr., Maude Latham, Robert Vignola, Jerry Mayer (and wife), Ann Haines (sister of William

Haines), Lorenz Jones, Mr. and Mrs. Alfred Yankawer of New York, Dr. Cyril Wright, and Carmen Samaniego (sister of Ramón Novarro).[80]

## Dating

Once Anita turned 21, she could date the men she wanted, though her reputation as the "no-date" girl still followed her. Reportedly, her first date without her parental chaperones was with Ben Maddox, a writer for *Screenland*, a popular fan magazine at the time. Naturally, he wrote about the date for his magazine.

When Maddox learned that Anita's parents had loosened their grip over their daughter's dating habits, he asked her out and to his surprise, she replied, "Yes, I'll go out with you *alone!*"

For Anita's first date unaccompanied, Maddox escorted her to the Roosevelt Hotel's Blossom Room. She wore a clinging black satin evening gown. From a ringside table, they danced until 2 a.m. and returned home to forage in the refrigerator. "On our first date, Anita proved to be the most perfectly poised young thing I've ever been out with," Maddox declared. It must have been successful for the couple went out on several more dates.[81]

But all those years of parental control still had a lingering effect. Several months after she came "of age," Papa Pomares (as the press liked to call him) told a reporter that if his daughter's future depended on "listening to dirty stories, petting, and indulging in cigarettes,

**Anita and a feline friend (MGM, 1931).**

she would quit the screen." That is why people were shocked when it was reported that she smoked a cigarette at a Hollywood party.[82]

Another of her steady dates was songwriter Nacio Herb Brown, whom she met while making *The Broadway Melody*. Brown was divorced and the two dated occasionally over the next few years, becoming friends. During that time, Brown fell in love with Anita and made his feelings known to everyone. However, she did not share his sentiment. "I was not interested in him personally at the time, except as a friend," Anita said. "My dad was crazy about him, though, and Herb was crazy about my father."[83]

Besides Brown, Anita courted movie mogul Carl Laemmle, Jr., son of Universal Studios founder Carl Laemmle and known to his friends as Junior. On occasion, he escorted her to parties at Universal where she met Boris Karloff and Bela Lugosi. As with Brown, Anita was not interested in Laemmle as a love interest but dated him for the publicity. She knew that socializing with important people helped her career.

For a time, Anita dated her *Reducing* costar, Buster Collier, who made a pass at her, but she spurned his advances. "I was going out with bigger fish at the time," she recalled. Those "bigger fish" included actors George O'Brien, Edmund Lowe, Charlie Farrell, and dance director Busby Berkeley.

After meeting at a party, actor Charles "Buddy" Rogers (future husband of Mary Pickford) invited Anita on a double date with actress Nancy Carroll and her escort. At Carroll's house, they waited while the actress got dressed. At one point, Carroll walked into the room to say hello. "What's the matter, honey?" she said to Anita, "Is Junior busy tonight?" Carroll's sarcasm shocked her. "Of course, Buddy was a perfect gentleman about it," Anita recalled. "He never said a word."[84]

Someone who never dated Anita—but wanted to—was the French chanteur Maurice Chevalier. They met at Charles Boyer's home where Anita captivated the singer; that evening, he taught her the tango. Chevalier had heard about Anita's parents' rules about dating, so he sent tickets for her and her mother to attend

**Portrait by Ferenc (Warner Bros., 1931).**

his concert in Los Angeles. "He was fascinating to watch. He had so much energy on stage," Anita recalled. "But yet at a party he'd sit quietly."[85]

Afterward, Chevalier asked Mrs. Pomares if he could escort Anita to dinner alone. But because he was married at the time, Mrs. Pomares told the singer, "No, Anita cannot go out with you." Chevalier was disappointed, but they saw each other at parties where they could dance.

Years later, Anita and her husband Herschel were in France and met with Chevalier. He took them to the Moulin Rouge, famous for its nude dancers. "I was keeping my head down," Anita laughed, "not looking at the stage because I didn't want to see anything off color. I wanted to be able to go to communion the next morning." Her gaze drifted around the theater, but no matter where she looked, her eyes fell on something that embarrassed her. Yet, she still went to communion the next day as planned.[86]

## *Fame and Popularity*

Anita had fans across the world. The studio claimed that at one time she received 10,000 fan letters a week, second only to Greta Garbo. Today, some historians dispute that number, claiming it was the studio "publicity machine" trying to create interest in her. It is true that MGM was an expert in publicity, making a player seem bigger, more popular, and better paid than was the truth. Whether the amount of weekly fan mail was hype or not, there is no question that Anita had her share of fame and popularity, making her feel like the most important star in the world.

There was one fan letter that stands out as "emotional verbosity, and seemingly superficial glitter"—as described by the author himself:

> Miss Page! You possess genius for the art that claims you, and an emanation of personality, far more important than the skillfully performed technicalities of ordinary talent, yet with a perfection of physical co-ordination, that fascinates and thrill the ever alert and watchful eye. Your ravishing and devastating beauty, the dainty loveliness of your shimmering dresses, combined with the magnetism radiated by your vivid personality, enslaves masculinity without a spoken word.[87]

People in high places were also fans. In Italy dictator Benito Mussolini saw *The Broadway Melody* and declared Anita his favorite actress. Reportedly, he sent the studio several requests for signed photos. Actress Marion Shilling recalled that at the time, Anita told her and another friend, Mona Rico, about getting "six letters from a gentleman called Mussolini. I only remembered the story when the war broke out and you heard about him and Hitler. I didn't think she knew who Mussolini was, though of course she knew he was important and most of all he hadn't sent a letter to Joan Crawford, so Anita was one up on her."[88]

Whether she knew who the Italian dictator was or not, she knew that he made multiple requests for a photo of her, "but they [MGM] wouldn't do it. However, when the studio eventually relaxed its policy of not lending me out and I made a film at Columbia, the Italian Embassy—after four years of frustrated effort—was able to obtain a picture."[89]

To take advantage of Anita's increasing popularity, the publicity department photographed her with major Hollywood celebrities. She posed with Jimmy Durante, W.C. Fields, and Clara Bow on "Hollywood Nights" at the Cocoanut Grove. She ran with the 1932 Olympic athletes and stood arm in arm with politicians including Los Angeles mayor George Cryer and governor of California James Rolph.

**Anita was the cover star on hundreds of magazines worldwide. She graced the cover of *The Movie Pictorial*, published in Japan, in May 1933.**

Once, photographers were present when Anita played badminton with Harpo Marx, the silent one of the Marx Brothers. Anita and Harpo, along with actress Martha Sleeper and tennis professional John Risso, formed a doubles match on the Marx courts. Another time she played tennis with Harpo's brother, Groucho, at his home. Because neither brother was wearing their on-screen attire and familiar make-up, Anita could not remember which of the four brothers was which. Years later, she met Groucho again in New York and told him, "Oh, I played tennis with your brother once."

Groucho looked at her curiously and said, "That was me!"[90]

Anita also appeared in product endorsements for fan magazines. She peddled everything from beauty secrets to full-length fur coats. There were Anita Page paper dolls and there was a perfume named after her. "They had me doing glamorous layouts for perfume, face powder and soaps," she said. "I think it was rather expected of a star to do this; it helped your alluring screen image." Her favorite endorsement was for Lux Soap in which she declared, "I always use Lux Toilet Soap. It keeps my skin so wonderfully smooth."

"After I did that ad," Anita recalled, "I received a case of Lux soap every month for about ten years! I guess they really liked me in it."[91]

In England, fans named Anita, Evelyn Brent, and Joan Crawford as their three favorite film actresses. In the United States, publicists voted Anita a 1929 WAMPAS Baby Star, and a poll of theater owners considered her as "one of her studio's highest drawing cards."[92]

Of course, there was an "Anita Page Fan Club." Their newsletter, called *Paging Anita Page*, reported the latest news and events to her fans. In one edition, Anita wrote: "I appreciate the interest that you have taken in me and my club and I only wish that I had the time to write you all personally and thank you. I want you to know that I will always be glad to hear from you."[93]

Anita in costume as silent star Barbara La Marr. Portrait by Elmer Fryer (Warner Bros., 1931).

## The Beginning of the End

Whatever popularity and likability Anita had, she lacked a business acumen that might have taken her career farther. Shortly before finishing *Our Modern Maidens*, Anita agreed to something that she would regret for the rest of her life. "I was getting so much publicity, that my agent did a dreadful thing," Anita recalled. Harvey Pugh reminded her of Mayer's promise to give her more money if she "clicked" with the public. Everyone agreed that Anita had "clicked," so Pugh scheduled a meeting with Mayer. Anita's father insisted on joining them to show his support.

"Harvey told me that I had to demand more money," she later

revealed. "He made it sound like it must be done!" At the meeting, Pugh laid out their stipulations to Mayer, threatening to take Anita out of *Our Modern Maidens* if he did not meet their demands. Pomares was silent, yet to Mayer his demeanor meant he supported Pugh's conditions. That angered him. To the mogul, they were bullies, and no one bullied Louis B. Mayer.

Mayer asked Anita, "Is this what you want?" Confused, Anita stared at him, saying nothing. As they were leaving his office, Mayer told her, "I'll never lift another finger to help you."

Anita models her star sign on a horoscope sweater (MGM, 1931).

Right away, Anita knew she had made a mistake—but it was too late. She got a new contract with a substantial pay increase, but it did not allow her a say in selecting her film parts or directors. "We won our point, they paid the money," Anita said. "But I never got a starring role again, which was the most important thing to me."

Anita later said that Pugh should have demanded better roles for her "like Bette Davis did later at Warners." MGM had never loaned her out before, but now they loaned her to Universal and other studios, and they continued that for the remainder of her contract.[94]

True to his agreement, Mayer ordered a new contract for Anita, and within a week Pugh and her attorney stood with her before Superior Judge Arthur Keetch. "Your honor," the attorney began, "Miss Page is not yet of age, and we would like to have you fix up her movie contract."

"With pleasure gentlemen, what are the terms?" Judge Keetch asked.

Harvey Pugh had negotiated $400 a week for the first year of her new contract, $600 the second year, $1,000 the third year and $1,500 the fourth year.[95]

In retrospect, Anita wished she had told Mayer the money was not

Superior court Judge Arthur Keetch of Los Angeles approves Anita's second year contract at MGM, February 1929.

important, but at 18 years old, she had much to learn. Two months later, she fired Harvey Pugh.

## James Rolph, Jr.: "Do you want to see the Queen?"

When Anita was in San Francisco doing publicity for *The Broadway Melody*, she attended a party at the Press Club Ruckus. At the event, she met San Francisco mayor James Rolph, Jr. Rolph, who would become governor of California in 1931, was infatuated with Anita after seeing her performance in *The Broadway Melody*—she was his favorite actress.

"Sunny Jim" Rolph was an overweight man in his 60s and one of California's most colorful governors, impeccably dressed to his polished high-heeled boots until rheumatism debilitated him the year before his death in 1934.

While in the governor's office, Rolph expressed his obsession with Anita, calling her the fair-haired beauty of the state. He sent her orchids on her birthday and had a large autographed photo of her on his desk in the

(From left) California governor James Rolph, Jr., Anita, and MGM boss Louis B. Mayer, April 1932.

governor's office. To everyone who visited, he asked, "Do you want to see the Queen?" and he would show them his framed photo of Anita as Queenie from *The Broadway Melody*.

In 1931, Anita used a bottle of sea water taken from San Francisco Bay by Rolph's son, James Jr., to christen a Robin monoplane that women flyers Edna May Cooper and Bobbie Trout were about to fly to shatter the world's endurance record. At another event, the National Ski Tournament at Lake Tahoe in 1932, Rolph was crowned king and Anita was crowned queen.

That same year, Anita was living at 3416 Manhattan Avenue in Manhattan Beach with her parents. One day, they were sitting on the front porch enjoying the California sunshine when an entourage of black limousines drove slowly through the narrow streets. The first car stopped in front of Anita's house and men in black suits jumped off the running boards to open the door. Rolph stepped out and greeted Anita and her parents. "I just wanted to say hello, dear." They chatted for several minutes and then Rolph returned to his limo and left. Because the governor's entourage had filled the entire street, Anita's neighbors complained. "Manhattan Beach was small then," Anita recalled. "The whole block was upset."[96]

## The Academy Awards: "The peas are canned"

While Anita was filming *The Little Accident* at Universal, the recently formed Academy of Motion Picture Arts and Sciences held their second annual awards ceremony. The year before, the Blossom Room of the Hollywood Roosevelt Hotel hosted the awards before a small gathering of film folk. That year, with a much larger crowd in attendance, they held the awards ceremony at the Coconut Grove in the Ambassador Hotel.

*The Broadway Melody* was in the running for Best Picture, as were Harry Beaumont for direction and Bessie Love for acting. In addition,

Clark Gable embraces Anita in *The Easiest Way* (MGM, 1931).

*Our Dancing Daughters* received nominations for Best Writing and Best Cinematography, but neither won.

Anita attended the ceremony dressed in an Adrian creation, escorted by Harry Crocker, a friend of Marion Davies and William Randolph Hearst. Anita was acquainted with him due to her visits to Hearst Castle.[97]

The academy served a delicious meal before the awards were presented at 10:30 p.m. While they were eating, a man at Anita's table interrupted the conversation, proclaiming, "The peas are canned!"

**Portrait by Tzamouzakis (MGM, 1932).**

"He was being funny," Anita recalled, "or so he thought."

Years later, Anita was living with her husband stationed at Cavite, Philippines Islands. One afternoon she received a telephone call—the voice on the other end said, "The peas are canned!"

"Uh-oh," Anita responded. "You were at the Academy Awards banquet, weren't you?" The man was living in Manila and had heard that Anita was in town and could not resist playing his practical joke.[98]

That evening of the second Academy Awards ceremony, *The Broadway Melody* competed against *Hollywood Revue of 1929* and won Best Picture of the Year. Harry Beaumont lost Best Director to Frank Lloyd (*The Divine Lady*) and Mary Pickford (*Coquette*) beat out Bessie Love for Best Actress.[99]

## A "Me-Too" Moment

In 1930, during filming of *War Nurse*, MGM hired a new casting director (Anita would not reveal his name). He scheduled a meeting with Anita to discuss a part he was considering her for. At the end of the working day,

Anita stopped at his office before going home. Her mother waited in the car, as did her *War Nurse* costar Robert Ames, who made a habit of seeing them home safely.[100]

In the casting director's outer office, Anita (carrying her make-up box) spoke with his two secretaries whom she knew. The casting director greeted her, and she took a seat in his office. Shortly, he buzzed one of the secretaries and told her, "You can go home now. I won't need you the rest of the day." The secretary paused for a moment and glanced at Anita. "But sir, I'm not finished with my work yet."[101]

"You can finish it tomorrow," he told her.

After that, he called in the remaining secretary. "You might as well leave too," he told her. "I'll be finished here soon." She explained that she also had work to do, but he assured her it could wait until morning.

Now that they were alone, the man complimented Anita's beauty and charm, which made her uncomfortable. Finally, she stood to leave but the man suddenly lunged at her, grabbing the make-up box from her hands. "You can't leave; I've got your makeup box."

"I don't need it," she replied as she rushed through the office and down the steps to the exit where he caught her, pushing her back against the door. He groped her, but she freed her hands and scratched his face, drawing blood. The man screamed as Anita broke free and ran from the building into the arms of Robert Ames, who was waiting at her car. Ames held her tight. "Anita, what happened?"

"He ... he tried to attack me," she stammered.

"Why, I'll kill him," Ames screamed.

"No, no, Robert. I'm all right. Let's just get out of here."

Ames helped Anita into her car and drove off before the casting director staggered out of the building wiping blood from his face. As they were leaving, Anita leaned out the window, waved and mockingly yelled, "Don't forget, we'll be expecting you for dinner on Sunday."[102]

Ames wanted to tell Mayer what happened, but Anita asked him not to say anything since she was not certain how close she was to the mogul since her contract dispute. Besides, she proved she could take care of herself and was sure the man would not bother her again.

## *Jean Harlow: A Sensitive Friend*

Anita had been in Hollywood one year and completed five pictures, all of them hits. It was no surprise that she became a WAMPAS Baby Star of 1929! The WAMPAS (Western Association of Motion Picture Advertisers) were a group of publicists who chose a "lucky thirteen" aspiring young actresses who were the most eligible for stardom. Among the other candidates that year that also made it were Loretta Young, Josephine Dunn, Jean Arthur, and Sally Blane.[103]

On February 12, 1929, while the 13 honorees were being photographed, Anita glanced across the lot and saw an attractive woman with platinum blonde hair in a slinky black dress. She could not stop staring at her, for she was more attractive than any of her fellow WAMPAS players. Later, she found out the "blonde bombshell" was Jean Harlow.

Harlow was doing extra work and had a featured role in Paramount's *The Saturday Night Kid* and was about to hit stardom in the Howard Hughes production of *Hell's Angels*. Afterward, Harlow's popularity rose with every film, so in 1932, MGM bought her contract from Hughes. Shortly after, Anita and Harlow became friends.

Irving Thalberg was casting *Red-Headed Woman*, a part that Anita wanted desperately. She was excited at the opportunity to test for a big lead and told everyone. She made multiple tests and was photographed in a dark wig. Executives and directors were impressed by her clear fitness for the role—a role that everyone agreed would make her a star.

Anita met with Thalberg and showed him the photographs. "So, Anita, you want to play the *Red-Headed Woman*?" he asked.

"Yes, Irving, very much," she replied.

"Well," he said, pausing, "what will you do for Papa?"

Anita was speechless. The way Thalberg looked at her she knew what he was proposing. She stood and said, "I'll give the best performance I can give in the picture." She walked out knowing she had lost the part.[104]

During filming of *Red-Headed Woman*, Harlow was walking to her dressing room when she passed Anita, who kept walking and did not acknowledge her. Sometime later, Harlow told Anita, "I walked down the lot and you just passed by me. I went to my dressing room, put my head on the table and cried. Then I looked at myself in the mirror and laughed. My hair was red, and I realized you didn't recognize me."[105]

They both had a good laugh, but Anita agonized at "how sensitive she was. She was a lovely person in so many ways." Months later at Harlow's wedding to Paul Bern, Harlow whispered in Anita's ear, "If I ever have a little girl, I want her to be just like you." Unfortunately, Harlow's marriage to Bern ended in tragedy. The following year, she married cinematographer Harold Rosson, a Bern look-alike who photographed several of her films. After that marriage ended in divorce a year later, Harlow had a long affair with actor William Powell.[106]

In 1936, Anita was in the powder room at Hearst Castle when behind her a voice said, "Have you ever given thirteen months of your life to one man?" Without looking, Anita laughingly replied, "Are you kidding? I

(From left) Anita, Madge Evans, and Joan Marsh in a publicity portrait for *Are You Listening?* (MGM, 1932).

wouldn't give them thirteen days." She turned, saw it was Harlow, and knew she was talking about William Powell. They sat on the couch and talked. "You know, Anita," Harlow began, "Bill has been good to me. He's teaching me to save. You know, I didn't want that big house on the hill, but Marino [Bello] and my mother wanted it."[107]

During her visits to the castle, Anita walked three miles around the estate every morning. Sometimes, William Powell joined her, and they chatted and looked at the animals Hearst had in captivity on the compound. "Jean knew I wasn't interested in him," Anita recalled, "but I thought he was a fascinating man."

At the time, Anita did not know what Harlow meant about giving herself to one man but could tell that she loved Powell deeply. It was not until she met her husband Herschel House that she knew of the love Harlow was referring to. After Harlow's death the following year, she recognized that they never had a chance. "I have the funniest feeling that after Bill lost her, he would have married her in a minute."[108]

## Adventures at Marion's

Anita was friends with actress Marion Davies since her early days at MGM. During the next seven years, Anita was a constant visitor at Hearst Castle and stayed in one of the three Mediterranean-inspired guest houses that bordered the main house. "There were few places that I wanted to go when I was working because I wanted to be in bed at nine o'clock sharp," Anita said. "But Marion's was different."

At Davies' beach house parties, Anita met Hollywood's biggest stars. Once, she saw Charlie Chaplin sitting in a corner, so she started a conversation with him. At the time, he was casting the female lead in *City Lights* and told her, "I'd like to test you. I think you'd be perfect." Anita was thrilled for the opportunity, but Mayer refused to loan her out.

Another time, a makeup-less Greta Garbo was sitting in a chair with love interest John Gilbert sitting at her feet, staring lovingly into her face. "Although she had attractive features," Anita said, "she was a disappointment." Garbo had that effect. Not until she went before the camera did the mystery begin. That evening, Anita was certain that Garbo was glaring at her. At the time, some were calling Anita "the young Garbo," which may have unnerved the Swedish star. In any event, Anita never met her. "One was never introduced to Garbo," she would say.[109]

Another mysterious celebrity was Howard Hughes, whose conversations were confusing. "I'd ask him something and he'd answer with something totally unrelated," she recalled. "He acted like he was hard of hearing."

Anita called Marion Davies—the only person she allowed to call her Annie—her best friend, leading to many weekends at Hearst Castle. The castle was enormous, and sometimes it was difficult to know who was there since guests were continually coming or going. One day, William Powell walked in the front entrance and Anita greeted him. "Oh, hi Bill, were you out playing tennis?"

"Anita, I just returned," Powell explained. "I've been gone for three days. Didn't you know that?"[110]

Davies also invited Anita to Hearst's other estate, Wyntoon. One weekend they were visiting with Davies' friends from her old Follies days. As they chatted, Marion told Anita, "You have the most beautiful bone structure."

"Well, I almost fell off my chair," Anita said. "And here she was so beautiful herself."

At the castle, Anita met a slew of celebrities, including Gloria Swanson and Claudette Colbert, who sat across the table from her at a dinner party. During the meal, Colbert wore dark glasses and never took them off. "I guess she didn't want to wear makeup," Anita reasoned. Actress Mary Carlisle once said that Anita was a fixture at Hearst Castle. "Anita was a vision," Mary recalled. "I loved to see her there."[111]

On one visit, Anita rode from the train station with Marlene Dietrich, who showed her a box of emeralds that she clutched on her lap. Later that evening, guests gathered around a piano to sing and Anita looked at Dietrich's face, noticing that she had penciled in eyebrows that were slightly higher than her own, which fascinated her.

At gatherings—which were practically every night—guests could have two cocktails before dinner and then a movie was shown. At midnight, Hearst allowed another small drink—if wanted.

Because of Davies' alcoholism, visitors could not bring alcohol to the estate, so valets searched suitcases, and if alcohol was found, the guest was escorted to the train station to return to Los Angeles. Hearst made every attempt to keep liquor from Davies but was not always successful.

One evening, Davies asked Anita to get her a shot of brandy. Anita could not refuse her, believing that one small drink would not be harmful. However, the liquor was in a locked cabinet and only Hearst and Fred, the head butler, had a key. Davies knew that Fred was fond of Anita. "Tell Fred you have a slight cold and ask for a shot of brandy," Davies told her. "Then bring it back here to me."

Dutifully, Anita asked Fred for a shot of brandy.

"Why, of course, Miss Page," Fred replied. "I'll get it for you right now. But you'll have to drink it here. Those are Mr. Hearst's rules." Caught off guard, Anita was not going to refuse the shot, Fred might get suspicious, so she drank it before returning to Davies' room.

"Do you have the brandy, Annie, dear?" Davies asked.

"Yes, it's right here," she grimaced, rubbing her stomach.[112]

Another time after a Hollywood dinner party, Anita returned with

Davies to her impressive MGM bungalow. She was spending the night there and wanted Anita to stay with her. "Charlie Chaplin's going to take us to lunch at the Brown Derby tomorrow," Davies told her, "so you might as well stay here tonight."

"Marion, I'm in evening clothes, and I don't have anything with me."

"Don't worry about that," Davies said, guiding Anita to her large dressing room where she opened the closet doors, revealing hundreds of outfits. "Take your pick, dear." Anita recalled that when Davies bought dress material, she was the only one who had it. She had one room filled with rolls and rolls of cloth ready for the dressmakers.[113]

However, Davies was also concerned with the needs of others, as Anita found out. At MGM, there was a little boy with a deformed eye who delivered newspapers to the stars' dressing rooms. Every day, Mrs. Pomares greeted the young man as he handed her a paper. Then, one day, he did not appear. Six months later, he returned, and his eye was normal. "Oh, my goodness, what happened to your eye," Mrs. Pomares asked the boy.

He explained that the "wonderful Marion Davies" paid for his operation, and "now I can see perfectly." Davies had not told anyone what she had done for the young man. "That's just the way she was," Anita remembered.[114]

In 1934, Davies' niece, Pepi Lederer, was visiting the castle with Anita. Doctors had diagnosed Lederer with emotional stress, and Davies was concerned for her health. They returned to Los Angeles, planning to go to the Trocadero nightclub that evening. However, Lederer's condition worsened and Davies had her admitted to the psychiatric ward of Good Samaritan Hospital, where, the next day, Lederer jumped to her death from a third-floor window. Anita attended the funeral and afterward went to Davies' Beverly Hills home where she met actress Carole Lombard, described by Anita as "lovely; she seemed to be sweet."[115]

William Randolph Hearst also had a fondness for Anita. In his newspapers, reviewers were usually kind—even if the film was terrible. Once, Louella Parsons' column reported that Anita had dinner with a well-known director soon after his divorce, making it sound sordid. In fact, the director was discussing a role with her during lunch in the studio commissary.

According to Anita, when Hearst found out, he pulled Parsons' column for one day as a reprimand. Parsons was furious, explaining that she was out of the office that day and her assistant wrote the piece without her knowledge. It was several months before Parsons mentioned Anita in her column.

Another time, guests were waiting for Hearst who was in a business meeting with several of his cronies. Davies knew they would be involved for hours, so she asked Anita to "go up to W.R. and tell him one of your corny jokes. That'll break the ice and then you can bring him down for the party."

As asked, Anita went to Hearst's office where a large crowd of men was surrounding their boss' desk. "I expected people to move when I came in," Anita recalled. "But I had to push my way to him. Once these people were with the 'Boss' they would stick to him like plaster."

When she reached Hearst, she sat on the desk in front of him. "Say, W.R., have you heard this one," she interrupted. "And then I'd tell him some story and he would howl like it was one of the funniest things he ever heard. Then he would say, 'Have you heard this one,' and would tell me a joke that was just as bad. But it would get him out of the business mood and into a party one."

After Anita's painful breakup from Nacio Herb Brown, Davies invited her to recover at the castle. "I wound up staying for five months," Anita laughed. "Marion wouldn't let me go. That's why I always say never invite me anywhere, because I'll never leave."[116]

Anita loved Davies and Hearst who were generous to her. One time, Anita repaid their kindness when Davies asked Anita to watch her niece, Patricia Van Cleve, who was dating the actor Arthur Lake, later known to audiences as Dagwood Bumstead in the *Blondie* series. "Would you watch her for me, Annie?" Davies asked. "You're the only one I trust."

Anita, who was the "one with the chaperones," now was one—albeit an undercover one. Without the couple knowing, Anita trailed them for a week as they went from one nightclub to another each evening. "I'd hop a cab every time they left so they wouldn't be suspicious," Anita recalled. "One night, though, Busby Berkeley walked into the Mocambo and almost blew my cover. He came to my table where I was sitting alone and said loudly, 'Are you having a good time, dear?'"

Luckily, the pair never caught on and Anita reported to Davies that all was well, thus doing her friend a favor. Pat and Arthur Lake were married at the castle in 1937. Years later, shortly before her death, Patricia Lake revealed to her children that she was the love child of Marion Davies and William Randolph Hearst. To Anita, this explained Davies deep concern for her. "It all makes sense now," she said.[117]

After Anita married in 1937, she never saw Marion Davies again. Years later, Anita asked her friend Randal Malone to find Davies' burial place so she could pay her respects. Michael Schwibs, a friend of Malone's, learned that the Davies' family mausoleum was at Hollywood Forever Cemetery. When they arrived at the cemetery, it was raining, and a brilliant rainbow appeared in the sky above Davies' resting place. "It was as if Marion was saying, 'I know you're here, darling,'" Anita said.[118]

## "What's the Matter with Anita Page?"

By mid–1931, Anita's career took a peculiar turn; she was playing minor roles at a star's salary. As a newcomer to the screen, she scored in *Our Dancing Daughters* and *The Broadway Melody*, but contrary to studio customs, solid performances were not rewarded with other meatier roles, and Anita Page became practically a "bit" player, yet she kept a steady popularity.

Though this is questioned by some historians, her fan mail at the time was reported as third in volume at MGM. In campus polls, college men chose her as their favorite actress. The year before, Mussolini had declared her as his favorite American star. But still, producers assigned her to uninteresting, uninspiring, minute roles.

Neither the studio nor her fans questioned her talent. What they questioned was why she was not a bigger star. She had the rudimentary talents for a successful career, including beauty, and, when the studio allowed it, glamour. She lacked the allure of Garbo, but her looks appealed to the average American boy who believed Anita was a girl he could take home to his mother. A young fan once wrote: "I wish there were more girls like you, but more than that, I wish I was one of the lucky guys to be invited over to your house. From now on, you are going to be the model for the kind of girl I want for a wife."[119]

The studio carpeted the fan magazines with photos and interviews. At one point, she was the most photographed person on the MGM lot. "In those days you made picture after picture without ever having a week off," Anita recalled. "Then, if

**Portrait by George Hurrell (MGM, 1931).**

you did have some time between filming, you spent it posing for studio portraits."[120]

One photographer that Anita posed for was George Hurrell. When they were not busy, Hurrell called Anita to his studio and would photograph her in various locales. "Up in the trees; out in the fields; splashing in streams; cuddling in silks," Hurrell recalled. Anita knew that working with Hurrell was a production—as though "you were getting ready to make a picture."[121]

Anita and Hurrell worked beautifully together. "He'd say something funny, and I'd start laughing and he'd snap me," Anita said. "One time I had tears in my eyes thinking of a scene; he knew just when to take you. He took some of me where I looked just like Barbara La Marr—though I think her mouth was prettier than mine."[122]

Despite her talents, some insisted that Anita did not have the ambition to become a big star. In 1932, a *Movie Mirror* article asked, "What's the Matter with Anita Page?" The author, Harriet Parsons (Louella's daughter), speculated why her career had stalled. "Anita has had four years in which to crash through," Parsons wrote, "yet she never seems quite able to make the grade. A few times, as in *Our Dancing Daughters*, *Broadway Melody*, and even in the atrocious *War Nurse*, she revealed flashes of decided potential ability—but somehow she never seemed to follow through."[123]

In addition, many believed that Anita's family hindered her growth in motion pictures. The fact that her father could care for her if she no longer had a salary was believed to be a disadvantage that Parsons noted: "Had Anita had to face Hollywood alone and unaided, knowing that her very bread and butter depended on her success, the story might have been different. Poverty is often an incentive."[124]

Pomares argued that when they came to Hollywood, Anita was still a child and they gave her the same care and attention that other parents concerned with the welfare of an only daughter would give her. "But when the talk that I was hindering her career became insistent—I went back East. I thought that now people wouldn't say that Anita doesn't do anything for herself, that she is a girl without a mind."

Gossip of her family's interference in her career angered Anita. "It isn't as if Dad hadn't made definite sacrifices for me," she insisted. She explained that her father had a thriving business in New York, and he relinquished that for her and her career. Her mother was careful not to be known as a studio mother, refusing to meet her directors (except for Sam Wood and Harry Beaumont). "Why, Dad and Mother can't even be at the same theater where I am without its being announced in gossip columns that Anita Page, beaued by Mr. X, was as usual chaperoned by her parents."[125]

## "I can kill Garbo's career just like that"

While these arguments had merit and could be correct, critics were not aware of other reasons for Anita's career not advancing. At first, she blamed her agent, Harvey Pugh, who insisted that she ask for more money after *The Broadway Melody* became a hit. Louis B. Mayer was a man of considerable power in Hollywood, and in his eyes, she had stabbed him in the back. He threatened that he would never help her again—and he did not.

The end came shortly before her contract expired and she publicly left the studio in January 1933. During a meeting with Anita and her mother, Mayer implied that he would help her career again, if only she would be "nice" to him. "What he actually meant was, if I slept with him, he would make me big," Anita declared. When neither Anita nor her mother responded, Mayer continued. "I can make you the biggest star on the lot in three pictures; and I can kill Garbo's career just like that," he said, snapping his fingers three times. "Things can be managed discreetly." Anita and her mother were horrified. She told Mayer that she "didn't play that way" and ran from the office followed by her mother. They never mentioned it again.[126]

Not long after, Anita was searching for a new agent when Ivy Crane, a friend in publicity, approached Michael Levee, one of the biggest and most powerful agents in Hollywood at the time. "Would you be interested in handling Anita Page?" she asked Levee.

"Well, I might," he replied. "Let me investigate it and I'll get back to you." Two days later, Levee called Crane and told her, "Drop her—she's the most dangerous woman in Hollywood."

"What had I done to become the most dangerous woman in Hollywood?" Anita asked. "I said 'no' to the boss, that's what I'd done. I could no more have gone to bed with Mayer than I could have stood on the ceiling."

Two years earlier, Anita was meeting with Mayer when his wife stopped by. As she was leaving, Mayer smiled and said, "Oh mother, it's getting dark out and I'll be here all alone with Anita. Aren't you worried?"

**Publicity portrait for *The Big Cage* (Universal, 1933).**

"No," Mrs. Mayer replied, "I trust Anita!"[127]

Years later, during World War II, Anita's husband was overseas, and she was living in Los Angeles. One night at the Mocambo, she was dancing with friends when the music stopped and she turned to see Louis B. Mayer, who appeared shocked to see her. Anita threw her arms around her former boss standing with his arms at his side. "You know L.B., I love you," she told him and returned to her seat. There was no animosity toward him—she was happily married and no longer under his power. Mayer never spoke but turned and walked away.[128]

## *Leaving Neverland*

In 1932, the studio ushered Anita into two more loan-outs: *The Big Cage* for Universal and *Soldiers of the Storm* for Columbia. Neither was memorable. When Anita's contract expired in February 1933, she chose not to have it renewed. "MGM never said they didn't want me," she recalled. "I just decided to move on." In the same press release, the studio announced that they were dropping Anita and actress Dorothy Jordon from their contract list. But Anita would not be idle. "I got an offer from Billy Rose to appear on Broadway in a revival of *Crazy Quilts*, a show he did a few years earlier."[129]

At the time, few people knew that Anita was leaving the studio. That is the way she wanted it. On her last day, her mother drove them off the lot—no parties and no farewells. Twenty-two-year-old Anita Page had been at MGM for five years.

Days later, when someone told Joan Crawford that Anita had left the studio, she said, "That's very sad. I thought she was a fine actress."[130]

## *Nacio Herb Brown: "You were meant for me..."*

The following year, Nacio Herb Brown, whom Anita was dating, tried to get MGM interested in her again but was not successful. Brown had been in love with Anita since he wrote and dedicated the *Broadway Melody* hit "You Were Meant for Me" to her.

Brown had separated from his second wife and was waiting for his divorce decree to be finalized. Brown's hits, including "Singin' in the Rain," "Pagan Love Song" and Anita's song, "You Were Meant for Me," were standards in the music world.

A close friend was silent film actress Pola Negri. She sang Brown's song "Paradise" in the film *A Woman Commands*. One day, Brown and Anita stopped by Negri's Beverly Hills house. The maid had them take a seat. Minutes later, she returned and said, "The *Negri* will be out in five minutes." Amused by the maid's announcement, Anita told Brown, "Well, I guess The *Page* will wait."[131]

Another time, the couple went to San Francisco with Brown's writing partner, Arthur Freed, and his wife. They went sightseeing by day and that evening attended a party at the St. Francis Hotel. After dinner, Herb asked Anita to dance, but because her ankle was hurting from walking around the city, she declined.

Later, the host of the party asked her to dance. Not wanting to be rude, Anita agreed. When Brown saw them dancing, he got angry and ordered several martinis. Meanwhile, at the next table, watching what was happening, was Bette Davis; at the time she was a young aspiring actress at Warner Bros. She sent a message to Brown to join her, which he did. "Herb, I think you are one of the most fascinating men in Hollywood," Davis told him. "I love your music."

Meanwhile, Anita returned to her table, and the group decided to go to the hotel's bar. "Come on, Herb, we're leaving," she told Brown as they passed him at Davis's table. Brown excused himself and, in the lobby, Anita explained that she did not want to insult the host by refusing his dance invitation. Brown understood, and they went to the bar. As they were having drinks, Anita glanced to the end of the bar and Bette Davis was standing there glaring at her. The two never exchanged words, and Anita never saw Davis again.[132]

Over the years, Brown and Anita's father became great friends. Once, however, their friendship was tested. Pomares had a strict rule that if Anita was living in his house she must be home from her date before sunrise.

One evening, the couple were on their way home, but Brown had forgotten his coat, so he returned to retrieve it. The sun was rising as the couple walked in the house and Pomares was waiting at the top of the stairs. "Never darken my door again," he dramatically told Brown, who left without saying a word. The next day, Brown returned and apologized. "Marino, you are a wonderful father. You were so right, and I was wrong. But I forgot my coat and it couldn't be helped." Within five minutes, they reconciled and remained friends for years to come.[133]

Over time, Anita and Brown became closer and he proposed on several occasions, but each time she refused. Brown believed that his divorce was now final, and he was free to marry again.

One evening at the Ambassador, Anita had several glasses of champagne and Brown once again popped the question. Later, claiming that the champagne had fogged her judgment, she replied, "I might." Encouraged, Brown coaxed her until she said "yes"; they decided to marry that night in

Tijuana. "I didn't want to," she later recalled. "But there wasn't anybody else I wanted to marry, and our families got along so well." The couple stopped in Manhattan Beach to have Anita's parents be their witnesses. "My dad was happy about the whole thing," Anita recalled. "But mother wasn't so happy."[134]

On July 26, 1934, at Tijuana City Hall, a justice of the peace performed the ceremony. The next day, the couple announced their marriage to the press at MGM studios. "You see," Brown told reporters, "the romance really began quite a long time ago. In fact, when I wrote 'You Were Meant for Me' for *Broadway Melody*, I dedicated it to Anita." A reporter asked Anita how she fell in love with the composer. "I really learned to love him when he taught me that new dance—the Carlo."[135]

Not surprisingly, all was not rosy from the start. Anita refused to live in the same house with Brown until they were married again in the Catholic Church—something she kept postponing. After nine months, Anita could not continue the way things were. "I don't love him, and I can't make myself," she told her mother.

In April 1935, Anita had the marriage annulled when she found out that Brown's divorce was not final at the time of their Mexican marriage. "Herb was wonderful to me and he was charming," Anita said, "but it wasn't meant to be."

About 10 years later, after Anita was married and had a daughter, she visited her parents' home and Brown was there, having an enjoyable time with Pomares. "Dad, you should have married him," she jokingly told her father.[136]

## *Hot Toddy*

On Sunday, December 15, 1935, Anita attended a party at the Studio City home of her friend actor Wallace Ford and his wife Martha. Anita and Ford had appeared in three films and they would socialize, often playing bridge. That night, Anita arrived early to help Martha prepare for the party. Shortly after 4 p.m., Martha received a telephone call. At first, she thought it was a friend of hers named Velma, but after a moment, she knew it was not her.

"Who do you think this is?" the caller asked.

"Velma," Martha replied.

"No, it's Hot Toddy." Thelma Todd, or "Hot Toddy", as her friends called her, was calling to let her know she would attend the party with a mystery guest. "You'll drop dead when you see who it is," Todd told her. Anita overheard the conversation and was eager to see Todd again. A few

Masquerade at Marion's. (From left) Anita dressed as a Spanish señorita, director Jack Conway as a Cossack and his wife Virginia Bushman at a Marion Davies costume party in 1931. Portrait by William Grimes.

years earlier, when Todd was married to Pat DiCicco, she tried to match Anita with his brother. "I took one look at him and decided there was no way," Anita said.

It had been more than a year since Anita last saw Todd, and she was looking forward to a reunion. However, Todd never showed for the party.

The next morning, Anita learned that police found Todd dead in her garage, slumped behind the wheel of her car. Mysteriously, the coroner said that she died on Saturday night, more than 12 hours before Martha received Todd's telephone call. "She couldn't have been dead then," Anita insisted. "I was there. I overheard the phone call."[137]

The murky circumstances surrounding Thelma Todd's death are a mystery to this day.

## The Comeback Trail?

When Anita returned to Hollywood in mid-1934 after the *Crazy Quilt* tour—an exhausting yet tremendous experience—it was the first time in six years that she was without a job. In time, she landed a screen test at Twentieth Century-Fox consisting of three scenes: one dramatic, one comedic and another where she is unhappy.

In the dramatic scene, Anita played a woman whose lover has spurned her, so she resolves to kill him. Furious, she searches the room until she finds a gun, turns to her lover, and shoots him. She sees what she has done and cries hysterically. When the scene was completed, she knew it was good. Anita's father had a friend at Fox who overheard an executive say that her test was one of the best he had seen. However, Fox never contacted her. They claimed they could not find her. "That was ridiculous," Anita insisted. "They knew where I lived. I didn't go anywhere." Not long after, she ran into a publicity person at Fox. "Why didn't you sign with us?" he asked her.

"Why don't you tell me?" she replied.

"It's funny," he told her. "They said to give you a big build-up and then just like that they said you were too much like Janet Gaynor."

Hoping to get her contract back at MGM, her agent showed them the Fox test and told them: "Do you know what you lost?" Another friend told Anita that Louis B. Mayer spoke about her to Daryl Zanuck, head of Twentieth Century-Fox, and thus the reason for the snub. "Mayer got to him," she assumed. Someone told her to leave town for a while and circumstances might change, but she could not see herself running away from the situation.[138]

After spending five months at Hearst Castle, Anita returned to Hollywood not knowing what her future held. In the press a rumor circulated that she was set to make a test at Universal for the Lillian Russell role in *Diamond Jim*, costarring with Edward Arnold. Critics noted that Anita was the most Lillian Russell–like type among those who auditioned. It is not certain if she tested for the role, but in any event, Binnie Barnes was cast.[139]

In the fall of 1935, Anita accepted a supporting role in *Hitch Hike to*

*Heaven*. Despite the fact that a Poverty Row studio was producing it, Anita was hopeful for a return to films and viewed *Hitch Hike to Heaven* as a comeback. Unfortunately, it did not work out, especially with major studios forbidden to hire her.

About the same time, she made a Technicolor test for *The Rest Cure* with her friend and former costar Dorothy Sebastian. Nothing came of this either and Anita was willing to leave Hollywood behind her. Except for a small role in the early 1960s, Anita would not appear before the cameras again for another 60 years.[140]

## Herschel House: Love at First Sight

In December 1936, Anita visited Coronado near San Diego for the Christmas holidays. She stayed at the Hotel del Coronado where, seven years earlier, she had filmed *The Flying Fleet* with Ramón Novarro. One day she went golfing at the Palos Verde Country Club with actor Monroe Owsley, whom she had briefly dated in Hollywood. Owsley usually played the best friend or brother in such forgettable MGM films as *Unashamed* and *Mr. Cinderella*.

In their group that day was Owsley's friend Lieutenant Herschel A. House, a young Navy flier on the USS *Ranger*. House, a native of Indiana, was the only son of James and Rebecca House. In 1926, he joined the U.S. Naval Academy, graduating in 1930. A somber nature, a dynamic mind and a good sense of humor helped him to climb the Navy ranks.[141]

The moment that Owsley introduced the couple, Anita said that something "clicked."

"We couldn't take our eyes off each other from the start," she recalled breathlessly.

"I proposed to her on the 10th hole," House admitted.[142]

Surprisingly, in 1929, then–Midshipman House saw Anita's picture on the cover of a theater program and kept it. "It's the only theater program I ever kept," House recalled. "On the cover was a picture of a beautiful girl in the arms of Douglas Fairbanks Jr."

House later asked Anita, "What did you mean giving yourself to Douglas Fairbanks Jr. that way?"

"It was only acting," she explained to her husband.

"But I told her she should have been saving herself for me."[143]

Sadly, Monroe Owsley was not happy for the couple and regretted introducing them. He loved Anita and begged her not to marry House. Of course, Anita told Owsley that she was going through with the marriage. "Well, if he ever mistreats you," he told her, "you let me know."[144]

Another person that Anita disappointed was Busby Berkeley. At the time, Anita was dating the dance director and the two were getting close. However, 19 days after meeting Herschel House, and three days after breaking her romance with Berkeley, Anita and House were married on January 9, 1937, at Yuma, Arizona. They kept the marriage a secret for two months until Anita finished public appearances in the East. "I'm through with the stage and screen," she told reporters. "Even though news of the marriage is out, we will go through with plans for a second ceremony..."[145]

On March 21, 1937, the couple married again in a religious ceremony conducted by Father Peter Conroy on the patio of Anita's Manhattan Beach home. Their romance was reminiscent of *The Flying Fleet*, where she meets a Navy flier at the Hotel del Coronado and they fall in love. "He was the handsomest man I ever saw," Anita said of her new husband. "He had the most chiseled nose."[146]

Less than three months later, Anita learned of the death of Jean Harlow on June 7, 1937. Another death went unnoticed that day because of the blonde bombshell's passing. The press reported the death of 36-year-old Monroe Owsley, who died in San Francisco from a heart attack. Owsley's friends said that he seemed not to care about anything during the last few months of his life and attributed his premature death to a broken heart.[147]

The Houses honeymooned in Japan and on the same boat with them was actor Fredric March. When they arrived at port, there were crowds waiting and cheering, and Anita thought the crowds were for March, but they were for her. She was still popular in their eyes.

After her marriage to Lieutenant House, Anita retired from motion pictures. This had been her plan—to work for a few years, and then marry and raise a family.

## *Anita's Second Career*

Over the next 20 years, Anita traveled extensively with her husband to such places as the Orient and the Philippines. In addition, they kept a longtime residence in Washington, D.C., partied at the White House and attended President Harry S. Truman's inauguration and inaugural ball.

Although Anita had a new life, it did not prevent her from meeting celebrities. Several months after her marriage, the newlyweds were at the Hotel del Coronado. One afternoon, she was on the beach wearing a white bathing suit when actor Errol Flynn saw her. He asked the cabana boy, "Who's the beautiful blonde in the white bathing suit?"

"That's the actress Anita Page," the boy replied. That evening, Flynn attended a party at the hotel and introduced himself to Anita. "He was a

**A 1940s snapshot of Herschel House and Anita during World War II.**

gentleman," Anita recalled. "He had the most incredible eyes when the light hit them."[148]

A year later, they were vacationing in Honolulu when a man approached them during dinner. "Excuse me," he said, "aren't you Anita Page?"

"Yes, I am," she said, not recognizing the stranger. Fortunately, House recognized him and asked the man to join them. "I'm Edward G. Robinson," the stranger said, holding his hand out to Anita. Later, after dinner, they returned to their hotel room and Robinson taught them parlor games. "He was a charming and wonderful man," Anita said.[149]

Anita settled into life as a naval wife, referring to it as a second career. Loving it, she oversaw naval parties at her home, entertaining admirals and such, but it was six years before they started a family.

However, not everything was as enjoyable. In December 1940, while they were stationed in the Far East, the military evacuated 1,342 Americans (including 904 wives and children of American naval personnel) because of tension between the United States and Japan. Anita was among those displaced. According to the *New York Times*, the attitude of the women was summed up by Anita, who told the reporter: "I hated to leave my husband, and that's true of every one of us Navy wives. But we were practically forced to leave. It didn't seem necessary to us. After all, in our little group, there's practically no war talk."[150]

In late 1942, Anita was living in Providence, Rhode Island, when she found out she was pregnant. Sadly, around the same time, doctors had diagnosed her mother with breast cancer. In early May 1943, despite being eight months pregnant, Anita flew to Manhattan Beach to her sick mother's bedside. After two weeks, she returned to Providence because crowded Los Angeles maternity wards had no room for her "in case her baby arrived early." A few days after Anita left, Maude Pomares died at her home on May 28, 1943. She was 49 years old.[151]

Portrait by Hessler, Washington, D.C., circa 1940s.

Anita was devastated by her mother's

**Anita is honored at the Festival of Film Classics in San Diego, which screened *The Broadway Melody* for two consecutive nights in November 1977.**

death, but two weeks later, on June 12, 1943, she gave birth to her daughter Anita Sandra House (everyone called her Sandra). Seven years later they welcomed another daughter, Linda.[152]

Anita's father remarried only a few years after his wife's death which greatly disturbed his daughter. She never forgave him, feeling he should have lived alone in her mother's memory. When he died in 1951, the family buried him next to Anita's mother at Holy Cross Cemetery, but to this day he has no headstone. Nine years later, tragedy struck again when Anita's younger brother Marino died from a brain tumor at the age of 37.[153]

Anita's husband, now a rear admiral, retired in March 1955 due to bad health. They returned to Coronado, California, where they first fell in love and built a house. The Houses blended into the community, with the admiral becoming chairman of the Coronado City Planning Commission and teaching political science at the University of San Diego. Anita became active in local civic and cultural organizations. In the late 1960s, she served as social director for the Coronado Community Theater, was chairperson of the annual Coronet Arts Ball and officiated over various galas and award dinners.[154]

Anita returned to MGM in 1970 for a film festival screening of *The Broadway Melody*. Afterward, at a luncheon held in the commissary, she dined with several of her former costars. When asked why she abandoned her career at age 26, she replied: "I enjoyed making pictures and always felt it was a fabulous experience. But the ultimate goal was a happy marriage,

Anita receives a special award for her contribution to motion pictures with Art Linkletter acting as master of ceremonies in November 1973.

and when this came along, it took priority over and replaced everything else."[155]

In 1988, Anita took part in a production number featuring representatives from each of the Best Picture winners at the 60th Annual Academy Award ceremonies. While on the red carpet on her way into the Shrine Auditorium, Anita collapsed. Paramedics treated her and a spokesperson for Good Samaritan Hospital reported that Anita had fainted due to "a combination of things—the heat, exhaustion, the excitement." From her hospital bed, Anita told a reporter, "I'm feeling much better and I want to thank my fans for all the kindness they've shown me."[156]

Anita returned to Coronado until the admiral's death on December 31, 1991. "I thought I'd never, never get over it. And I never will. But I appreciate the beautiful daughters he gave me." Shortly after, Anita suffered a stroke. Part of her therapy included returning to the limelight that she had forsaken nearly 60 years earlier. She moved to Los Angeles, attended film conventions, and made personal appearances.[157]

In 1992, the Screen Actors Guild invited Anita to a showing of *While the City Sleeps*, the 1928 film she made with Lon Chaney. At the conclusion, the audience gave her four standing ovations. "Afterward, I must have signed over three hundred autographs," she said.

At all of her appearances, Anita's daughter Linda recalled that her mother was "a real pro and never blinked when all the cameras flashed."[158]

At the age of 85, Anita returned to the screen as an aging silent film star in the 1996 independent production *Sunset After Dark* opposite her friend actor Randal Malone. Malone created a successful career in such films as *Alien Force* and *Blood Legend* and had a stint on the popular MTV series *Singled Out*. Because of their friendship they had hoped to work together. "It was marvelous being in front of the camera again after all these years," Anita said. "I had a ball working with Randy—he was great. And the director, Mark Gordon, was so patient and helpful in working with me."[159]

"She never grew weary of acting," Malone said. "She wanted to work. She wanted to see herself in color, which she did in *Sunset After Dark*. She loved working again."[160]

Anita also never "grew weary" watching herself in one of her own films, especially *Our Dancing Daughters*. "Oh, I love to do that! I'd rather see my old films than any of the new ones today." As for today's films and actors, Anita called them "terrible." She did not "admire them" or have any "wish to see them."[161]

After her MGM career, Anita went on to have a happy marriage and two children. That was gone now; there was only her return to the limelight

(From left) Daughter Linda, husband Herschel, Anita, and daughter Sandra as Anita accepts an award in the 1980s. The portrait of Anita in the foreground was painted by Sandra, an artist who at one time worked for Disney.

and some occasional independent film work, which she enjoyed. Nobody loved being a movie star more than Anita Page.

Sadly, on April 4, 1998, Anita's daughter Sandra died from breast cancer, the same disease that took her grandmother. She was 54 years old. Sandra had been a talented artist and worked for Walt Disney Studios. Sandra's

Sandra House, Anita, and *Playboy* founder Hugh Hefner at Anita's 83rd birthday party at the former St. James Hotel on the Sunset Strip, August 1993 (courtesy Randal Malone).

daughter, Elizabeth Young (Anita's only grandchild), also died from the same disease.[162]

## Final Days

By 2008, Anita was no longer making personal appearances due to her health. She had several bouts of pneumonia which confined her to bed in the home of her caregiver, manager, and friend Randal Malone. She developed congestive heart failure, and after several hospital admissions, Anita's doctor, Angela Adelman, decided that it was too exhausting for her and she would check on her at home.

Late one evening, Malone, holding Anita's hand, and Michael Schwibs sat at her bedside as Dr. Adelman checked her vitals. At about 3 a.m. on Saturday, September 6, 2008, Anita Page drew her last breath surrounded by those who loved her. She was 98 years old. "I didn't want to let go," Malone said. "I know she'd had the greatest full life and a wonderful career. I had loved her so much and she became a part of our family."

(From left) Randal Malone, Mary Brian, Anita, and Charles "Buddy" Rogers, who dated Anita in the early 1930s, at the Cinecon film festival held at the Hollywood Roosevelt Hotel, September 1993 (courtesy Randal Malone).

When the attendants arrived to remove her body, they noticed the framed photos of Anita hanging on her bedroom wall depicting her film career. "Oh, she was an actress," one of them said. Dr. Adelman smiled and said, "She was a star."[163]

Anita's funeral was at Van Nuys' Praiswater Mortuary with her burial at Holy Cross Cemetery in San Diego, next to the admiral.[164]

A few days after her death, Academy Award winner George Clooney paid tribute to Anita: "She looked like a cross between Miss Havisham and Norma Desmond. She had the oomph of a star who believed herself to still be big. She could walk into a party and the whole room would spin around. She'd talk about old movies and stars like Rudolph Valentino and Greta Garbo and weekends with Randolph Hearst."[165]

One evening during Anita's renascence, she was with Randal Malone traveling to a showing of one of her films where she was the guest of honor. As their car approached the theater, there was a throng of people standing in front. "I wonder why all these people are crowding around the limousine?" she asked Malone.

"They've come to see you, honey," he told her. "They haven't forgotten you."

**Anita on the steps of her first Hollywood apartment at 7566½ De Longpre Avenue where she resided in 1928 and revisited in the mid-1990s with Randal Malone and author Allan R. Ellenberger.**

"I was so moved," Anita recalled. "So grateful! So honored. I signed autographs and blew kisses until they nearly had to carry me into the theater. The people were so kind. This was one of the most wonderful moments of my career, and to experience it at this time in my life when I never dreamed anything like this would ever happen at my age."[166]

Thanks to film festivals, television, and DVDs, the world and her fans can enjoy the films of Anita Page for years to come.

# THE FILMS

# A Kiss for Cinderella

Famous Players–Lasky Corp.
Paramount Pictures Corp.
A Herbert Brennon Production
1925

## Statistics

Silent / Black & White / 35mm / Fantasy. Runtime: 10 reels, 9,686 ft., 100 min. © Famous Players–Lasky Corp., 11 Jan 1926; LP22254. New York premiere: Rivoli Theater, December 25, 1925. Los Angeles and Chicago premiere: December 26, 1925. Release date: December 1925.

## Credits

Produced by Adolph Zukor and Jesse L. Lasky; directed by Herbert Brenon; scenario by Willis Goldbeck and Townsend Martin, based on the play *A Kiss for Cinderella* by James M. Barrie (London, March 16, 1916); cinematography by J. Roy Hunt; art direction by Julian Boone Fleming.

## Cast

Betty Bronson (Cinderella), Tom Moore (Policeman), Esther Ralston (Fairy Godmother), Henry Vibart (Richard Bodie), Dorothy Cumming (Queen), Ivan Simpson (Mr. Cutaway), Dorothy Walters (Mrs. Maloney), Flora Finch (Second Customer), Juliet Brenon (Third Customer), Marilyn McLain (Gladys), Pattie Coakley (Marie-Therese), Mary Christian (Sally), Edna Hagen (Gretchen), Barbara Barondess (uncredited), Anita Pomares (Lady in Waiting).

## Plot

A young girl who dreams of a Prince Charming is named Cinderella by an artist whose studio she cleans because she always talks of wonderful things that will one day befall her. A police officer, who at first suspects her of being a German spy, hears about her dreams at supper. The police officer leaves Cinderella waiting in the bitter cold. Then comes the dream, big ball and later her recovery from an illness caused by exposure; the police officer proposes, and she accepts.

## Behind the Scenes

One day, Mrs. Pomares received a telephone call from the mother of

Betty Bronson, who was visiting New York with her family. Bronson was filming *A Kiss for Cinderella* at Paramount's Astoria Studios and was staying at the Plaza Hotel; she invited Mrs. Pomares and Anita for a visit.[1]

Dressed in a new brown velvet suit, Anita was excited to meet Bronson, who took a liking to the 15-year-old. Bronson knew that Anita aspired to be an actress and asked what steps the young hopeful had been taking to attain her dream. Anita explained that she was a "second-place winner" in a beauty contest, but that was the extent of her endeavors.

Mrs. Bronson reminded her daughter that she was about to film a scene for *A Kiss for Cinderella* that takes place at the royal ball. "Maybe you could use Anita," she suggested.[2]

"Well, Anita, I've never won a beauty contest," Bronson told her, "but I'm doing very well in the movies. Would you like to try it?"

"I'd love it," Anita said, her eyes bugging out, trying to hide her excitement. Then came the voice of gloom—Anita's mother. "Mrs. Bronson, I don't know. I don't want her wandering around on a movie set." Anita begged, "Please, Mother, please!" Ignoring her daughter, Mrs. Pomares continued, "I'll tell you what I'll do. I'll go to her school, and if they say her work is good enough that she can take a week off, I'll let her do it." Mrs. Bronson assured her that she would be on the set to watch over her.[3]

So when Washington Irving's principal gave his consent, it opened the door for Anita to move into the world of motion pictures. In the film, Anita played one of several ladies-in-waiting to Cinderella.

Anita was disappointed that director, Herbert Brenon, did not allow the younger girls to wear make-up, since her mother never let her wear it. One day, Mrs. Bronson left Anita alone in the dressing room. Fascinated by the jars of make-up on the dressing room table, she gave into temptation and applied layers of greasepaint to her face. When Mrs. Bronson returned, she saw Anita and laughed. "No, no, Anita dear, come here," she said, washing the make-up off Anita's face.[4]

*A Kiss for Cinderella* received mixed reviews with the *Exhibitor's Herald* calling Betty Bronson's performance "worse than ever." Unfortunately, audiences agreed with critics and stayed away from theaters, making it a financial disappointment for Paramount.[5]

## Reviews

"Betty Bronson as the little waif living in wretchedness and poverty, registers poignant pathos. Later, in her transition to the role of a princess, dressed in royal raiment and chosen by the prince for his future bride, she is equally touching and certainly lovable."—*Exhibitor's Trade Review*, January 9, 1926.

"Elegant production but not the entertainment that *Peter Pan* was."— *The Film Daily*, February 1, 1926.

# *Love 'Em and Leave 'Em*

Famous Players–Lasky Corp.
Paramount Pictures Corp.
A Frank Tuttle Production
1926

## Statistics

Silent / Black & White / 35mm / Comedy-drama. Runtime, 62 min. © Famous Players–Lasky Corp., 3 Dec 1926, LP23404. Production dates: January 3, 1926, to January 29, 1926. New York premiere: Paramount Theatre, December 4, 1926. Release date: December 6, 1926.

## Credits

Produced by Adolph Zukor and Jesse Lasky; associate producer, William Le Baron; directed by Frank Tuttle; screenplay adapted by Townsend Martin, based on the play *Love 'Em and Leave 'Em, a Comedy in Three Acts* by John V.A. Weaver and George Abbott (New York: February 3, 1926); production editor, Ralph Block; cinematography by George Webber; edited by Julian Johnson

## Cast

Evelyn Brent (Mame Walsh), Lawrence Gray (Bill Billingsley), Louise Brooks (Janie Walsh), Osgood Perkins (Lem Woodruff), Jack Egan (Cartwright), Marcia Harris (Miss Streeter), Edward Garvey (Mr. Whinfer), Vera Sisson (Mrs. Whinfer), Joseph McClunn (August Whinfer), Arthur Donaldson (Mr. McGonigle), Elise Cabanna (Miss Gimple), Dorothy Mathews (Minnie), Anita Pomares (Flirting French girl).

## Plot

Mame and Janie are employees in a large department store. Janie uses club funds to bet on the races and throws suspicion on Mame. Mame gets the money back and wins the sweetheart Janie stole from her but Janie wins the boss.

### Behind the Scenes

While filming *A Kiss for Cinderella*, Anita noticed a young man staring at her. She assumed he was flirting so she returned his gaze with her best coquettish look. By the end of the week, she discovered, to her embarrassment, that he was an assistant director looking for a girl to do a bit in Louise Brooks' latest film, *Love 'Em and Leave 'Em*.

The part called for a flirtatious French girl and clearly Anita was perfect for the part. When she completed her scene, Anita thought it would end up on the cutting room floor because it had nothing to do with the story. But upon seeing the completed film, to her delight, the scene was intact. Afterward, the assistant director gave her some advice: "You're only fifteen, but if you take dancing lessons and acting classes, and you come back in two years, you'll knock 'em cold!"[6]

While critics liked the cast and thought it was good entertainment, the film did not draw audiences like expected (but patrons did not miss much, according to several critics).

### Review

"Louise Brooks is enough like Clara Bow to appeal to most of the men, even when playing a mean part, and she sure 'leaves 'em' faster than most girls can 'catch 'em.'"—*Exhibitor's Herald*, January 8, 1927.

# Beach Nuts

## Kenilworth Production Co., Inc.
## 1927

### Statistics

Silent / Back & White / 35mm / Comedy. Runtime: 20 min. © Kenilworth Productions Co., Inc., 16 Sep 1927, LU24415.

### Credits

Produced by Harry K. Thaw; directed by Harold Forshay; screenplay by Tom Bret.

### Cast

Tommy Albert, Anita Rivers, Susan Hughes.

## Behind the Scenes

Two months after she signed with the John Robert Powers modeling agency, Powers called Anita into his office. A new film company at Pathé was looking for a second lead and he was sending her to audition, along with 18 of his other girls. "But I think you'll get the part," he encouraged her.[7]

Five minutes into the audition, Anita had the part. The producers were so impressed that, a week later, they revised the story and assigned her the lead. She signed a contract and received a new name—Anita Rivers.

The newly-formed Kenilworth Productions was bankrolled by the infamous Harry K. Thaw and operated for more than six months at Fort Lee, New Jersey. Reportedly, Thaw never interfered, nor made suggestions, only supplied financing.

Kenilworth made only three films: *A Noisy Noise*, starring Willie Brown "of Boston," which was described as a "very good two-reel comedy"; *Beach Nuts*, a bathing beauty comedy short that Anita appeared in with their other discovery, Susan Hughes (a former Thaw employee called the short "bad"); and *The Spirit World* (the only feature), which starred Wilfred Lytell (Bert's brother) and was "pretty fair." According to *Variety*, Anita Rivers "appeared in all the pictures wearing curls."[8]

Within a week, Harold Foshay, a former actor and *Beach Nuts*' director, told Anita the company was moving their operations to California. Anita was excited. The studio would pay her mother's and brother's expenses to chaperone her and 17-year-old costar Susan Hughes on their trip to California.

When Thaw met with United Artists executives to discuss distributing his films, they explained they would release them if Thaw's name was not on the films. They feared his reputation would be bad press. Their perceived audacity infuriated Thaw; if the studio would not use his name, he would shelve the films.

"But the worst of the whole thing," Anita recalled, "was that as soon as his name was related to us, no one took us seriously. It all became a joke, and everyone laughed at us." Until Thaw settled his dispute with United Artists, Anita and her mother stayed at the Ambassador Hotel and waited. "Mr. Thaw could not seem to make up his mind what he wanted to do."[9]

They were at a standstill. United Artists refused to allow Thaw's name on his films, so Thaw had no recourse but to return to New York with his entourage. Subsequently, *Beach Nuts* and the other two films remained unreleased. It was reported that Thaw kept the three negatives in his possession in Paris, yet today they are presumably lost. After that, Kenilworth Productions ceased to exist.

# *Telling the World*

Metro-Goldwyn-Mayer Corp. (Loew's)
1928

Tagline: "EXTRA! William Haines as an 'Up and at 'Em' Newspaper Man in *Telling the World!*"

## Statistics

Alternate title: *He Learned About Women*. Silent / Black & White / 35mm / Comedy-Drama. Runtime: 8 reels, 7,184 ft., 72 min. © Metro-Goldwyn-Mayer Distributing Corp., 23 Jun 1928, LP25397. New York premiere: Capitol Theatre, the week of July 14, 1928. Release date: June 30, 1928.

## Prologue

Hollywood: Egyptian Theater. Benny Rubin appeared with Juanita Connors and Her Girl Friends.

## Credits

Produced by Bernard Hyman (uncredited); directed by Sam Wood; scenario by Raymond L. Schrock; story by Dale Van Every; titles by Joseph White Farnham; cinematography by William Daniels; edited by Margaret Booth and John Colton; settings by Cedric Gibbons; wardrobe by Gilbert Clark; poster art by Glenn Cravath.

## Cast

William Haines (Don Davis), Anita Page (Chrystal Malone), Eileen Percy (Mazie), Frank Currier (Mr. Davis, Don's father), Polly Moran (Landlady), Bert Roach (Lane), William V. Mong (City Editor), Matthew Betz (The Killer), Sôjin Kamiyama (as Sôjin), Miki Morita (uncredited), Billy Wise (uncredited), Katharine Irving (Society Editor).

## Plot

Disinherited and missing, Don Davis tricks the *Telegram* into giving him a job as a reporter by offering to reveal the location of the missing man. The editor learns that the would-be reporter is in fact the missing man but keeps to his word and assigns Don to interview his father as to why he was thrown out. The newspaper plays a joke on Don and sends him to investigate an imaginary murder. When an actual murder takes place, a

**With William Haines in** *Telling the World* **(MGM, 1928) (courtesy Joseph Yranski).**

young dancer named Chrystal sees the killing. Don and Chrystal strike up a friendship and she falls in love with him. Don is preoccupied with becoming a reporter in Paris, and Chrystal, feeling discouraged, joins a show in the Orient. Don realizes that he is in love with Chrystal and travels to Shanghai to marry her. A powerful governor hires the show troupe, but an ambitious general murders the governor and frames Chrystal as the murderess.

Chrystal is sentenced to death, but Don comes to the rescue by sending messages from the military wireless room. The news that an American girl is to be beheaded in China is broadcast worldwide, and the governments of United States of America, Great Britain and Japan send out rescue teams. The young newlyweds are set free.

## *Behind the Scenes*

Anita's first film for MGM was *Telling the World*. According to Sam Wood, what won her an MGM contract and the lead opposite William Haines was her screen personality. "[It] is unlike that of any other leading woman on the screen and is, at the same time, appealing."[10]

Anita recalled that when she first walked onto the studio lot, she was terrified. "I prayed that no one would see how scared I was." During that first week, she was anxious. William Haines told her that it was not "so deadly serious, after all, the best thing to do is to take it easy." He recommended that she be natural but remember that "the camera wants to see your face, not the back of your head. Forget worry—and have a good time, baby!"

"That was the best possible advice for a scared beginner," Anita laughed. "Bill introduced me to the camera and made me feel at home."[11]

As for director Sam Wood, Anita grew to respect him. "I'm so green at this game and I try to watch everyone else work and listen to every word Mr. Wood says," Anita said. "I'm just learning about timing. But everyone is so nice to me. If Mr. Wood shouted at me, I'd die, but he's so patient and Billy is so good and gives me a wonderful chance in his scenes."[12]

Wood, admiring Anita's loveliness, asked everyone if they wanted to see "the most beautiful girl in the world." Naturally, curiosity brought out the stars to meet Anita, including Ramón Novarro, Norma Shearer and Marion Davies.

One day, Bernard Hyman, the film's producer, told Anita that one of the "biggest stars" at MGM expressed to Louis B. Mayer that she "wanted to look like" Anita. "Who is it?" she insisted, but Hyman would not tell her. However, years later, Marion Davies revealed that she was the one. By that time, she and Davies were close friends.[13]

In one scene Anita had to cry, but hard as she tried the tears would not flow. With take after take, she thought about the wasted money while the cast and crew waited for her to "turn on the tears." Wood suggested that she use the menthol blower, a device used by actors that blew menthol into their eyes, causing them to water and appear to be crying. "Norma Shearer uses it," he admitted. Anita would not have it. "Sam, I have to cry on my own. If I don't, I'll never be able to do it."

"What's holding you back?" he asked.

**With William Haines in *Telling the World* (MGM, 1928).**

Anita explained that everyone standing around waiting for her to cry was costing the studio money, and it bothered her. Wood had an idea. The following Sunday, he brought Anita and cinematographer William Daniels into the studio to film the scene. With only two people on the set, Anita was at ease and the tears flowed.[14]

When she saw the rushes and how she appeared on screen, she gave the credit to cinematographer William Daniels, who she called "wonderful."

"I'm so amazed that Mr. Daniels can make me look like that on the screen," she said. "He's marvelous and I keep telling myself, 'That isn't you, Anita it's just awfully good photography.'"[15]

Anita was grateful for the understanding and extra effort that Daniels and Wood took arranging the private filming session. After that, Anita could cry at the drop of the proverbial hat.

In another scene, Anita was not happy with her costume and told Haines. "Bill, I'm going to the front office. This dress is too revealing."

"No, you're working on my picture," he told her. "You don't have to go to the front office. I'll do it." Anita was fond of Haines and over the next four years, she appeared in four films with him. "When I first worked with him I was almost afraid to go on the set. Bill was such a joker that I expected to find tacks on the chairs. But I don't think he liked to play tricks on people unless they were the sort that could take it big."[16]

*Telling the World* was a critical success and reviewers considered it William Haines' best work since *Brown of Harvard*. *Variety* liked the picture and wrote: "Wood's direction, Farnham's titles and Haines' familiar conception of male ego, spiced by a couple of new mannerisms, can plead guilty to queries on why this is a good picture."

The critics lauded Anita's performance, especially New York critic Norbert Lusk:

> "Considering that Miss Page makes her motion-picture debut in this film, she gives a surprisingly good account of herself in what is nothing less than a leading role. She has magnetism, piquant prettiness, and some individuality, surely a great deal to be found in this year of overnight discoveries which disclosed little or nothing. It requires no undue optimism to see that Miss Page, with more experience, will become a valuable addition to the ingénue leads, if, indeed, she is not that already."[17]

Anita watched her first leading performance on the big screen at the downtown Grauman's Metropolitan Theater. "It's only been previewed in a few small towns, yet I am getting all these fan letters already." Sadly, *Telling the World* is considered a lost film; however, a fragment (roughly 40 minutes) is archived at London's British Film Institute (BFI).[18]

## *Reviews*

"Here's the newest picture girl—and she's a treat. You're going to fall for Anita Page as hard as Haines does in the picture, only it won't take you as long as it did him. Anita is so young and fresh and pretty and radiant you can't believe she is actually a movie actress in a studio working at a director's orders. She might have wandered in from some girls' select seminary on a lark."—*Screenland*, September 1928.

"Miss Page both looks good and every so often gets a chance to do a little trouping. MGM is understood to have fair sized expectations about this girl and with this as evidence, seems to have a good chance of having its prophecy fulfilled."—*Variety*, July 18, 1928.

"...the production is further embellished by the presence of Anita Page, a newcomer on the screen. *Telling the World* is her first picture, but as Haines' leading lady she is pleasingly effective in a role that might have taxed the talents of one far more experienced in the ways of camera technique."—*Los Angeles Times*, June 3, 1928.

"Whatever good work there is seems due to Anita Page, the pretty and attractive leading lady."—Mordaunt Hall, *New York Times*, July 22, 1928.

## *Academy Award Nominations*

Joe Farnham, Best Title Writing.

# While the City Sleeps

Metro-Goldwyn-Mayer Corp. (Loew's, Inc.)
1928

Tagline: "*Now!* The man of 1,000 faces in a picture with 1,000 *Thrills!*"

## Statistics

Alternate titles: *China Town*; *Easy Money*; *Underworld Melodrama*. Synchronized musical score and sound effects (Movietone) / Black & White / 35mm / Crime-Melodrama. Runtime: 9 reels, 7,231 ft., 70 min. © Metro-Goldwyn-Mayer Distributing Corp., 29 Sep 1928, LP25705. Production date: April 14, 1928. Release date: September 15, 1928.

## Prologues

Los Angeles: Loew's State Theater. Ted Doner featured in Fanchon and Marco's revue, with Bobbie Thomson aiding. Contortion and acrobatic acts included. Fox Movietone News featured evangelist Aimee Semple McPherson, and in the same newsreel, Rabbi Wise addressed the season for Jewish faith.

New York: Capitol Theater. Fox Movietone News; Marion Harris, "blues" singer; Chester Hale ballet; "In the Clouds," with Joyce Colet; Sylvia Miller, Paul Clayman, and others; Hal Roach's comedy *Imagine My Embarrassment* with Charley Chase.

## Credits

Produced by Bernard Hyman (uncredited); directed by Jack Conway; story and scenario by A.P. Younger; titles by Joseph White Farnham; cinematography by Henry Sharp; edited by Sam S. Zimbalist; settings by Cedric Gibbons; wardrobe by Gilbert Clark; original music by William Axt and Edward Cupero (uncredited); set musicians, Jack Feinberg and Sam Feinberg (uncredited); technical advisor, Roy Harlacher.

## Cast

Lon Chaney (Dan Coghlan), Anita Page (Myrtle), Carroll Nye (Marty), Wheeler Oakman (Skeeter), Mae Busch (Bessie), Polly Moran (Mrs. McGinnis), Lydia Yeamans Titus (Mrs. Sullivan), William Orlamond (Dwiggins), Richard Carle (Wally), Sidney Bracey (Short Order Cook), Jack Feinberg (Man on Street), Sam Feinberg (Man on Street), Joseph W. Girard

(Captain of Detectives), Eddie Kane (Skeeter's Gang Member), Fred Kelsey (Detective in Shadow Box), Clinton Lyle (Skeeter's Gang Member), William H. O'Brien (Apartment Tenant), L.J. O'Connor (Police Officer in Hallway), Bud Rae (Skeeter's Gang Member), Angelo Rossitto (Skeeter's Gang Member), Scott Seaton (District Attorney), Eddie Sturgis (Skeeter's Driver), Leo Willis (Skeeter's Gang Member).

### *Plot*

Plainclothesman and keeper of the peace Dan Coghlan suspects gang leader Skeeter of murder and robbery and sets out to prove him guilty. When Skeeter takes an interest in the young Myrtle, whom Dan has known since she was a girl and is secretly in love with, Dan does everything in his power to protect Myrtle and have Skeeter and his gang put behind bars.

### *Behind the Scenes*

Lon Chaney, a leading MGM star, was famous for his odd and bizarre portrayals and was instrumental in choosing his own films. For his next part, he wanted to play a non-monster role. At the time, Anita was involved

(From left) Lon Chaney, Anita and Carroll Nye in *While the City Sleeps* (MGM, 1928).

in filming *Our Dancing Daughters*, whose success would bolster her career and make her one of the most sought-after actresses on the lot.

Chaney saw the rushes from the still unreleased *Our Dancing Daughters* and was impressed by Anita's performance. He asked Thalberg to cast her in his next film, *While the City Sleeps*, but her next film was to be *The Bellamy Trial* with Leatrice Joy so Thalberg reassigned her.[19]

Chaney was fascinated at how Anita used her eyes to express emotion. He knew that being camera-friendly was important, but for him, acting came through the eyes, telling the young actress that the "eyes are the window to the soul."[20]

Still, Chaney knew this was only her third film (the studio did not release the already-completed *Our Dancing Daughters* until after the release of *While the City Sleeps*), and she needed an education in the art of filmmaking. Speaking to her as if she were an ambitious daughter, he explained the importance of make-up and taught her to conserve her energy, not to overplay, but to be sincere and cultivate an enthusiastic love for her work. "Great and vital lessons," she agreed. "Whether for a star or a beginner."[21]

Chaney's advice continued: "Never act purely on impulse in important matters. Think things over carefully. Then, when you're sure that you're right, go ahead. And don't let anything swerve you from that decision."

Chaney's acting method fascinated her. In one scene, she sat transfixed as he manipulated his hat, handing it off from one hand to another. "The way he worked that hat and made it work for him."[22]

One morning they worked on a scene where she had to cry real tears. Chaney told her to "always believe what you're doing." He added that "sincerity is the key-note of success in this business. Don't spread your emotions all over the screen. Conserve them and make them genuine." By working with Chaney, and watching him, Anita tried to learn to eliminate "sloppiness and haphazardness." He was never too absorbed or too busy to stop and advise her.[23]

Through studio chatter, she heard that Chaney could be distant with costars. "Of course, he was a big, big star," she recalled. "I had read that sometimes he didn't even say good-bye to people, but he was marvelous to me."[24]

Critics called *While the City Sleeps* a "well-knit story, exceptionally cast and directed" and called Chaney's performance "excellent" with a strong supporting cast headed by Anita.[25]

## *Reviews*

"Anita Page was the girl in the case, and she did very good work. She is more at ease before the camera than she has been hitherto, and her work reveals a polish which augurs well for her future."—*The Film Spectator*, November 3, 1928.

"Myrtle, played by Anita Page, who was one of the dizzy girls in *Our Dancing Daughters* ... is quite good."—*New York Times*, October 22, 1928.

"Not until Anita Page enters as the heroine-bound-to-get-into-difficulties does the action really pick up. Miss Page's presence alone is sufficient to lend a concentrated purpose to the meanderings of the film, and though her portrayal is not as sparkling as in *Telling the World*, she established the winning quality of her personality."—Edwin Schallert, *Los Angeles Times*, September 24, 1928.

# *Our Dancing Daughters*

Metro-Goldwyn-Mayer Corp. (Loew's, Inc.)
A Cosmopolitan Production
A Milestone Film Release
Cosmopolitan Productions
1928

Tagline: "On with the Dance! Wild Youth Intoxicated with Life. Is Pleasure Bent. What's a Wedding When the Jazz Horn Sounds a Call to Arms?"

## Statistics

Alternate titles: *The Dancing Girl*; *Dancing Feet*. Synchronized musical score and sound effects (Movietone) / Black & White / 35mm / Drama. Runtime: 9 reels, 7,652 ft., 86 min; © Metro-Goldwyn-Mayer Distributing Corp., 1 Sep 1928, LP25605; New York premiere: Capitol Theatre, October 7, 1928. Release date: October 1928.

## Prologues

Los Angeles: Loew's State Theater. Fanchon and Marco's *Hollywood Studio Girls Idea* appeared with Charlie Murray. George Sidney performed a varsity drag take off. Lucille Page was a contortionist dancer deluxe. Other musical attractions included the Three Gobs, Charles Rozella, Mary Miles, Mildred Perlee, and a well-trained chorus.

New York: Capitol Theatre. The pre-show included *Under the Sea*, a stage spectacle, with Walters and Ellis, Mario Naldi, and the Chester Hale dancing girls. Fox Movietone News of Van and Schenck.

## Credits

Produced by Hunt Stromberg (uncredited); directed by Harry Beaumont; assistant director, Harry S. Bucquet; story and scenario by Josephine Lovett; titles by Marian Ainslee and Ruth Cummings; cinematography by George Barnes; settings by Cedric Gibbons; wardrobe by David Cox; music by William Axt (uncredited); edited by William Hamilton and Margaret Booth (uncredited); Dave Friedman (unit manager).

*Song(s)*: "I Loved You Then as I Love You Now" words and music by Ballard MacDonald, William Axt and David Mendoza. "Ain't We Got Fun?" words by Raymond B. Egan and Gus Kahn, music by Richard A. Whiting. "Broken Hearted," composer unknown.

## Cast

Joan Crawford (Diana "Di" Medford), John Mack Brown (Ben Blaine), Nils Asther (Norman), Dorothy Sebastian (Beatrice "Bea"), Anita Page (Ann "Annikins"), Kathlyn Williams (Ann's mother), Edward Nugent (Freddie), Dorothy Cumming (Diana's mother), Huntly Gordon (Diana's father), Evelyn Hall (Freddie's mother), Sam De Grasse (Freddie's father), Robert Livingston (Party Boy), Helen Brent (uncredited), Geraldine Dvorak (Party Guest), Mary Gordon (Scrubwoman), Lydia Knott (Scrubwoman), Fred MacKaye (Diana's admirer), Alona Marlowe (Party Girl), Bert Moorhouse (Diana's party friend), Gordon Westcott (Diana's party friend).

An un-retouched proof of Anita in a costume designed by Adrian for *Our Dancing Daughters* (MGM, 1928).

## Plot

Young and carefree socialite Diana meets Ben at a party and falls in love.

Ann, a beautiful yet amoral blonde, steals Ben's affections and marries him for his money. Heartbroken Diana stays with her friend, Bea. Diana receives a letter from Ann describing how happy she is with Ben. Bea's brother Freddie also receives a letter from Ann explaining her unhappiness and her wish to be with Freddie. Bea and Diana learn of the secret letter. Diana plans to travel for a year and holds a farewell party. After a quarrel with Ann, Ben unexpectedly attends the party, reconciling with Diana. Soon after, Ann arrives at the party to confront the two lovers. At the end of the night, Bea attempts to send Ann home, but she drunkenly falls down a flight of stairs to her death. After Diana returns from a year away, she and Ben are free to pursue a relationship.

## *Behind the Scenes*

Joan Crawford, who had been at MGM for two years, stole a copy of the script for *Our Dancing Daughters* and begged producer Hunt Stromberg for the part of Diana. Crawford, who was brought to Hollywood by Harry Rapf after he saw her in a Broadway chorus line, knew if she got this part it would make her a star—something the studio was trying to do since they held a nationwide contest to change her name from Lucille Le Sueur.

Louis B. Mayer assigned the part of the conniving greedy blonde to Anita, infuriating Harry Beaumont, the film's director. "L.B., what are you doing?" Beaumont protested. "Page has only done one film. We need a consummate actress for this part. The whole picture depends upon her performance."

Mayer remembered the day Anita stormed into his office and defended herself when the studio was about to dismiss her because of her association with Harry Thaw. Because of her raw, gutsy nerve, he knew she would be right for the part. He smiled at Beaumont and said, "You take her. She's a Bernhardt."[26]

Production began on *Our Dancing Daughters* with former All-American halfback turned actor Johnny Mack Brown added to the cast. Though Beaumont still disagreed, Anita was cast as Ann, the bad girl who steals Johnny Mack Brown from Joan Crawford.

Anita was still filming *Telling the World* when production began on *Our Dancing Daughters*. Beaumont received a memo that Anita would be available around March 12, but it added, "Their production is now four days behind schedule and if they lose any more time, Miss Page will finish later than expected." This did not make Beaumont any happier with his new star.[27]

"Beaumont was of French descent," Anita recalled, "a great technician but also an emotional director who knew better than to let the technical

(From left) Anita, Joan Crawford, and Dorothy Sebastian in *Our Dancing Daughters* (MGM, 1928).

end get in the way of filming. If he thought you were relaxing a bit, he would buzz you."[28]

Beaumont believed that the character of Ann was important to the plot and felt that Anita had neither the talent nor experience to pull it off. To show his contempt, he tried discouraging her, hoping she would quit. In one scene, Anita was having problems hitting her mark. "Fortunately, film acting was easy for me," she recalled. "About the only thing I had trouble with was the close-up. I would forget about the camera and go right out of the scene."

Finally, in desperation, Beaumont asked Harry Bucquet, his assistant director, to build a small box frame around Anita to remind her to stay within range. Anita stood in front of the cast and crew boxed in by the small wall. Embarrassed and angry, Anita swore under her breath, "I'll show you, Mr. Beaumont. I'll show you."

Unfortunately, the story was leaked to a reporter and the following blurb appeared in print: "Directors have a terrible time getting Anita to stand still for her close-ups. So now they have solved the problem by putting Anita in a soapbox, so that she can't run around while her close-ups are being filmed."[29]

Dorothy Sebastian felt compassion for her younger costar and embraced her when she completed the scene. "Anita, don't be upset or nervous. I saw the rushes last night and you are going to be great in this part." Anita was grateful for Sebastian's encouragement but wanted to prove herself to Beaumont.[30]

Another cast member who was helpful was Nils Asther. "Johnny Mack Brown and I were the babes in the woods of that class," she remembered. "We sat at the feet of Nils Asther and tried to learn from him." Asther taught her repression and poise, quite different from William Haines' ease and gaiety. "Emotions repressed are often more significant than emotions obviously expressed," Asther told her. From that, she tried to restrain her feelings.

"I watched Nils, whom I think is one of the greatest actors of the screen," Anita confessed, "watched him thinking himself from one mood into another. Just watching him work was a priceless lesson in screen technique."[31]

Eventually though, she proved to Harry Beaumont that she could manage the part. When the film wrapped, she asked why he was so tough on her. "Anita, you are a fighter," he told her. "You're magnificent when your back's against the wall."[32]

Besides Beaumont's near harassment, Anita had to deal with Joan Crawford's upstaging attempts. Anita's character (Ann) is an alcoholic, and she crashes the bon voyage party of Crawford's character (Diana) and finds her with her husband Ben (Brown). The script calls for her to become hysterical and beat on him. While preparing for the scene, Crawford told Anita to be "careful when you do this scene with Johnny. Don't hit him too hard. You don't want to hurt him."

Anita was prepared to go all the way, but Crawford's warning disturbed her. Before filming the scene, she told Brown about Crawford's advice. "Should I hold back?" she asked the former fullback. Brown shook his head. "No way, honey. You give it everything you got. I know how to take care of myself."

Anita chose not to follow Crawford's instruction and was effective in the scene. From then on, Anita was convinced that Crawford wanted to hold back her performance. But she proved she could be as smart as Crawford. "Her little ploy didn't work," she told her mother.[33]

At the end of the film, an intoxicated Ann falls to her death down a flight of stairs. "I had to get drunk in *Dancing Daughters*. I did not know a thing about it, because I never even had a tiny drink. But they say I did it all right..."[34]

Louis B. Mayer did not approve of Anita's character's behavior, but he was a businessperson and knew he had to present the "new morality."

**With Johnny Mack Brown in *Our Dancing Daughters* (MGM, 1928).**

Therefore, to balance the good and the evil, he invoked the "sinner must pay" code: Anita's character had to die at the end of the picture.

To set the mood for the death scene, the on-set orchestra played "Can't Help Lovin' That Man of Mine" to achieve the proper emotional pitch. The emotions of the scene overcame Anita, and before going down the stairs, she lost control. To bring her out of it, Beaumont slapped her. "He's the only man who ever hit me," she said.[35]

However, there were still problems. Beaumont directed that Anita fall the first four steps, then a stunt woman would finish the act. However, the stairway fall was treacherous, and the stunt woman could not do it. Finally, a stunt man dressed in a blonde wig and dress performed it.

Per the script, Anita would lie at the bottom of the stairs where four scrubwomen were mopping the floor. Beaumont wanted realism, so he had the scrubwomen use dirty water which Anita had to lie face down in while Beaumont filmed reaction shots from different angles. "I felt as if I had to shower for a week."[36]

At the *Our Dancing Daughters* preview at the Fox-Wilshire Theater, 500 people waited in line, so a second showing was planned. When the film broke, editor Margaret Booth had "to race back to the studio to fix a reel while they started on reel one."[37]

Nevertheless, *Our Dancing Daughters* was a hit and made Joan Crawford a star. *Variety* said of the film's success: "It's mainly because of Joan Crawford and Anita Page, who seesaw for cast honors..." A *New York Times* reviewer added: "Anita Page runs away with the acting honors in what is technically an unsympathetic role, but she brings to it beauty, humor and magnetic unselfconsciousness."[38]

"I don't care about the other films I did," Anita insisted years later. "*Our Dancing Daughters* was *my* picture. I say that because I did the acting. Joan Crawford danced her way through it; I acted my way through it."[39]

*Our Dancing Daughters* made $40,000 on its first weekend at New York's Capitol Theatre. Lines outside were five deep waiting for standing-room-only space.

Fortunately, no cuts were needed by the New York censors, but in Philadelphia the famous scene where Crawford strips down to her undies while doing the Charleston was more than the City of Brotherly Love could handle; it and a heavy love-making scene along the Carmel shore line were deleted.

Anita made personal appearances at theaters across the country. At one theater, there was an opening in the stage floor with a rug placed over it. When Anita walked on the rug, her leg fell into the hole. The opening was not deep, and Anita was unhurt—except for her ego. "Well, I certainly fell for you," she told the shocked audience. "I hope you'll fall for me." The audience applauded wildly. Anita's quick thinking saved what could have been an awkward and dangerous moment.

*Variety* spotlighted Anita's "lengthy drunk sequence" where she gave "abundant authenticity," ending in her death after a fall down a flight of stairs.[40]

## Reviews

"All the reviewers have singled her out for uncommon praise and consider her a potential star."—Norbert Lusk, *Los Angeles Times*, October 14, 1928.

"One thrill you won't forget, nor the girl—Anita Page. Hers would be the outstanding performance if Joan Crawford and Dorothy Sebastian were not also in the picture."—*Photoplay*, August 1928.

"And the big thrill is the small new blonde, Anita Page, who, in her second part, steals the picture from Joan Crawford and gives a performance that would be unusually good even for a big star."—*Motion Picture Magazine*, September 1928.

"Anita Page gives a fairly good portrayal of a dancing daughter."—Mordaunt Hall, *New York Times*, October 8, 1928.

*Academy Award Nominations*
Josephine Lovett, Best Writing.
George Barnes, Best Cinematography.

# The Flying Fleet

Metro-Goldwyn-Mayer Corp. (Loew's, Inc.)
1929

"Dedicated to the officers and men of Naval Aviation whose splendid co-operation made this production possible."

Tagline: "*Sound!* The whir of racing blades. The roar of speeding motors. The whistle of passing wind— These will quicken your pulse in this thrilling tale of Knights of the Air!"

## Statistics

Alternate title: *Gold Braid*. Synchronized musical score and sound effects (also silent version) (Movietone) / Black & White / 35mm / Drama. Runtime: 11 reels, 9,044 ft., 72 min. © Metro-Goldwyn-Mayer Distributing Corp., 16 Jan 1929, LP37. Production date: August 5, 1928. New York premiere: Capitol Theater, the week of February 9, 1929. Release date: January 19, 1929.

## Prologues

Los Angeles: Loew's State. Rube Wolf led the stage show. The Page Sisters, Will Stanton, Jue So Tai, Ethel Osep, and the Eight Torpedoes also appeared.

New York: Capitol Theater. The pre-show included *Miami Nights*, produced by Arthur Knorr, with Dave Schooler, the Capitoliens, the Runaway Four, and the Chester Hale Dancers.

## Credits

Produced (uncredited) and directed by George Hill with the sanction of the United States Navy; screenplay adapted by Richard Schayer, based on an original story by Lieutenant Commander Frank Wead, U.S.N. and Byron Morgan; titles by Joseph White Farnham; cinematography by Ira Morgan;

aerial photography by Charles Marshall; art direction by Cedric Gibbons; edited by Blanche Sewell; wardrobe by David Cox.

*Song(s)*: "You're the Only One for Me," words by Raymond Klages, music by William Axt and David Mendoza; "The Oceana Roll," words by Roger Lewis, music by Lucien Denni; "Where Do We Go from Here," by Howard Johnson; "Sailing, Sailing (Over the Bounding Main)," by Godfrey Marks; "Anchors Aweigh," words by R. Lovell and Alfred Hart Miles, music by Charles A. Zimmerman.

## Cast

Ramón Novarro (Ens./Ltn Tommy Winslow), Ralph Graves (Ens./Ltn Steve Randall), Anita Page (Anita Hastings), Edward J. Nugent (Dizzy), Carroll Nye (Tex), Sumner Getchell (Kewpie), Gardner James (Specs), Alfred Allen (Admiral), The Three Sea Hawks (Themselves), Wade Boteler (Shipwrecked Crewman), Bud Beary (Admiral's Aide), Roscoe Karns (Shipwrecked Radio Operator), Claire McDowell (Mrs. Hastings, Anita's Mother).

## Plot

Best friends Tommy and Steve graduate at Annapolis to become part of the U.S. Navy's Flying Fleet. When both aviators meet the beautiful Anita at the Hotel del Coronado in San Diego, they vie for her affections and competition ensues. With their friendship now strained, Steve is sent on a long-distance flight to Honolulu, but his plane crashes at sea. The fleet send out a rescue team, but after days of no luck, it is ordered to abandon their search. Tommy pleads for one more try and finds Steve and his crew, and the men are rescued. Anita joins the hospital ship and is reunited with Tommy, whom she genuinely loves.

## Behind the Scenes

Ramón Novarro, the star of *The Flying Fleet*, first met Anita when he visited the set of *Telling the World*, when director Sam Wood encouraged everyone to see "the most beautiful girl in the world." Novarro, one of MGM's leading male heartthrobs, liked Anita's vitality and requested her services for the film.[41]

Anita looked forward to working with Novarro. The front office, however, had their concerns. Novarro's height was 5'8" and executives felt that Anita was too tall, so they would recast her with Josephine Dunn, another MGM starlet. That was "nonsense" to Novarro. At a preproduction meeting, he told producer Bernie Hyman that he could "wear lifts in my shoes." He reminded them that he appeared with Joan Crawford in *Across to Singapore* and that "she's as tall as Miss Page." Afterward, Anita was waiting in the hallway. "Thank you very much, Mr. Novarro. I hope I get the part."

"I think you will," he replied. And she did.⁴²

The week before her 18th birthday, *The Flying Fleet*'s cast and crew traveled to San Diego to film at the naval base and the Hotel del Coronado. Naturally, Anita's parents went with her, but the studio would only pay for Mrs. Pomares' expenses, so her father rented a cottage nearby while Anita and her mother stayed at the Hotel del Coronado.

One day, Anita had finished location filming and was waiting in a studio limousine when an attractive young man approached her. "I'm going down to Mexico for the weekend," he told her, "would you like to come with me?"

**With Ramón Novarro in *The Flying Fleet* (MGM, 1929). This portrait was taken September 26, 1928 (courtesy Joseph Yranski).**

"Why, of course not," Anita replied. "I never heard of such a thing." The quick-thinking limo driver told Anita that her father was waiting for her. "I'll drive you there now," he said. As the limo pulled away from the curb, the young man tried to get in, but Anita was able to push him out.

A few days later in the hotel lobby, she sensed that someone was following her, but dismissed it. In her room, she answered the telephone and a voice said: "Miss Page, I'm a friend of your father's attorney. I met you when you came back from Europe recently." She knew something was wrong. "I'm sorry," she told him, "I've never been to Europe. I think you have the wrong Miss Page," and hung up the phone.

Recalling the strange man at the limousine, she locked the door and called the front desk, asking to speak to the hotel detective. "I'm sorry, Miss Page, I don't know where he is now," the clerk replied.

"You've got to find him," she pleaded. "I think a man may be trying to get into my room." Five minutes passed and she called again.

"We haven't been able to find the detective," he told her.

**The filming of *The Flying Fleet* (MGM, 1929). Ramón Novarro and Anita Page can be seen in the center beneath the plane's propeller (courtesy Joseph Yranski).**

When her mother arrived, Anita explained what happened, so they checked out and moved into her father's rented cottage. Within a few days, the police apprehended the young man, who had a history of mental illness and recently had a nervous breakdown. Anita would not press charges if he promised not to bother her again. That was the last she heard from him.[43]

From Novarro, Anita learned the lesson of singleness of purpose and diligence. "Always finish whatever you start," Novarro told her one day on the set, "never leave loose ends, Anita. They are so hard to pick up again." He also taught her to neglect no detail, no matter how small. He would stop a scene to correct a bad light which was making a shadow across her cheek or to suggest a more graceful movement.[44]

One evening, Novarro took Anita to a dance given by the San Diego naval officers who were working with the film crew. Anita was feeling quite self-important over the attentions they were giving her. During their dance, Novarro said, "Don't let flattery turn your head, child, or make you forget the hard work ahead of you. It has ruined more than one beginner. You owe to the public, which is making you, the giving of the very best and most serious efforts of which you are capable."[45]

At *The Flying Fleet*'s San Diego premiere, the manager of the Pantages Theatre asked Novarro and Anita to appear. Typically, Novarro did not attend premieres. He believed that fans would be disappointed to see him in person. "We are an illusion," he told Anita. "The audience does not look at us as real. We are just an image on a giant screen that can never live up to their expectations in person." However, Anita convinced him to attend.[46]

The naval air station crowded 130 planes into the air, flying in review for the event. At the theater, Novarro and Anita walked into the theater arm in arm before a crowd of screaming fans. As the picture began, Novarro's name appeared on the screen and the audience applauded wildly. When Anita also applauded, Novarro glared at her, shocked. "What are you doing?" he demanded. "Stop it!"

Novarro's reaction surprised her. However, she was not taking orders from anyone and continued her applause. Anita was furious. The couple entered the theater arm in arm but left with five feet separating them; she did not speak to Novarro for three days. She never understood the reason for his unusual reaction. "Maybe he thought I was being nice to him because he was a movie star," she later wondered. But if so, it was not true; she had a profound respect for him.[47]

"Ramón was a wonderful influence for me," Anita said. "It is pretty hard for any girl to keep her head when she is tasting the first drops of a little success. When I'd begin to think I was pretty good, I'd look at Ramón, who had let nothing interfere with his constant study and his progress, and remember that I was still a rank beginner with nothing accomplished to give me the right to self-pride."[48]

Technically, *The Flying Fleet* was a wonder. The aviation sequences were among the best filmed at the time, showing how the Navy evaluated and trained aviators to receive and condition airplanes at sea in full action, with astonishing aerial maneuvers. Ramón Novarro and Ralph Graves, each having the most quietly dramatic but most strenuous roles of their careers, acted with charming youthful fervor. Anita supplied whatever "It" is.

## *Reviews*

"Anita Page, whose popularity is increasing in leaps and bounds as pictures in which she has appeared get into circulation, is the damsel on the sidelines waiting to be grabbed for the final clinch by Novarro."—*Variety*, February 13, 1929.

"Anita Page does well as the heroine, with whom the hero as well as one of six musketeers falls in love."—*Harrison's Reports*, February 16, 1929.

"Miss Page's importance does not save her from being sacrificed to a blah role which any extra could have played."—Norbert Lusk, *Los Angeles Times*, February 17, 1929.

# *The Broadway Melody*

Metro-Goldwyn-Mayer Corp. (Loew's, Inc.)
1929

Tag lines: "The pulsating drama of Broadway's bared heart speaks and sings with a voice to stir your soul!"

"ALL TALKING ALL SINGING ALL DANCING!"

### Statistics

Sound (Movietone), (also silent) / Black & White with Technicolor sequences / 35mm / Musical. Runtime, 10 reels, 9,372 ft. (silent version, 5,943 ft.), 111 min. © Metro-Goldwyn-Mayer Distributing Corp., 5 Mar 1929, LP183. Production date: October 19, 1928. Hollywood premiere: Grauman's Chinese Theater, February 1, 1929. New York City premiere: Astor Theater, February 8, 1929. Release date: June 6, 1929.

### Prologues

Hollywood: Grauman's Chinese. Sid Grauman produced a long, spectacular, veritable Follies called "Broadway Nights," which included airplane glimpses of New York, with George M. Cohan's "Give My Regards to Broadway" going full force. The introduction of the song "Broadway Melody" with Charles King warbling it energetically. Grauman brought in famous stage actors of the day to perform: Buster West, Alfred Latell, and the Pasquali Brothers.

New York: Astor Theatre. *Confession*, a short sound feature based on a playlet by Kenyon Nicholson and directed by Lionel Barrymore. Robert Ames, Carroll Nye, Christian Yves, and Yvonne Stark were the featured actors.

### Credits

Produced by Irving Thalberg (uncredited), and Lawrence Weingarten (uncredited); directed by Harry Beaumont; continuity by Sarah Y. Mason; story by Edmund Goulding; dialogue by Norman Houston and James Gleason; titles (silent version) by Earl Baldwin; cinematography by John Arnold; art direction by Cedric Gibbons; film edited by Sam S. Zimbalist and William LeVanway (silent version, uncredited); wardrobe by David Cox; recording engineer, Douglas Shearer; sound technicians, Wesley C.

Miller, Louis Kolb, O.O. Ceccarina and G.A. Burns; ensemble numbers staged by George Cunningham.

*Song(s)*: "The Wedding of The Painted Doll," "Broadway Melody," "Love Boat," "Boy Friend," "Harmony Babies" and "You Were Meant for Me," music by Nacio Herb Brown, lyrics by Arthur Freed. "Give My Regards to Broadway," by George M. Cohan. "Truthful Deacon Brown," music and lyrics by Willard Robison.

## Cast

Anita Page (Queenie Mahoney), Bessie Love (Harriet "Hank" Mahoney), Charles King (Eddie Kearns), Jed Prouty (Uncle Jed), Kenneth Thomson (Jock Warriner), Edward Dillon (Stage Manager), Mary Doran (Flo), Eddie Kane (Francis Zanfield), J. Emmett Beck (Babe Hatrick), Marshall Ruth (Stew), Drew Demarest (Turpe), Nacio Herb Brown (Pianist), Arthur Freed (Bystander in Rehearsal Room), James Burrows (Singer), Ray Cooke (Bellhop), William Demarest (Bit Part), James Gleason (Music Publisher), Carla Laemmle (Oyster shell), Joyce Murray (Specialty dancer), The Angeles Twins (Chorus Girls), Betty Arthur (Chorus dancer), Eddie Bush (Quartet Guitarist and Singer), Eddie Lang (Guitar Player in Band), Carl M. Leviness (Party Guest), The Mawby Triplets (Angella, Claudette, Claudine), Charlotte Merriam (Flapper in Pearl Necklace), Blanche Payson (Wardrobe Lady), Alice Pitman (Chorus Girl), Bill Seckler (Quartet Guitarist and Singer), Diana Verne (Chorus Girl), Dorothy Vernon (Hotel Housekeeper), Alice Weaver (Chorus Girl), Dorothy Coonan Wellman (Chorus Girl).

## Plot

A small-town sister act on the vaudeville circuit, Hank and Queenie, professionally known as "The Mahoney Sisters," travel to New York seeking success on Broadway. Eddie Kerns, a songwriter and Hank's boyfriend, writes a new song, "The Broadway Melody," with the intention of the sisters performing it in Zanfield's new revue. After their first rehearsal, Zanfield cuts the act, and only Queenie earns a new place in the show as a model. Queenie catches the eye of Jacques Warriner, a financier for the show. Warriner courts Queenie, while Eddie falls in love with her. Hank tries to deter Queenie from Jacques' advances but fails. An altercation between the sisters leads to Eddie confessing his love for Queenie. Hank disguises her heartbreak and encourages Eddie to fight for Queenie. Hank takes a touring job with a chorus girl, and reconciles with Queenie and Eddie, who settle down to married life.

## Behind the Scenes

In *The Broadway Melody*, Anita received top billing. Her costar

(From left) Bessie Love, director Harry Beaumont and Anita on the set of *The Broadway Melody* (MGM 1929).

Bessie Love was a film veteran since 1915, when she was an extra in D.W. Griffith's *The Birth of a Nation*. After an extended search, the part of the song-and-dance man was handed to Charles King, who was on the road in the musical comedy *Hit the Deck*. Benny Thau, a booker for Loew's vaudeville circuit, recommended King to Louis B. Mayer, who signed him for *The Broadway Melody* and hired Thau for the MGM casting office.

Screenwriter Edmund Goulding pitched the story of *The Broadway Melody* during a meeting with Thalberg and production supervisor Lawrence Weintgarten, the husband of Thalberg's sister Sylvia. Weintgarten recalled that Goulding was "very inventive and was loaded with ideas"; however, he would tell a story in the morning and totally forget it by that afternoon. To help with Goulding's flawed memory, Weintgarten had Vivian Newcom (Thalberg's secretary) write down everything Goulding suggested.[49]

Weintgarten assigned screenwriters Sarah Mason and Norman Houston to adapt Goulding's story with actor James Gleason contributing dialogue. Broadway producer Billy Rose initially was to compose the music, but at the last minute, Thalberg selected MGM's recently hired songwriting team Arthur Freed and Nacio Herb Brown.

The new "sensation" of sound brought terror into the hearts of many of Hollywood's most talented actors. Even though most actors had normal sounding voices, when translated to the still inferior soundtrack, it was a different story; men might sound effeminate and the slightest accent or speech impediment became amplified.

For example, when Marion Davies attended the Los Angeles premiere of *The Jazz Singer*, she was not happy hearing the film talk. Unknown to the public, Davies had a slight stammer. That evening, she told her escort, studio publicist Hubert Voight, "M-m-m-mister Voight, I-I-I have a problem!" However, when Davies memorized a script, she could speak without difficulty.[50]

Clara Bow was a different story. She dreaded the "talkies" because of her Brooklyn accent, which most admitted was not that bad. A few years later, when a fire broke out on the Paramount lot, Bow ran into the street and yelled, "I hope to Christ it was the sound stages!"[51]

Actors working in Hollywood for years found themselves on the streets. Studios sent representatives to New York to hire seasoned, voice-trained stage actors. The dawn of sound ruined careers daily.

Anita, too, was concerned if her voice would make the grade. "I was so nervous I could scarcely speak during the first days of that picture. The microphone scared me to death." Fortunately, her costar Charles King taught her the real "audience feel"—the first fundamental lesson in the "talkies."

"Don't be scared, Anita," King told her. "Learn to think of the mike as a living thing, a real flesh-and-blood audience. Play to it. Please it. Sell your voice and your songs to it. Make it like you." King taught her countless things about using her voice.[52]

Determined to correct any flaws, Anita underwent a three-hour evaluation on the University of Southern California's new "voice dissector," which found faults in a subject's voice. The overall comments on her

**Charles King sings "You Were Meant for Me" to Anita in *The Broadway Melody* (MGM, 1929).**

performance noted, "Very good material, hard worker, intelligent, ambitious, learns quickly."[53]

"That voice test was nearly as much of a thrill as my first day in pictures," Anita remembered. "I was so excited that I scarcely remember what I did first. I do remember mother and I went down to USC where I enrolled in a class for voice culture."

Anita was the first pupil to enroll for the course. After working all day at the studio, she attended school for two hours studying the enunciation of difficult words. For the first time she had to memorize lines, which came easily. "At home, I went through my dialogue script with mother, dad and little Marino and we had great fun," Anita said.[54]

Because the studio had only one operable sound stage, *The Broadway Melody* shared space with MGM's first all-talking dramatic film, *The Trial of Mary Dugan*, starring Norma Shearer. During the morning and early afternoon, the *Mary Dugan* company used the studio, and in the evening, *The Broadway Melody* cast and crew moved in. This odd scheduling compensated for the elevated temperatures that filled the unventilated studio due to the hot California sun. Sometime after 5 o'clock, Anita arrived at the studio and worked into the early morning hours.

*The Broadway Melody* was originally planned as a part-talkie, and its dailies had impressed Thalberg to make it the studio's first all-sound picture. "Thalberg quickly discerned that something special was being made," Anita recalled, "so he put the picture on higher priority. I remember he visited the set every day; something he never did with other pictures." This change created added pressure for *The Broadway Melody*'s director, Harry Beaumont.[55]

"*Broadway Melody* was one of the earliest talking movies produced," Beaumont later said, "yet in it we were able to overcome the usual handicaps of primitive equipment and techniques and come up with several technical 'firsts' in movie making."

The addition of sound was revolutionary not only for the country but also for the studios, discarding all conventional movie-making techniques. One example was soundproofing the camera motor's whir by placing it in a small room so the microphone could not pick it up. The camera was now stationary and could not move. Cinematographer John Arnold solved the problem by mounting a large soundproofed box on a movable truck with the camera and camera operator inside; two men in stocking feet carried the microphones.[56]

Anita recalled more problems. "That microphone heard everything," Anita said. "In one scene, I was wearing a taffeta skirt with petticoats, and every time I walked, there was a terrible rustling noise on the soundtrack. So I had to take off the petticoats before we could go ahead with the scene."[57]

The mechanics of sound improved on a weekly basis. When a problem arose, they solved it, but it wasted valuable time. Bessie Love recalled one specific incident: "I remember listening to the playback of one scene, and we heard this echo in the background. So, the sound experts said, 'Everybody out'; they laid carpets and covered the entire area with nails. Back we went and reshot the scene; and listened to the playback. The echo was still there. So out we went, in they came, hanging the place with heavy curtains and material to drown the echo."[58]

After several attempts, they made it as good as they could and filmed it.

In another scene, Anita was filing her nails, but microphones were picking up a tapping noise. They searched everywhere and could not find it. "At last someone noticed that it was me!" Anita said. "As I filed my nails, I was tapping my foot without even thinking of it. In a silent picture, no one would have noticed."

Even though sound was exciting, Anita felt that silents were better than talkies. "In silent pictures, it was all face and expression," she said. "The camera could follow you around, and you had to be able to get yourself over on the screen without talking. Silent pictures were much

(From left) Bessie Love, Charles King and Anita in *The Broadway Melody* (MGM, 1929).

easier for me. If you didn't get your lines quite right, it didn't make much difference."[59]

*The Broadway Melody* was exhausting, as the cast worked hard on the musical numbers. To worsen matters, the flu had struck members of the cast and crew. Harry Beaumont was ill and directed from a couch so the production would stay on schedule. "At least that picture cured my mike fright," Anita later said. "I was so tired and so glad to just be able to keep on my feet that I forgot to be afraid of the mike."[60]

After the film was completed, Thalberg was impressed and added one more musical number, "The Wedding of the Painted Doll," filmed in Technicolor. But upon seeing the rushes, Thalberg was furious. "It's much too static," he told Beaumont. "Refilm it!"

The picture was over budget, so the studio's new sound engineer, Douglas Shearer (Norma's brother), suggested replaying the recording through loudspeakers on the stage and having the actors mouth the words. This would save technicians from bringing in an entire orchestra again. Technicians could then dub it onto the film. "Will that work?" Thalberg asked his brother-in-law. Shearer was certain it would—and it did. From then on, dubbing prerecorded music and ending the need for an orchestra on the set became the standard. Another first for *The Broadway Melody*.[61]

When the film premiered at Hollywood's Grauman's Chinese Theater on a rainy February 1, 1929, it was a sensation. The studio placed gigantic signs outside the theater proclaiming, "All-Talking! All-Dancing! All-Singing!"

Anita arrived dressed in an original Adrian gown made of white tulle trimmed in a leaf pattern of sequins with white gardenias, accented by a dark fox fur with a cape of transparent velvet draped over her shoulders.

John Gilbert hosted the evening and introduced Charles King and Anita Page—each receiving hearty applause—but when Bessie Love appeared, the applause was deafening. Gilbert also welcomed costar Jed Prouty and director Harry Beaumont. Also attending that night were Cecil B. DeMille, Renée Adorée, Gloria Swanson, Joan Crawford, Josephine Dunn, Raquel Torres, Corinne Griffith, Sue Carol, Billie Dove, Marion Davies, Lois Wilson, Adolphe Menjou, and scores of others.

In New York City, *The Broadway Melody* played at the Astor, while Anita's recent film, *The Flying Fleet* with Ramón Novarro, was at the Capitol Theater.

*The Broadway Melody* was a hit, but Anita admitted that she did not like the film. "I hated saying things like 'gee, ain't it elegant?' Besides, *Broadway Melody* was Bessie Love's picture. Bessie had hopes that she would make quite a bit out of it, spent a lot of time taking dancing lessons, and she gave a beautiful performance. At first, I didn't like it at all, but I do like it now."[62]

MGM produced *The Broadway Melody* on a budget of $280,000, but the film made a whopping $4,000,000 at the box office.

Anita's performance in *The Broadway Melody* earned her fans from many levels of society including dictator Benito Mussolini, California governor James Rolph, and a young comedian who would make his own mark in the entertainment business—Milton Berle. "I was twenty years old at the time and it [*The Broadway Melody*] was showing at a theater at 45th Street and Broadway in New York City," Berle said. "I remember watching this beautiful blond on the screen and thinking how gorgeous she was; I fell in love with her right away. I recall her, along with Bessie Love and Charlie King who sang 'You Were Meant for Me' to her. From then on I was thrilled every time I saw her on the screen."[63]

The *New York Times*' Norbert Lusk said of Anita's performance: "Though it is scarcely necessary to dilate on the prodigious hit registered by Anita Page with the first night audience, it is nevertheless a delight to applaud her freshness, charm and amazing expertness, which is all the more disarming because her naturalness conceals the least hint of technique either in projecting her charm or depicting the emotions of her role. By many of us she is considered the outstanding find, of not one, but several years."[64]

### Reviews

"Anita Page … is blonde and she is beautiful. Her acting, especially her voice, does not enhance her personality. Notwithstanding, it must be admitted that there are girls who talk as though she is made for the screen. Miss Page, however, fails to give one an impression of spontaneity, for she recites rather than speaks her lines."—Mordaunt Hall, *New York Times*, February 9, 1929.

"Anita Page adds beauty and charm to the production—plenty of it and her voice records exceptionally. She will be a great success in this production, because she invests with such a variety of qualities her portrayal has the dash of youth besides."—Edwin Schallert, *Los Angeles Times*, February 4, 1929.

### Academy Awards

Best Picture

### Academy Award Nominations

Harry Beaumont, Best Director
Bessie Love, Best Actress

# *Speedway*

Metro-Goldwyn-Mayer Corp. (Loew's, Inc.)
A Harry Beaumont Production
1929

"The producers acknowledge with thanks the co-operation of the Indianapolis Speedway Association and the actual participation of the world-famous racing drivers in recording scenes for this production."

Tagline: "*Speed* was his middle name! On the track—in love—the sky was the speed limit!"

## Statistics

Sound (Western Electric System) (also Silent) / Black & White / 35mm / Melodrama. Runtime: 8 reels; 6,962 ft., 7,075 ft., 82 min. © Metro-Goldwyn-Mayer Distributing Corp., 9 Sep 1929, LP664. Release date: September 7, 1929.

## Prologues

Los Angeles: Loew's State. Fox Movietone Newsreel; a Hal Roach comedy, *Dad's Day*; and on stage a colorful Fanchon and Marco revue, "Art in Taps."

New York: Capitol Theatre. Walt Roesner and his captivating Capitolians in Arthur Knorr's "Shanghaied," with 40 Chester Hale Girls and other headline entertainers. Yasha Bunchuk conducted the Capitol Grand Orchestra—New York's most popular musical ensemble.

## Credits

Directed by Harry Beaumont; story by Byron Morgan; adaptation by Alfred Block, Ann Price, Byron Morgan; titles by Joseph White Farnham; cinematography by Henry Sharp; edited by George Hively; art direction by Cedric Gibbons; wardrobe by David Cox; musical synchronization under the direction of Dr. William Axt (uncredited); stunts by Leon Durray (stunt driving double for John Miljan) and Deacon Litz (stunt driving double for William Haines).

## Cast

William Haines (Bill Whipple), Anita Page (Patricia "Pat" Bonner), Ernest Torrence (Jim MacDonald), Karl Dane (Dugan), John Miljan (Lee Renny), Eugenie Besserer (Mrs. MacDonald), Polly Moran (Waitress), Alfred Adam (Doctor), Harry Hartz (Harry Hartz, driver).

## Plot

Car mechanic Bill Whipple helps veteran race driver Jim MacDonald at the Indianapolis speedway. While at the race, Bill meets aviatrix Patricia, and she takes an interest in him. Patricia is a guest of Lee Renny, Jim's rival in the race. Bill gets a piece of machinery for the race and told to fly. During the flight, Patricia takes Bill up in the air, but when the plane becomes disabled, he saves himself and Patricia using one parachute. At the racetrack, Jim's bad heart disqualifies him, so Bill steps in to drive on his behalf. Bill fakes an eye injury so that Jim takes over on the last lap and wins. Patricia understands and admires Bill for letting Jim fulfill his ambition.

## Behind the Scenes

The studio sent Anita on location for her next picture. *Speedway*, a

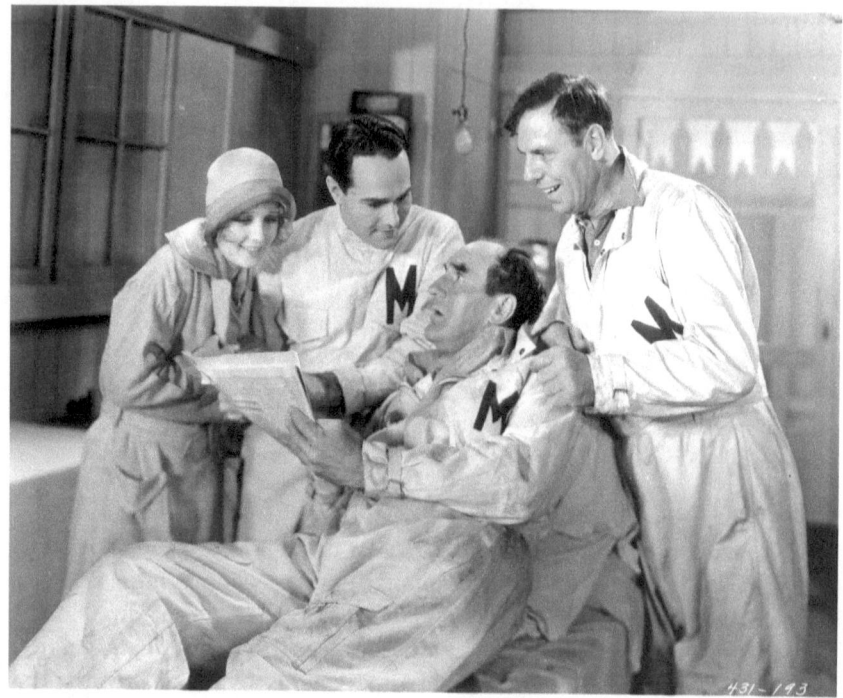

(From left) Anita, William Haines, Ernest Torrence and Karl Dane in *Speedway* (MGM 1929) (courtesy Joseph Yranski).

racing story, was filmed at the Indianapolis Motor Speedway during the Memorial Day holiday. William Haines costarred and Harry Beaumont once again directed Anita in their third film together.

Anita was cast as an aviator, and to prepare herself, she took flying lessons at Central Airport near Burbank where the aerial scenes were filmed. At Indianapolis, when she was not filming, she watched the drivers racing at breakneck speed. She was thrilled how costars Haines, Ernest Torrence, John Miljan and Karl Dane managed their cars. However, she had hoped for a 108 mile-an-hour spin around the famous racetrack herself, but the rules would not allow women on such risky rides—so Anita had to watch from the sidelines.

Anita's popularity was growing steadily since her debut in films the year before, resulting in appearing at personal appearances and big Hollywood parties. Because of her overindulging at these events, Anita was steadily gaining weight. Her appearance was important and any deviation from her studio-approved 118 pounds meant going on a diet. There was a scale in her bedroom and every Saturday her father would weigh her. The results could mean two things: two pounds over her approved weight meant going light on sweets and starches for a while. Two pounds under meant building up.

To lose the extra weight, Anita consumed only coffee and fruit for several weeks. Her goal was to lose enough weight so she could eat "cream cheese and nut sandwiches like Connie Bennett."[65]

During her stay in Indianapolis, her insufficient diet got the better of her and she became ill. Her mother sent for a doctor, but he did nothing for her. "I'm going to die," she moaned as she paced across her hotel room. "I know I'm going to die."

Mrs. Pomares was concerned, but she refused to show Anita how worried she was. "Now that will be all, young lady," she told her daughter. "You just pop into this hot tub and you'll be all right in a shake."

"Mother kept kidding me about dying until the second doctor got there," she mused. "I just wouldn't have been able to die with her laughing at me."[66]

Critics found *Speedway* "okay" but were offended by Haines' "offensive-stuff" with considerable footage devoted to his "sickening smart-aleck tricks." The public was growing tired of the "wisecracker's" constant gags. As for Anita, in reviews, critics barely mentioned her performance, except noting that she was in the film.[67]

### Reviews

"As a story *Speedway* rates good entertainment. The most serious defect in the production is the clowning and wisecracking of its star, who cannot, apparently, appear in a single scene with any semblance of naturalness.... Anita Page plays the part of the girl for whom Haines cares..."—*Los Angeles Times*, October 5, 1929.

"Haines is his usual breezy self but does not win our sympathy as much as Ernest Torrence, who gives a typically effective performance. The rest of the cast are competent."—*Film Weekly*, January 31, 1930 [UK].

# *Our Modern Maidens*

Metro-Goldwyn-Mayer Corp. (Loew's, Inc.)
A Jack Conway Production
1929

Tagline: "An All-Talking—singing and dancing jazz party!"

## Statistics

Alternate title: *The Big Brass Band*. Silent with sound sequences (Western Electric Sound System) / Musical score and sound effects by Movietone (also silent) / Black & White / Drama. Runtime: 8 reels, 6,976 ft., 70 min. © Metro-Goldwyn-Mayer Distributing Corp., 12 Aug 1929, LP591. New York premiere: Capitol Theater, September 7, 1929. Release date: September 8, 1929.

## Prologues

Los Angeles: Loew's State. Fanchon and Marco's *Hollywood Studio Girls Idea*. The main attraction was the Three Gobs, hoofers whose vocal efforts are à la Paul Whiteman's Rhythm Boys. Charles Rozella, Mary Miles, Mildred Perlee, and a well-trained chorus divide the other turns.

New York: Capitol Theatre. "Atop of New York," devised and staged by Arthur Knorr. Frank Cambria's stage offering "The Jazz Clock Store" and Abe Lyman and his Californians. Overture: "The Glory of Russia," Yasha Bunchuk conducting.

## Credits

Produced by Jack Conway (uncredited) and Hunt Stromberg (uncredited); directed by Jack Conway; story and continuity by Josephine Lovett; titles by Marian Ainslee and Ruth Cummings; cinematography by Oliver T. Marsh; art direction by Cedric Gibbons; edited by Sam S. Zimbalist; gowns by Adrian; musical score by William Axt (uncredited) and Arthur Lange; dance direction by George Cunningham.

*Song*: "Wedding March (Bridal Chorus)" from the opera *Lohengrin* by Richard Wagner.

## Cast

Joan Crawford (Billie Brown), Rod La Rocque (Glenn Abbott), Douglas Fairbanks, Jr. (Gil Jordan), Anita Page (Kentucky Strafford), Edward Nugent (Reg), Josephine Dunn (Ginger), Albert Gran (B. Bickering Brown), Adrienne D'Ambricourt (Annette), Edwina Booth (undetermined role), Carrie Daumery (Wedding Guest), Geraldine Dvorak (Garbo Look-a-like), Anita Garvin (Bridesmaid), Stuart MacChesney (Child in the Wedding), Earl McCarthy (Party Guest).

## Plot

Carefree socialite Billie is engaged to young diplomat Gil. Billie meets senior diplomat Glen Abbott and proceeds to enchant him with the aim of aiding Gil's career using Abbott's influence. Billie's friend Kentucky stays for the summer and falls in love with Gil, becoming pregnant by him. Not

(From left) Josephine Dunn, Joan Crawford, and Anita as they appear in *Our Modern Maidens* (MGM, 1929).

knowing of Kentucky's pregnancy or Billie's feelings for Abbott, Gil feels duty bound to marry Billie though he loves Kentucky. Abbott learns of Billie's engagement, and after an intense argument, he leaves her. Billie and Gil go ahead to marry, but when Billie learns the truth from Kentucky at the wedding, she reunites her with Gil. Billie leaves for Paris, and while there she meets Abbott whom she really loves.

## Behind the Scenes

It was not long before MGM tried to recoup its success and popularity of *Our Dancing Daughters* by bringing back members of the original cast for a follow-up film entitled *Our Modern Maidens*. It reunited Anita and Joan Crawford, while adding Rod La Rocque and Douglas Fairbanks, Jr., to the cast. At the time, Fairbanks was engaged to Crawford and many saw it as a way for Joan to keep an eye on her betrothed.

However, Crawford and Fairbanks' public display of affection for each other irritated Anita. The couple created their own language, understood only to them, which they cooed to each other during breaks in the filming. "After a while, the whole thing became very annoying to everyone on the set," Anita said, adding to her already strained relationship with Crawford.[68]

*Our Modern Maidens*, just as its predecessor, was a silent film with musical synchronization. In April 1929, Thalberg announced the studio's policy for making silent films: "Where a story lends itself to silent treatment, we will produce a complete silent version as well as a talking version."[69]

Part of the reason were the difficulties they had filming sound pictures. For months, passing planes had disturbed open air sequences. To solve the problem, studio executives met with the Department of Commerce and the California Aircraft Operators Association. They agreed that whenever a captive red balloon floated over the studio, it was a warning to planes that talkies were filming. Then, pilots would avoid their airspace by 2,500 feet.

*Our Modern Maidens* gave Anita the chance to once again be dramatic and emote in several scenes, something she enjoyed. "I guess hysteria must be almost a second nature with me. I cried and cried, you remember, in the part of the unhappy Kentucky in *Our Modern Maidens*. It was grand. Three days of it—and I couldn't stop sobbing when Mr. Conway, our director, called 'Cut!'"[70]

Anita did not believe that an actor had to experience outrageous extremes in their personal life before one was qualified to play-act them. It was more the ability to project oneself into any given situation. "I have always been able to lose myself," she said, "sometimes embarrassingly so, in the sufferings of heroes and heroines of a make-believe world."

In fact, her release of emotions was not only for the screen. She once recalled how she became so wracked with sobs watching Lillian Gish's plight in *La Bohème* that people in the audience turned around and stared at her in shocked disapproval. "And it is even easier to get worked up about a character I am playing myself," she added.[71]

A practice Anita started on *Our Modern Maidens* was sketching

On set of *Our Modern Maidens* (MGM, 1929). The cast included (third from left) Josephine Dunn, Douglas Fairbanks, Jr. (seated), Joan Crawford (seated), Anita (standing behind Crawford), director Jack Conway (to the right of Anita with fingers in vest pockets), and Edward Nugent (looking over Conway's left shoulder).

her costars and presenting them with the pastel drawing as a gift. Anita sketched actress Vilma Banky when she visited her husband Rod La Rocque, but Banky did not take the sketch with her.

*Our Modern Maidens* garnered complimentary reviews. It was an ultra-modern story filled with snappy action and a fine story that all enjoyed. The film appealed mostly to younger viewers as it dealt with their problems. As a team, Crawford and Fairbanks were a good exploitation angle. Once again, Anita received praises for her performance.

## Reviews

"Joan Crawford is the star and has the meatiest role, but Anita Page, the *Broadway Melody* girl, runs away with the picture. Miss Page is truly a trouper."—*Variety*, September 11, 1929.

"From an acting standpoint, Anita Page shows that she really has something more than she has shown heretofore."—*Motion Picture News*, September 14, 1929.

"Anita Page has several scenes in which she becomes almost hysterical, and she enacts such scenes splendidly."—*The Film Spectator*, September 7, 1929.

"Miss Page in particular contributes an authentic and moving portrayal of Kentucky.... As the weaker of the two girls, she naturally wins greater sympathy in her part, though this should not be construed as minimizing the star's abilities."—Philip K. Scheuer, *Los Angeles Times*, August 23, 1929.

"Miss Page is pretty, but her portrayal of intense grief is not especially impressive."—Mordaunt Hall, *New York Times*, September 7, 1929.

# *The Hollywood Revue of 1929*

Metro-Goldwyn-Mayer Corp. (Loew's, Inc.)
1929

Tagline: "25 of the screen's greatest stars—chorus of 200—amazingly revolutionary motion picture!"

## Statistics

Alternate title: *Gus Edwards' M-G-M Review*; *The MGM Revue of Revues*. Sound (Movietone) / Black & White with Technicolor sequences / 35mm / Variety; Runtime: 13 reels, 11,669 ft., 113 min. © Metro-Goldwyn-Mayer Distributing Corp., 23 Sep 1929, LP800. Production date: March 1929. Hollywood premiere: Grauman's Chinese Theater, June 20, 1929. New York premiere: Astor Theatre, August 14, 1929. Release date: November 23, 1929.

## Prologue

Hollywood: Grauman's Chinese. "Curiosities," Movietone News, Symphony Orchestra.

## Credits

Produced by Harry Rapf (uncredited) and Irving Thalberg (uncredited); directed by Charles F. Reisner; first assistant director, Lionel

## The Hollywood Revue of 1929    115

Barrymore (uncredited); assistant directors, Jack Cummings, Sandy Roth and Al Shenberg; dialogue by Al Boasberg and Robert E. Hopkins; skit by Joseph White Farnham; cinematography by John Arnold, Irving Reis, Maximilian Fabian, John M. Nickolaus; art direction by Cedric Gibbons and Richard Day; edited by William S. Gray and Cameron K. Wood; costumes by David Cox, Henrietta Frazer and Joe Rapf; musical arrangement by Arthur Lange, Ernest Klapholtz and Ray Heindorf; sound by Douglas Shearer (recording engineer), Russell Franks (sound assistant), William Clark (sound assistant), Dr. Wesley C. Miller (sound assistant), A.T. Taylor (sound assistant), dance ensembles by Sammy Lee and George Cunningham; specialty dancer, Joyce Murray; production manager, Joe Cohn; electrician, Louis Kolb.

*Song(s)*: "Singin' in the Rain," "You Were Meant for Me," "Tommy Atkins on Parade," words by Arthur Freed, music by Nacio Herb Brown. "Low Down Rhythm," words by Raymond Klages, music by Jesse Greer. "For I'm the Queen," words and music by Andy Rice and Martin Broones. "Gotta Feelin' for You," by Joe Trent and Louis Alter. "Bones and Tambourines," "Strike Up the Band," "Tableaux of Jewels," by Fred Fisher. "Lon Chaney Will Get You If You Don't Watch Out," "Strolling Through the Park One Day," "Your Mother and Mine," "Orange Blossom Time," "Minstrel Days," "Nobody but You," "I Never Knew I Could Do a Thing Like That," by Joe Goodwin and Gus Edwards.

### Cast

Conrad Nagel (Master of Ceremonies), Jack Benny (Master of Ceremonies), John Gilbert (Romeo), Norma Shearer (Juliet), Joan Crawford, Bessie Love, Lionel Barrymore, Cliff Edwards, Stan Laurel (Magician's Assistant), Oliver Hardy (Magician), Anita Page, Nils Asther (Specialty), Edward J. Nugent, The Brox Sisters (Bobbe, Lorraine and Kathlyn Brox), Natacha Natova and Co., Marion Davies, William Haines, Buster Keaton (Princess Raja), Marie Dressler (The Queen), Charles King, Polly Moran, Gus Edwards, Karl Dane, George K. Arthur, Gwen Lee, Albertina Rasch Ballet, The Rounders, The Biltmore Quartet (Paul Gibbons, Ches Kirkpatrick, Eddie Bush, and Bill Seckler), Nacio Herb Brown, Ernest Belcher's Dancing Tots, Carla Laemmle, Angella Mawby, Claudette Mawby, Claudine Mawby, Myrtle McLaughlin, Ray Cooke (Messenger), Ann Dvorak (Chorus Girl/Stage Assistant who slaps Jack Benny), Nora Gregor, June Purcell (Singer), Arthur Lange (Orchestra Leader).

### Plot

*Hollywood Revue of 1929* was the first musical extravaganza production without any attempt at a plot.

Conrad Nagel serenades Anita with her swan song "You Were Meant for Me" in *The Hollywood Revue of 1929* (MGM, 1929).

## *Behind the Scenes*

The first song and dance film with no pretensions as to plot but with all sorts of airs as to the number of stars involved, quality of songs, and the glamour of the chorus girls was *The Hollywood Revue of 1929*. Other studios passed up this radical step until later attempts came with *Fox Movietone Follies* and *Paramount on Parade*, among others. Credit for starting the departure from all accepted production standards is given to producer Harry Rapf, who had fostered a number of outstanding films in the silent and talking era.

Songwriter Arthur Freed started out as a song plugger for a music publisher. Later, in vaudeville, he appeared with the Marx Brothers before joining forces with Nacio Herb Brown and becoming one of the top teams in Hollywood. He later became successful as a producer at MGM with his own unit.

Brown, Freed's partner, was a former real estate man when Thalberg hired him in 1929. While working on *The Broadway Melody*, he met and became enamored with its star—Anita Page. Brown became friendly with Anita and her parents, becoming great friends with her father. Anita was the inspiration for the song "You Were Meant for Me," which became a big hit and was used again in *The Hollywood Revue of 1929*, a musical extravaganza with an all-star cast.

The entire star and featured player list at MGM was used (everyone but Garbo and Ramón Novarro) in the film, in addition to vaudeville and musical comedy names. Jack Benny and Conrad Nagel were emcees, and Joan Crawford performed her famous Charleston dance number while singing "Gotta Feelin' for You." Marion Davies tap-danced on a drum, and Norma Shearer and John Gilbert performed the balcony scene from *Romeo and Juliet*—in 1920s jive and Technicolor!

Anita appeared in a cameo with Conrad Nagel who serenaded her with "You Were Meant for Me." Some sources say that Charles King's voice was dubbed over Nagel's, but Anita insists that Nagel sang the song. In fact, all cast members signed affidavits to assure audiences that they were hearing their real singing voices in the film. Years later, Conrad Nagel's daughter recalled her father walking around the house singing the song to her in preparation.[72]

The consensus of audience opinion was that the screen was beginning to show the stage what it could do in sheer entertainment. Mark Hellinger, the *New York Daily News* film critic, said of *The Hollywood Revue*: "If this film doesn't catch on like wildfire, I am Calvin Coolidge's old electric horse."[73]

## Reviews

"[*Hollywood Revue*] has the ingredients that make for financial success, a long list of names, plenty of talent, a great bunch of songs and elaborate staging."—*Hollywood Filmograph*, June 22, 1929.

"Colorful settings, catchy musical hits and the results of the efforts of the country's most noted stage showmen are attractive feature."—*Los Angeles Times*, January 20, 1930.

## Academy Award Nominations

Best Picture
Cedric Gibbons, Interior Decoration

# *Navy Blues*

### Metro-Goldwyn-Mayer Corp. (Loew's, Inc.)
### 1929

Tagline: "Ahoy! The Joy Fleet Is in Port!"

## Statistics

Alternate titles: *The Blue Jacket, The Gob*; Sound (also Silent) / Black & White / 35mm / Comedy. Runtime: 9, reels, 6,936 ft., 75 min. © Metro-Goldwyn-Mayer Distributing Corp., 2 Jan 1930, LP959. Production date: July 20, 1929. New York premiere: Capitol Theatre, January 10, 1930. Release date: December 20, 1929.

## Prologue

Los Angeles: Loew's State. Fanchon and Marco in "Manila Bound," an elaborate display of mantillas and multicolored shawls are a feature in the finale. Popular song hits of 1929; a Charley Chase comedy with Thelma Todd and Anders Randolf; Fox Movietone News.

## Credits

Produced by Clarence Brown (uncredited); directed by Clarence Brown; adaptation by Dale Van Every; story by Raymond L. Schrock; dialogue by J.C. Nugent, Elliott Nugent, and W.L. River; cinematography by Merritt Gerstad; art direction by Cedric Gibbons; editing by Hugh Wynn; wardrobe by David Cox; music by William Axt (uncredited); recording engineers, Gavin A. Burns (uncredited) and Douglas Shearer.

*Song*: "Navy Blues," words by Roy Turk, music by Fred E. Ahlert.

## Cast

William Haines (Kelly), Anita Page (Alice), Karl Dane (Sven Swanson), J.C. Nugent (Mr. Brown), Edythe Chapman (Mrs. Brown), Gertrude Sutton (Hilda), Wade Boteler (Higgins), Jack Pennick (Kansas), Gino Corrado (Headwaiter), Frank Genardi (Unknown role), Clarence Brown (Roller Coaster Rider), Shorty English (Sailor at Canteen), Adolph Faylauer (Cabaret Dancer), Christian J. Frank (Cabaret Doorman), Pat Harmon (Bouncer at Garden Cabaret), Lew Hicks (Policeman), Maxine Elliot Hicks (Girl in Sweatshop), Frank McLure (Cabaret Dancer), Charles McMurphy (Policeman), King Mojave (Cabaret Dancer), Marshall Ruth (Chubby Blonde Sailor), Richard Tucker (Man Dancing with Alice), Jacques Vanaire

**Anita and William Haines are directed by Clarence Brown in *Navy Blues* (MGM, 1929).**

(Cabaret Dancer), Adele Watson (Head of Ladies Uplift Society), Frank Yaconelli (Organ Grinder).

## Plot

Sailor Kelly meets Alice while on shore leave. That night, Alice invites Kelly to her family home, but when her parents wake, they order him to leave. Alice pleads with her mother but in the end the two lovers both leave. Kelly returns to his ship and travels away, and on his return, he visits Alice's home to marry her. Realizing Alice has never been back home, he searches for her and finds her working as a dancer in a cheap cabaret. Kelly begs forgiveness and persuades Alice to go home to reconcile with her parents and to be his wife.

## Behind the Scenes

Three days after completing *Our Modern Maidens*, Anita started filming *The Gob* with her *Telling the World* lead William Haines. Directed by Edward Sedgwick, the film was to be silent except for musical synchronization. The wharf at San Pedro served as location filming as it closely resembled a naval facility.

A few days after the production started, the studio halted work and discarded *The Gob* footage, announcing it was "re-vamping" it as an "all-talker." The studio had underestimated the public's response to talking films, due in part to *The Broadway Melody*'s success, feeling that audiences would no longer accept silent films.[74]

On July 20, 1929, production resumed under the new title *Navy Blues* with the same cast except for the actor who played Anita's father. Clarence Brown, who had the envious moniker of "Garbo's director," replaced Edward Sedgwick. But before completing the film, David Burton and Sam Wood directed various scenes.[75]

Now over her fear of crying, Anita could, at any time, turn on the tears for the camera. So when Clarence Brown told Anita that "we're going to film a scene in which I want you to cry," Anita thought to herself, "That's not a problem," until he added: "I only want to see one tear falling down your cheek." Anita lay awake all night wondering how to cry one tear on cue. The next day, Polly Moran jokingly suggested that she turn her profile to the camera; however, that was not what Brown wanted.

When it came time to shoot the scene, the stage was quiet as the camera caught a close-up of Anita's face and one tear slowly rolled down her cheek. Then, abruptly, someone opened an outside door and ruined the take. "Let's do it again," Brown screamed. Amazingly, Anita came through and did the one tear again, this time without any interruptions.[76]

*Variety* and *Film Daily* complained of the film's "weak plot" and "forced comedy"; however, critics raved about the effective pictures of life on board ship and the realistic settings. *Navy Blues* was William Haines' first talking picture, but it was Anita that critics paid attention to.[77]

## *Reviews*

"Blonde Anita Page plays the heroine. And how she plays her. Essentially of the baby-face type, Anita Page is anything but a vapid baby-doll. She can act with genuine grace and intelligence. Some of her scenes are so direct and natural she gives you the sensation of unintentional spying."— *New York Mirror*, January 12, 1930.

"Anita Page also enhances her reputation more than he [Haines] in *Navy Blues*. The girl is simply gorgeous in some of her close-ups and continues to surprise with the depths of her dramatic talent."—*New York American*, January 11, 1930.

# *Free and Easy*

Metro-Goldwyn-Mayer Corp. (Loew's, Inc.)
1930

Tagline: "A SCORE of stars make whoopee in this comedy carnival!"

## Statistics

Alternate titles: *On the Set*; *Easy Go* (TV). Spanish version title: *Estrellados*. French version title: *Le Metteur en Scene*. Sound (also Silent) / Black & White / 35mm / Comedy. Runtime: 10 reels, 8,413 ft., 73 min. © Metro-Goldwyn-Mayer Distributing Corp., 2 Apr 1930, LP1193. Release date: March 22, 1930.

## Prologues

Los Angeles: Loew's State. Fanchon and Marco's *Milky Way* idea, with Vernon Stiles Norce, Stohe and Lee, Bert Faye and others taking part.

New York: Capitol Theatre. "Varieties" with the Michon Brothers, Sydell Sisters, the Chester Hale Dancers, and others.

## Credits

Produced by Buster Keaton (uncredited) and Edward Sedgwick (uncredited); directed by Edward Sedgwick; production manager, Edward Brophy (uncredited); assistant director, Jack Mintz (uncredited); scenario by Richard Schayer; adaptation by Paul Dickey; French titles by Alexander Stein and Allen Byre; dialogue by Al Boasberg; cinematography by Leonard Smith; art direction by Cedric Gibbons; edited by William LeVanway and George Todd (uncredited); wardrobe by David Cox; music by William Axt (foreign version, uncredited); recording engineers, Karl E. Zint and Douglas Shearer; sound assistant, Jack Jordan; dance director, Sammy Lee; assistant choreographer, Ann Dvorak; still photographer, George Hurrell, Sr. (uncredited).

Song(s): "The Free and Easy" and "It Must Be You," words by Roy Turk, music by Fred E. Ahlert.

## Cast

Buster Keaton (Elmer Butts), Anita Page (Elvira), Trixie Friganza (Ma), Robert Montgomery (Larry), Fred Niblo (Director), Edgar Dearing (Officer), Gwen Lee (Herself), John Miljan (Himself), Lionel Barrymore

**With Buster Keaton in *Free and Easy* (MGM, 1930).**

(Himself), William Haines (Himself), William Collier, Sr. (Himself, Master of Ceremonies), Dorothy Sebastian (Herself), Karl Dane (Himself), David Burton (Himself), Jack Baxley (Train Conductor), Edward Brophy (Benny), Richard Carle (Eunuch Crowning Elmer), Louise Carver (Big German Woman), Emile Chautard (undetermined role), Jackie Coogan (Himself), Cecil B. DeMille (Himself), Drew Demorest (Larry's Valet), Ann Dvorak (Chorine), Joseph Farnham (Himself), Pat Harmon (Doorman at Premiere), Lottice Howell (Vocalist), Arthur Lange (Conductor), Theodore Lorch (Himself), Billy May (Himself), Doris McMahon (Singer and Dancer).

### *Plot*

Elmer, a garage man of Gopher City, Kansas, becomes the publicity agent of Elvira, a beauty prize winner, and takes the girl to Hollywood to launch her film career. While in the film capital, it is Elmer who gets noticed and becomes successful. Elvira confesses that she has no desire to be in movies and falls in love with a film star. Elmer realizes he is in love with Elvira, but too late to win her affections, he continues his new life in show business.

## Behind the Scenes

In 1928, Buster Keaton—by his own admission—made the worst mistake of his career. After his remarkable success with *College* and *Steamboat Bill, Jr.*, Keaton sold his studio and signed a contract with MGM. His first two films for the studio were silent and well received. His third film, *Free and Easy*, a musical farce, would be his first talkie and Anita his leading lady. The film included cameos from the biggest celebrities on the lot including director Cecil B. DeMille, Lionel Barrymore, and Jackie Coogan.

Keaton had a bungalow on wheels on one corner of the back lot and Anita would join him there for lunch on most days. She was amazed at his talent and considered him a comic genius. Anita was quick to recognize the similarities and the differences between Keaton and Charlie Chaplin: "Chaplin was more humorous. He was a fascinating man to talk to—and very funny—he thought funny. Keaton's comedy was more physical." She enjoyed working with Keaton so much that she repeated the experience a year later in *The Sidewalks of New York*.[78]

By now, Keaton's career was failing, as was his marriage to Natalie Talmadge. Alcoholism had its grip on his life, and even though he continued

(From left) Anita, Robert Montgomery and Trixie Friganza in *Free and Easy* (MGM, 1930).

to work, he was soon forgotten until he made a cameo in Charlie Chaplin's *Limelight* in 1952, which was the beginning of a nonstop revival that lasted until his death 14 years later.

Critics called *Free and Easy* well produced, sometimes tuneful, unusually amusing, but never the scream that most of Keaton's silent films were. The addition of sound diminished that certain something that made Buster Keaton unique.[79]

### Reviews

"Anita Page, regarded by many as the most beautiful girl in Shadowland, on and off the screen, turns in a dandy portrayal of a stage-struck bucolic. Her naïve sweetness is illusively hit off in her love scenes with Larry, and she is arresting attractive in several close-ups."—*Hollywood Filmograph*, April 19, 1930.

"Despite the presence of the good-to-look-at and seldom-seen Anita Page, this must be counted as one of Mr. Keaton's minor efforts, in fact as quite an off-day at the studio."—*New York American*, March 28, 1930.

"Mr. Keaton's voice is all right; it coincides with the slow-minded, earnest-faced little comedian in whom it is contained."—*Los Angeles Times*, April 12, 1930.

## *Caught Short*

Metro-Goldwyn-Mayer Corp. (Loew's, Inc.)
Cosmopolitan Productions
1930

Tagline: "You'll drop into your seat, crazy from laughing at the antics of these two comedy queens!"

### Statistics

Sound (Movietone) / Black & White / 35mm / Comedy. Runtime: 8 reels, 6,873 ft., 75 min. © Metro-Goldwyn-Mayer Distributing Corp., 22 May 1930, LP1315. Release date: May 10, 1930.

### Prologues

Los Angeles: Loew's State. The "City Service Idea," about the various civil guardians of Los Angeles, played. A performance by a man on a ladder twirling a rope and three axes in the air. Also performing were the Eddie Mack Dancers, Shapiro and O'Malley, DeQuincy and Stanley, Seb Meza, Laddie la Monte, and Frank Sterling.

New York: Capitol Theatre. Metrotone News; "Cheer Up," a stage contribution with Teddy Joyce, Evelyn Wilson, the Chester Hale Dancers, and others.

## Credits

Directed by Charles F. Reisner; book by Eddie Cantor; story by Willard Mack; continuity by Willard Mack, Robert E. Hopkins and Joseph H. Hopkins (uncredited); dialogue by Willard Mack and Robert E. Hopkins; cinematography by Leonard Smith; art direction by Cedric Gibbons; edited by George Hively and Harold Palmer; wardrobe by Henrietta Frazer; recording engineers, Fred R. Morgan and Douglas Shearer.

*Song(s)*: "Going Spanish," words by Raymond B. Egan, music by Dave Snell; "Somebody," words and music by Roy Turk and Fred E. Ahlert.

## Cast

Marie Dressler (Marie Jones), Polly Moran (Polly Smith), Anita Page (Genevieve Jones), Charles Morton (William Smith), Thomas Conlin (Frankie), Douglas Haig (Johnny), Nanci Price (Priscilla), Gretta Mann (Sophy), Herbert Prior (Mr. Frisby), T. Roy Barnes (Mr. Kidd), Edward Dillon (Mr. Thutt), Alice Moe (Miss Ambrose), Gwen Lee (Manicurist), Lee Kohlmar (Peddler), Greta Granstedt (Fanny Lee), Roscoe Ates (Bit part).

## Plot

Marie Jones and Polly Smith are both proprietors of boarding houses on opposite corners of the street in New York. Marie, a widow of a gambler, is conservative and has a daughter, Genevieve. Polly, a take-a-chance type, has a son William, who is in a budding romance with Genevieve. Polly decides to try her luck at the stock market and becomes rich. She does not convince Marie to follow her example, and the two ladies quarrel, causing a divide between Genevieve and William. Polly takes her son to the seaside, and while away Marie decides to try her luck on Wall Street. Marie buys stocks in American Cheese and becomes successful. Marie and her daughter visit the same seaside resort as Polly and her son, but the fighting continues, and William becomes engaged to a stage star. Just as the marriage is about to take place, the stock market crashes, and the two mothers are united in grief. The actress ditches William and the two young lovers are reunited.

(From left) Charles Morton, Polly Moran, Marie Dressler and Anita in *Caught Short* (MGM, 1930).

## *Behind the Scenes*

*Caught Short* was the first of three films that Anita made with the comedy team Marie Dressler and Polly Moran. The veteran actresses had been successfully paired in *The Callahans and the Murphys*, *Bringing up Father*, *The Hollywood Revue*, and *Chasing Rainbows*. That same year, Dressler won a Best Actress Academy Award for her portrayal in *Min and Bill* opposite another frequent costar, Wallace Beery.

Cosmopolitan Productions, the corporation of Anita's friend, newspaper mogul William Randolph Hearst, produced *Caught Short* which began filming on January 28, 1930. The story was based on an Eddie Cantor gag-book; however, when Fred Whitbeck, MGM's publicist, previewed the finished film, he told Thalberg that it was a "criminal waste of talent of a grand old lady, Marie Dressler." Critics agreed; however, the theater-going public did not.[80]

When Thalberg asked Whitbeck how *Caught Short* was performing at Loew's State, Whitbeck resolutely replied that it "broke records." The film opened to sensational box-office success: with an investment of $171,000, the film grossed $1,027,000. Crowds equaled those of *Anna Christie*'s opening. The *Detroit Times* reported: "Never such a riotous comedy. Miss it and you'll regret it to your dying day." Audiences' responses declared Dressler and Moran the greatest comedy team of many years.[81]

While Dressler was pleased with the film's financial success, she too was uncertain about *Caught Short*'s contemporary humor aimed at the stock-market disaster, believing there was a place "for the *Caught Shorts* of the industry; but there's a bigger need for the real stories that people live."[82]

## Reviews

"Marie Dressler makes this picture, although the comedy material given her is sometimes thin. Polly Moran is also good, as a rival boarding-housekeeper, and Charles Morton and Anita Page are good as their two children."—*The Picturegoer*, January 1931 [UK].

"Anita Page, Charles Morton, Herbert Prior and many other clever players, including some attractive children do very well with scant material."—*The Bioscope*, May 28, 1930 [UK].

"Miss Page is attractive as the romantic Genevieve."—Mordaunt Hall, *New York Times*, June 21, 1930.

"Anita Page and Charles Morton are just a nice ingenue and juvenile couple, fitting nicely enough into the grooves assigned them."—*Inside Facts of Stage and Screen*, May 10, 1930.

# Our Blushing Brides

Metro-Goldwyn-Mayer Corp. (Loew's, Inc.)
A Harry Beaumont Production
1930

Tagline: "Shall They Become Blushing Brides or Girls Without Blushes?"

## Statistics

Sound (Western Electric Sound System) / Black & White / Melodrama. Runtime: 11 reels, 88 min. © Metro-Goldwyn-Mayer Distributing Corp, 7 Jul 1930, LP1439. New York premiere: Capitol Theater, week of August 1, 1930. Release date: August 1930.

## Prologues

Hollywood: Pantages Theatre. Fanchon and Marco's *Rhythm-A-Tic Idea* with the Georgia Lane dancers. Slim Martin offered a tuneful musical novelty with the orchestra.

New York: Capitol Theatre. The on-stage act, *The Invitation to the Dance*, created by Chester Hale, with Joyce Coles, Ivan Triersault, Carlo Ferretti, and the Capitol Ballet Corps, with newsreel.

## Credits

Directed by Harry Beaumont; dialogue and continuity by Bess Meredyth and John Howard Lawson; additional dialogue by Edwin Justus Mayer; titles by Helen Mainardi (uncredited); cinematography by Merritt Gerstad; art direction by Cedric Gibbons; edited by George Hively and Harold Palmer (uncredited); costumes by Adrian; sound by Douglas Shearer (recording director) and Russell Franks (recording engineer, uncredited); choreography by Albertina Rasch.

## Cast

Joan Crawford (Jerry March), Anita Page (Connie Blair), Dorothy Sebastian (Francine "Franky"), Robert Montgomery (Tony Jardine), Raymond Hackett (David Jardine), John Miljan (Martin "Marty" W. Sanders), Hedda Hopper (Mrs. Russ-Weaver), Albert Conti (Monsieur Pantoise), Edward Brophy (Joe Munsey), Robert Emmet O'Connor (the Detective), Martha Sleeper (Evelyn Woodforth), Gwen Lee (Dardanelle—a Mannequin), Mary Doran (Eloise—a Mannequin), Catherine Moylan (A Mannequin), Norma Drew (A Mannequin), Claire Dodd (A Mannequin), Walda Mansfield (A Mannequin), Polly Ann Young (A Mannequin), Ernie Alexander (Elevator Operator), Oscar Apfel (Floorwalker), Louise Beavers (Amelia—the Mannequins' Maid), Ann Dvorak (One of the "Quartet" of Models with Tony), Clarence Geldart (Store Manager), Mary Gordon (Mrs. Mannix), Maude Turner Gordon (Mrs. Daniels Jardine), Sherry Hall (Theater Patron Behind Jerry), Doris Lloyd (Miss Hartley), Jacques Lory (Andre), Wilbur Mack (Flirting Customer with Cane), David Mir (Emile), Broderick O'Farrell (Dr. Foster), Sarah Padden (Mrs. Hinkle), Leo White (Gaston).

## Plot

Three shop girls share an apartment and work together at Jardine's department store. Francine meets Martin, a customer who spends extravagantly and asks her out on a date. Connie has a romance with David Jardine, a son of the store owner. Tony, the eldest son of the Jardine family, admires Jerry, lead model in a fashion show. After the show she goes with

**Joan Crawford consoles Anita in a scene from *Our Blushing Brides* (MGM, 1930; courtesy Richard Adkins).**

him to his "nest." Cautiously Jerry escapes and scorns Tony as a wild boy. Connie moves to a plush apartment financed by David, whom she is now engaged to. Tony still pursues Jerry, but she turns down his advances. Francine marries Martin, who turns out to be a thief, and Francine is subsequently arrested. While visiting a cinema, Jerry spies David with a society girl and overhears that they are to be married. Jerry visits Connie to break the news, and they both return to the boarding house, where heartbroken Connie commits suicide. Realizing that Tony is a good man, Jerry accepts his proposal and they later marry.

### Behind the Scenes

In 1930, the studio tried a third installment of the "jazz baby" series with the all-talking—and most expensive of the trio—*Our Blushing Brides*. In this one, Dorothy Sebastian rejoined Anita and Crawford, adding Robert Montgomery. Anita recalled a running joke on the set, saying, "I used to laugh and say that we're going to be *Our Galloping Grandmothers* at the rate we're going."[83]

Unusual features of the film included a spectacular fashion show held in the gardens of a Long Island estate and an Albertina Rasch ballet, filmed at night. The ballet sequence required a six-week training course in Greek dancing by Joan Crawford.

*Our Blushing Brides* was a hit and turned in a profit of $412,000, the highest of the three films. *Film Daily* described it as "another of those pretty screen stories made for the shop-girl vote…" Another film reviewer thought a better title would be *Our Dizzy Divorcees*. Fortunately, that title was not necessary since this would be the last film incarnation.[84]

### Reviews

"Dorothy Sebastian as Francine is excellent and so is Anita Page as the blond Connie."—*New York Times*, August 2, 1930.

"As usual in these pictures, Miss Page seems to be the outshining brightener. She hasn't as much footage as the moralizing Miss Crawford, but her role is the more colorful of the two. As in both earlier pictures, she is the weaker character. She takes the glitter for gold and eventually manages to lend a heart throb to the story."—Edwin Schallert, *Los Angeles Times*, August 4, 1930.

# *The Little Accident*

### Universal Pictures Corp.
### 1930

Tagline: "Imagine his embarrassment! The stork arrives … just before the wedding! Oh, sweet baby daze. What a situation!"

## The Little Accident

### Statistics
Sound (Movietone) (also Silent) / Black & White / 35mm / Comedy-Drama. Runtime: 9 reels, 7,897 ft. (silent, 7,289 ft.), 82 min. © Universal Pictures Corp., 2 Aug 1930, LP1455. Production date: May 20, 1930. New York premiere, August 1, 1930. Release date: September 1, 1930.

### Credits
Produced by Carl Laemmle, Jr.; associate producer, Albert De Mond; directed by William James Craft; screenplay by Gladys Lehman, based on the play *The Little Accident* by Floyd Dell and Thomas Mitchell (New York, October 9, 1928), and the novel *An Unmarried Father* by Floyd Dell (New York, 1927); dialogue by Anthony Brown; cinematography by Roy Overbaugh; edited by Harry W. Lieb; supervising editor, Maurice Pivar; art direction by Walter R. Koessler; costume design by Johanna Mathieson; recording supervisor, C. Roy Hunter; synchronization and score by David Broekman.

### Cast
Douglas Fairbanks, Jr. (Norman), Anita Page (Isabel), Sally Blane (Madge), ZaSu Pitts (Monica), Joan Marsh (Doris), Roscoe Karns (Gilbert), Slim Summerville (Hicks), Henry Armetta (Rudolph Amendelara), Myrtle Stedman (Mrs. Overbeck), Albert Gran (Mr. Overbeck), Nora Cecil (Dr. Zernecke), Bertha Mann (Miss Hemingway), Gertrude Short (Miss Clark), Dot Farley (Mrs. Van Dine), Walter Brennan (Milkman), Grace Cunard (Nurse).

### Plot
On the morning of his wedding to Madge, Norman Overbeck receives a letter from a maternity hospital in Chicago. Fearing exposure, Norman visits the hospital and discovers that he is father to a three-week-old baby. His ex-wife Isabel has allowed the baby to be placed for adoption, but Norman disagrees and tries to persuade Isabel to keep the child. Without any luck, Norman smuggles the baby from the hospital and tries to raise the child himself. In desperation, Norman plans to marry Monica who is employed to look after the baby. Isabel decides she wants to keep her baby and searches for Norman. Though complications arise between her and his fiancée Madge, Norman's affections for the child prompt him and Isabel to try matrimony again.

### Behind the Scenes
Up to this point, MGM had refused to loan Anita to another studio—including Charlie Chaplin. However, since her falling out with Mayer over

(From left) Anita, Douglas Fairbanks, Jr., and Sally Blane in *Little Accident* (Universal, 1930).

her new contract, things changed for her at the studio. Carl Laemmle, Jr., whom she had been dating for two years, requested Anita for a Douglas Fairbanks, Jr., film he was producing. "They'd never loaned me out before," she recalled, "but now they gave me to Universal, put my name as number two, and people began to wonder. There was nothing I could do."[85]

# The Little Accident

Anita and Fairbanks were good friends and got along famously. Fairbanks was married to Joan Crawford at the time, but even though she was not around, Crawford's presence was clear on the set.

One day, Fairbanks received a telegram from Crawford. Upon reading it, he crumpled it and stormed off the set. Later, Anita learned that Joan was warning him to stay away from that "blonde siren" which confused her since her only feelings toward Fairbanks were friendly. Not long afterward, Crawford and Fairbanks were divorced.

In *The Little Accident*, Anita had a crying scene. She removed her mascara so it would not run and performed the scene with no problems. After it was over, she replaced her make-up. A few minutes later, Fairbanks had close-ups of the same scene, so Anita read her lines to him from behind the camera. Anita began crying again. Suddenly, Fairbanks let out a howl and began laughing. "What are you laughing at?" Anita sobbed.

"Look at yourself," he laughed. When the make-up girl brought a mirror, Anita looked in horror as her mascara was running. Fairbanks laughed as Anita cleaned her face.[86]

When *The Little Accident* completed filming, Anita did not see Fairbanks again until the Cinecon Film Festival held on Labor Day Weekend, 1993, at the Hollywood Roosevelt Hotel; both actors received lifetime achievement awards. Afterward, they met in the lobby. "Anita, you're still beautiful," Fairbanks whispered as he kissed her on the cheek. The two talked briefly about the old days and Anita sat on his lap to the delight of the fans who gathered to watch and take photographs.[87]

*The Little Accident* was a slickly-produced light comedy, fairly amusing in spots, but it was a film that some critics said was not worth traveling far to see. The dialogue was also not exciting, with the liveliness lowered by the necessity of keeping outside the range of Will Hays' censors. Yet other critics called the dialogue bright with capable acting, thoroughly amusing entertainment.[88]

## Reviews

"Mr. Fairbanks does his best and acts as if he believes in 'Little Accident,' and the other members of the cast—from Anita Page down—are creditable in their roles."—*New York Times*, August 4, 1930.

"Anita Page has little to do but gains all the sympathy as the unhappy young mother."—*The Bioscope*, August 20, 1930 [UK]

# War Nurse

Metro-Goldwyn-Mayer Corp. (Loew's, Inc.)
1930

Tagline: "Now it is told! The woman's side of the war!"

## Statistics

Sound (Movietone) / Black & White / 35mm / Drama. Runtime: 9 reels, 7,333 ft., 79 min. © Metro-Goldwyn-Mayer Distributing Corp., 13 Nov 1930, LP1724. New York premiere, October 23, 1930. Release date: November 22, 1930.

## Prologues

Los Angeles: Loew's State. Eddie Peabody, The Band-Joy-Boy, performed, also Fanchon and Marco's *Gondoliers Idea*.

New York: Astor Theater. *Dogway Melody*, a comedy with dogs, was presented.

## Credits

Directed by Edgar Selwyn; scenario by Becky Gardiner; added dialogue by Joseph White Farnham; cinematography by Charles Rosher; art direction by Cedric Gibbons; edited by William LeVanway; wardrobe by René Hubert; costume jeweler, Eugene Joseff; recording engineer, Douglas Shearer.

## Cast

Robert Montgomery (Wally O'Brien), Anita Page (Joy), June Walker (Babs), Robert Ames (Robin), ZaSu Pitts (Cushie), Marie Prevost (Rosalie), Helen Jerome Eddy (Kansas), Hedda Hopper (Matron), Edward Nugent (Frank), Martha Sleeper (Helen), Michael Vavitch (Doctor), James Bush, (Frank and Wally's Buddy), Ann Dvorak (Nurse in VA Hospital), Louis Mercier (Wounded French Soldier), John Miljan (French Medical Officer), Sandra Ravel (French Chanteuse).

## Plot

A group of American women enlist as nurses in France during World War I. Seeking romance and adventure, Barbara "Babs" Whitney and friends arrive in France to find the realities of the war. A young woman named Joy leaves a convent and joins the group, working within a makeshift

**With Robert Ames in *War Nurse* (MGM, 1930).**

hospital; the nurses' days and nights are spent looking after wounded soldiers. Romance blossoms for Babs and Joy when they meet aviator Wally and soldier Robin. Wally is captured on a solo flight over Germany. Robin and Joy become engaged before Robin leaves for duty. Joy finds out Robin has a wife and transfers to a hospital near Paris. Disillusioned, she gets drunk and sleeps with a married soldier. Ordered to return to America in case of scandal, Joy instead flees to Babs and begs to keep working as a nurse. There she meets Robin on his deathbed, who confirms his true love for her. An air raid destroys the hospital, and Joy collapses in a nearby barn. Shortly after giving birth, Joy dies, and Babs looks after the baby. A few years later, she reunites with Wally and they take Joy's son as their own.

## Behind the Scenes

*War Nurse* was based on an anonymous work about a group of female volunteers for nursing duty in France during the Great War (World War I). For unknown reasons, Anita replaced Loretta Young mid-way through the film. Costars included Robert Montgomery, ZaSu Pitts and Robert Ames who, not unlike his character in the film, developed quite a crush on his blonde costar. At the end of the workday, he would escort Anita to her home to make sure she arrived safely.[89]

*War Nurse* was the first Hollywood assignment for stage actress June Walker and the second film production for Edgar Selwyn. It was also a reunion for Walker and Selwyn, whose association as star and producer in the Broadway show *Gentlemen Prefer Blondes* was one of the most successful productions of the recent theatrical season.

Shelling a war hospital and staging an airplane machine gun attack on a column of trucks and ambulances were two of the main technical problems during production. In one scene, heavy powder was used in the stunt with the charges blowing huge holes in the walls of a ruined church. Many of the extras were war veterans, some missing arms or legs, and were unable to move quickly from the shelling and bursting walls.

In one part of the set, Anita was standing within three feet of a section which explodes. Fortunately, she was not hurt by flying particles, protecting her head with her arms, but an extra some distance away was struck and injured on the chest and arms.

On a more pleasant note, singer Lawrence Tibbett was filming *New Moon* on another sound stage and visited the *War Nurse* set. He began joking with Hedda Hopper, and a moment developed into an imitation love scene in which Tibbett sang love lyrics, culled from various operas. Anita and the cast gathered around and were treated to an impromptu concert.

Despite the $600,000 budget, critics noted that used stock footage from *The Big Parade* was used, but it was the poorly-written script that made *War Nurse* Anita's first real flop of her career.

At the film's end, Anita's character is pregnant and dies giving birth during a bombing raid. This was the second picture where she bears an illegitimate child and the third where she dies at the film's finale. Critics noticed that Anita was becoming the personification of wronged womanhood. *Variety* wrote: "Miss Page is again ruined and dies ... this repeat routine for Miss Page unquestionably gives her filmdom's record mileage on the wayward path. It's gotten so that patrons know what this girl must go through as soon as they see her on a screen."[90]

Anita delivered two unintentional laughs in the film; the first was when, in her hysteria, she said she wanted her mother, and the other was when June Walker brought in the baby and said to Anita, "This is your son." However, most critics agreed that the blame lay in the dialogue and sloppy editing. In fact, critics praised her performance in an otherwise dreadful film.

*The Herald Tribune* remarked: "It is the misfortune of Miss Anita Page that it was chiefly her scenes which caused last night's discourtesy; but it would be entirely unfair to blame her for that. As a matter of fact, she provides, in the role of the innocent girl nurse, who is, as they say, taken advantage of, so fine and touching a performance that she strikes an effective blow on behalf of cinema trained players."[91]

Despite the negative reviews, Anita enjoyed working on *War Nurse*. "The role was exacting," she said, "like all good ones. The story tells of the woman's part in the war, which hadn't been touched on until now. The nurse group in the film include several different types of girls. I liked ZaSu Pitts's work especially well."[92]

## Reviews

"Anita Page, who has the role of the erring girl, is hardly equal to the situation when registering hysterical outbursts at the horror of the situation."—*The Bioscope*, December 17, 1930 [UK].

"It is a Hollywood conception of nurses and the World War, something written to give Anita Page a chance to reveal her attractive presence."—Mordaunt Hall, *New York Times*, October 24, 1930.

"In this highly emotional and difficult part, the attractive player [Anita] gives a rather surprising performance. She suffers heartbreak and dies in first rate fashion."—*Standard Union*, October 30, 1930.

"Anita Page, as the junior nurse, is at her best in a role that provides greater range than any of the others…"—*Picture Play Magazine*, January 1931.

# *Reducing*

Metro-Goldwyn-Mayer Corp. (Loew's, Inc.)
1931

Tagline: "There's Too Much Waste in their Waist Lines!"

## Statistics

Sound (Western Electric Sound System) / Black & White / 35mm / Comedy-Drama. Runtime: 8 reels, 75 or 77 min. © Metro-Goldwyn-Mayer Distributing Corp., 12 Jan 1931, LP1881. Production date: October to mid November 1930. Release date: January 3, 1931.

## Prologues

Los Angeles: Loew's State. A troupe of trim, clean-cut German acrobats.

New York: Capitol Theatre. "Crinolines," stage show, with Hyde and Burrell, Andrew and Louise Carr, Yvette Rugel, Joyce Coles, and a newsreel.

### *Credits*

Directed by Charles F. Reisner; assistant director, Sandy Roth (uncredited); dialogue continuity by Willard Mack and Beatrice Banyard; additional dialogue by Robert E. Hopkins and Zelda Sears; cinematography by Leonard Smith; art direction by Cedric Gibbons; edited by William LeVanway; wardrobe by René Hubert; recording director, Douglas Shearer; Eugene Joseff (costume jeweler).

### *Cast*

Marie Dressler (Marie Truffle), Polly Moran (Polly Rochay), Anita Page (Vivian Truffle), Lucien Littlefield (Elmer Truffle), Buster Collier, Jr. (Johnnie Beasley), Sally Eilers (Joyce Rochay), William Bakewell (Tommy Haverly), Billy Naylor (Jerry Truffle), Jay Ward (Marty Truffle), Roscoe Ates (Stuttering Ticket Agent), Sidney Bracey (Beasley's Butler), Jules Cowles (Man on Train with Big Mustache), Edward Dillon (Train passenger), Bobby Dunn (Train Station Extra), Herbert Prior (Man on Ticket Line in a Hurry), George Reed (Train Porter).

### *Plot*

Polly Rochay owns a prominent beauty parlor in New York and invites her penniless sister Marie and family to stay, supplying a job for Marie at the parlor. Polly's daughter Joyce is engaged to Johnnie Beasley, a young millionaire. Marie's daughter Vivian has a boyfriend back home in Indiana who wishes to marry her. Johnnie and Vivian become acquainted and soon begin to date. A confrontation between the two daughters creates a family rift and Polly orders Marie and her family to leave. Johnnie continues to date Vivian, but one night Joyce visits her aunt Marie and explains that she is pregnant with Johnnie's baby. Marie orders Johnnie to marry Joyce, and Vivian reconciles with boyfriend Tommy. Learning the truth, Polly visits Marie on Thanksgiving and the two sisters embrace.

### *Behind the Scenes*

According to director Charles Reisner, writers searched for a story which would be a worthy successor to *Caught Short*. The search ended when MGM executives read the synopsis of *Reducing*, about the happenings in a weight-loss salon for excess avoirdupois.[93]

Dressler had returned from a European vacation and Moran from the Mt. Clemmons, Michigan, baths where she went to cure an intestinal ailment.[94]

Anita (left) with Marie Dressler (center) and Polly Moran in *Reducing* (MGM, 1931).

Anita had completed *War Nurse* and planned to take a short vacation when Dressler and Moran asked that she play the young girl lead in *Reducing*. This was the sixth film in which Anita appeared with Moran. "Oh, Polly was a fun gal," Anita told Dressler biographer Matthew Kennedy. "She and Marie had a certain magic together. They worked together like a dream."[95]

Once again, Anita played Dressler's daughter. Certain plot twists made it necessary for mother and daughter to look as much alike as possible. Dressler asserted that if one copied exactly the way another used their hands and eyes and how they walked, you could make people see a resemblance between the "fat lady and the living skeleton!" In *Reducing*, Dressler said that she imitated Anita's "eyes and the walk."

"Miss Page has a distinctive gait," Dressler stated, "but more important she widens her eyes in a very individual manner. By widening my eyes similarly, the illusion was created. Of course, Miss Page is much lighter, has no wrinkles, and is er—well, we won't say how many years younger, but by a few acting tricks it was possible to make myself resemble her sufficiently for the purposes of the story."[96]

Once again, critics did not see the humor of forcing Dressler into performing "grotesque slapstick," even though noting a genuine "laugh or two" sandwiched between "reels of stale wheezes," but in the end they admitted that it was only fair to report that the laughter which greeted *Reducing* was "prolonged and loud."[97]

### Reviews

"…the Dressler-Moran duo have a hilarious time. Assisting them in carrying out the love side of the piece are four very personable young players, Anita Page, Sally Eilers, William Bakewell and 'Buster' Collier, Jr."—*Brownsville Herald*, February 13, 1931.

"Anita Page, who played the principal supporting role in *Caught Short*, is again seen in a prominent part…"—*Nevada State Journal*, March 8, 1931.

# *The Easiest Way*

Metro-Goldwyn-Mayer Corp. (Loew's, Inc.)
1931

Tagline: "A story that beggars description. A frank, fearless drama of a woman who sinned!"

### Statistics

Sound (Western Electric Sound System) / Black & White / 35mm / Drama. Runtime: 8 reels, 73 min. © Metro-Goldwyn-Mayer Distributing

Corp., 19 Feb 1931, LP1987. New York premiere: Capitol Theater, the week of February 27, 1931. Release date: February 7, 1931.

## Prologues

Los Angeles: Loew's State. Fanchon and Marco's *Submarine Idea*.
New York: Capitol Theatre. *Novelettes*, with Barton and Mann, the Chester Hale dancers, and others.

## Credits

Produced by Hunt Stromberg; directed by Jack Conway; assistant director, Al Shenberg and Robert A. "Red" Golden; screenplay adapted by Edith Ellis, based on the play *The Easiest Way* by Eugene Walter (New York, December 19, 1909); cinematography by John Mescall; art direction by Cedric Gibbons; edited by Frank Sullivan; gowns by René Hubert; sound by Douglas Shearer and Russell Franks.

## Cast

Constance Bennett (Laura Murdock), Adolphe Menjou (William Brockton), Robert Montgomery (Jack "Johnny" Madison), Anita Page (Peg Murdock Feliki), Marjorie Rambeau (Elfie St. Clair, Brockton Model), J. Farrell MacDonald (Ben Murdock), Clara Blandick (Agnes Murdock), Clark Gable (Nick Feliki, Laundryman), Hedda Hopper (Mrs. Clara Williams), Richard Bishop (Hotel Clerk), Lynton Brent (Brockton Associate), Noel Francis (Woman at Cook-Out), Jack Hanlon (Andy Murdock), John Harron (Chris Swoboda), Dell Henderson (Bud Williams), Charles Judels (Mr. Gensler), Elizabeth Ann Keever (Tillie Murdock), William H. O'Brien (Alfred, Brockton's Butler), Andy Shuford (Bobby Murdock), Michael Stuart (Office Boy), Francis Palmer Tilton (Artist).

## Plot

Growing up in a poor working-class family, shop girl Laura seeks a better life and decides not to marry the boy next door. Laura takes a job as a model and quickly catches the attention of her boss Brockton, soon becoming a "kept woman." Meanwhile, sister Peg marries hardworking laundry man Nick; they have a baby and settle down. Nick disapproves of Laura's lifestyle and makes it clear she is not welcome in their home, much to Peg's dismay. Problems arise when Laura falls in love with a young journalist named Jack. Jack leaves on a business trip, and Laura promises to leave her life of luxury and make good. Laura takes a job at a department store but is unable to pay her hotel bills and reluctantly goes back to Brockton. After a long business trip, Jack returns to marry Laura, but Brockton makes sure Jack finds out the truth. Heartbroken, Jack leaves her. Laura turns up

**Anita (right) with Constance Bennett in *The Easiest Way* (MGM, 1931).**

uninvited at Peg's home during Christmas. Nick realizes that Laura has returned to her roots and welcomes her in.

### Behind the Scenes

*The Easiest Way* was based on Eugene Walter's 1909 play and took several years to finally get to the screen. Between 1927 and 1930, First National, David O. Selznick, Joseph Schenck and one of the DeMille brothers all expressed an interest in bringing the play to the screen.

The problem was that it was a touchy story line, especially since the newly formed Hays Office was checking the content of every film coming out of Hollywood. After First National bought the rights in 1927, Jason S. Joy of the AMPP wrote to producer David Fink to convince him not to produce it. "If the story is not already on the list of unacceptable material, it ought to be," Joy wrote to Fink.

Fink was confused as to why *Sadie Thompson* could be produced and not *The Easiest Way*, since both films dealt with similar subject matter. Fink eventually abandoned the project after the Hays Office warned that his film could run into "censorship problems."[98]

Universal bought the story and offered it to William de Mille, who refused after speaking with Will Hays about the play. Later, another producer bought the rights and received a letter from a Hays Office official: "It would be best if you did not undertake a thing which other responsible companies have already decided would not be good for the industry."[99]

A similar letter went out to Fox when they bought the rights. When Pathé inquired about the property, the Hays Office insinuated that the cost-conscious studio would lose money because no theater would run it.

Next, Columbia rejected it after the Hays Office insisted that they change the title and make other changes to bring the story into conformity with the Producers Code. Finally, MGM bought the property and gave an adaptation to the Hays Office. They also received resistance from the censor and in a letter to Irving Thalberg wrote, "The trouble with the [MGM] adaptation is that it builds up audience sympathy for Laura Murdock and supplies her with the means of securing sympathetic excuses for, if not actual approval of, her weakness of character. Also, this adaptation is much more dangerous than the original play, which for a long time has itself been considered dangerous motion picture material ... and did not go far enough in building up the idea that Laura is being punished."[100]

To placate the Hays Office, producer Hunt Stromberg promised to revise the screenplay. "We will insert a scene," Stromberg informed the Hays Office, "in which Laura makes it plain that the life she has been leading has been hideous, destructive, shameful and unhappy."[101]

Because of Thalberg's influence, the Hays Office relented and made no further objections. Production began on December 4, 1930, with Constance Bennett cast in the role of Laura Murdock. Thalberg cast Anita as Bennett's sister Peg who marries Nick, the local laundryman, at her parents' insistence, because he makes a good living.

Clark Gable, who recently signed with MGM, was given the role of Nick. *The Easiest Way* was his first film for the studio and Anita Page was his first leading lady. "I thought he was charming," Anita recalled. "but there was never in my mind any romantic feeling. People can't understand that, but he just wasn't my type."[102]

Well, if he was not Anita's type, he was for many girls in the audience and at the studio where executives originally laughed at his big ears. However, after the film opened, there was something about his screen persona that caused people on the lot to whisper: "There goes what's-his-name from *The Easiest Way*."[103]

When the film previewed at Glendale's Alex Theater, Thalberg stood outside and asked people as they were leaving how they liked "that new fellow that plays the brother-in-law." From audience reaction, Thalberg told studio executives: "We've got ourselves a new star!"[104]

Gable befriended Anita and her mother, whom he doted on. Every

**Clark Gable's first leading lady. Clark Gable and Anita as a young married couple in *The Easiest Way* (MGM, 1931).**

morning he stopped by Anita's dressing room to greet her mother. "How nice to see you again, Mrs. Pomares," he would say, then talk with her while Anita prepared for that day's filming. Gable's attention made him a favorite of Mrs. Pomares.

Once he offered to drive Anita and her mother home, but because she had her car and a chauffeur at the studio, she politely refused. Word spread around the studio that Anita had turned down Clark Gable. People taunted her: "There goes the girl that said 'no' to Clark Gable!"

"He just wanted to give me a ride home, not marry me!" Anita protested.[105]

Whenever Gable had not seen Anita for more than two weeks, he would ask someone, "Where's Anita Page?" In 1953, when he was making *Mogambo*, Gable told a reporter: "Grace Kelly reminds me of my first leading lady, Anita Page."[106]

"Of course, I loved Grace Kelly," Anita said, "so that didn't hurt my feelings at all!"[107]

Anita's experience with Constance Bennett was a little more disconcerting. She had met Bennett on several occasions and at one point went on a diet so she could "eat cream cheese and nut sandwiches like Connie Bennett."[108]

For her part as the plain sister, director Jack Conway had Anita wear no make-up except for face powder. Even with minimal make-up, Anita was stunning. After seeing the previous day's rushes, Bennett asked Anita, "Are you sure you're not wearing makeup?" Then she wiped her hand over Anita's face. When she saw that she was only wearing powder, Bennett left without saying a word.[109]

*The Easiest Way* received mixed reviews by the critics, yet some described it as the best translation of a play-to-the-screen they ever saw. *Variety* wrote: "A solid piece of screen production containing all the strong story appeal of the stage play and with a world of splendid touches that were not possible in a stage presentation and that in the new form enhance the original. Quite as strong in appeal is the prestige of its players ... [including] Anita Page, in the minor sister part, completes a flawless aggregation."[110]

Columbia head Harry Cohn was furious that the Hays Office had prevented them from producing the film by forcing changes to the script including the title while allowing MGM to make only minimal changes. They complained to Will Hays' office that Cohn was "incensed because he had his heart set at the time on making *The Easiest Way*."[111]

While the film received complimentary reviews in the United States, it was different in other parts of the globe. Censor boards in Ireland, Nova Scotia, and Alberta rejected *The Easiest Way*. Because the film had to be edited in Alberta to meet their standards, the chief censor wrote: "The film had been cut so badly to try to make it decent ... that we had to stop in the middle of it, because we thought we were looking at the wrong reels."[112]

## *Reviews*

"A solid piece of screen production containing all the strong story appeal of the stage play and with a world of splendid touches that were not possible in a stage presentation and that in the new form enhance the original."—*Variety*, March 4, 1931.

"Clark Gable, as the brother in law, and Anita Page, as the sister, handle their respective roles capably."—*New York Morning Telegraph*, March 2, 1931.

"Anita Page is charming as the heroine's respectable little sister."—*Standard Union*, February 28, 1931.

"Anita Page, always a good actress, makes a real character of the heroine's sister..."—*New York Herald-Tribune*, February 28, 1931.

"Clark Gable and Anita Page are likewise tangible assets."—*New York Sun*, February 28, 1931.

# Gentleman's Fate

Metro-Goldwyn-Mayer Corp. (Loew's, Inc.)
1931

Tagline: "Once a Gentleman.... Always a Gentleman? Or Turned into a Bum Overnight?"

## Statistics

Sound (Western Electric Sound System) / Black & White / 35mm / Drama. Runtime: 10 reels, 90 or 93 min. © Metro-Goldwyn-Mayer Distributing Corp., 19 Feb 1931, LP1991. Production date: November 24, 1930. Release date: March 7, 1931.

## Credits

Produced by Harry Rapf (uncredited); directed by Mervyn LeRoy; dialogue continuity by Leonard Praskins, based on the short story "A Gentleman's Fate" by Ursula Parrott in *Household* (Mar-Jul 1931); cinematography by Merritt Gerstad; art direction by Cedric Gibbons; edited by William S. Gray; wardrobe by René Hubert; recording director, Douglas Shearer.

## Cast

John Gilbert (Jack Thomas aka Giacomo Tomasulo), Louis Wolheim (Frank Tomasulo), Leila Hyams (Marjorie Channing), Anita Page (Ruth Corrigan), Marie Prevost (Mabel), John Miljan (Florio), George Cooper (Mike), Ferike Boros (Angela), Ralph Ince (Dante), Frank Reicher (Francesco), Paul Porcasi (Papa Mario Giovanni), Tenen Holtz (Tony), Sam Appel (Waiter at Banquet), Leila Bennett (Lunch Counter Attendant), James Dime (Mug at Peace Banquet), Edward LeSaint (Detective Meyers), Dick Rush (Detective), Harry Tenbrook (Lunch Room Customer).

## Plot

Jack, a gentleman, discovers his father and brother are both gangsters and takes the blame for a necklace stolen by the duo. Disillusioned, his society fiancée breaks their engagement. Jack soon becomes a bootlegger with his brother, but disaster strikes when a rival gang member is murdered. The gang sends a beautiful moll named Ruth to uncover Jack's hiding place. Jack treats Ruth like a lady and she soon reveals her identity. The rival gang traps Ruth but during a shootout both the gang leader and Jack are

Gangster's moll Anita with John Gilbert in *Gentleman's Fate* (MGM, 1931).

fatally wounded. After Jack's death, his brother and Ruth both vow to leave the racket.

## Behind the Scenes

Film historians have suggested that Louis B. Mayer produced *Gentleman's Fate* as a punishment for several actors who had crossed him, including John Gilbert and Anita Page. Both were assigned to this gangster potboiler, along with Louis Wolheim, Leila Hyams, and Marie Prevost.

The studio borrowed Mervyn LeRoy from Warner Bros. to direct *Gentleman's Fate* which was based on Ursula Parrott's short story that appeared in *Household* magazine.

The Hays Office protested after reading the script, warning the studio that the Code would not allow representations of police officers as friends of gangsters. They also pointed out that the script made gangland activities too attractive and suggested they cut the police from the script entirely.

Anita and John Gilbert became friends during filming and would have lunch together in his bungalow. "Jack was very trustworthy," Anita recalled. "He was a gentleman. I knew the people I could trust. He never once tried anything."

During their long conversations, Gilbert never mentioned Garbo, but he did speak of Virginia Bruce, with whom he was having an affair at the time. "I felt so sad for him," she said, "but I think he was happy with Virginia Bruce. He loved to tell me about how happy John Barrymore was with Dolores Costello."

According to Anita, in one scene, Gilbert had to cry. Anita was intrigued. She had never seen a man cry so profusely on cue before. "Jack, little girls are allowed to cry, but little boys aren't supposed to," she told him. "How in the world can you just lie down and cry buckets?"

"If the scene plays false and I don't believe it, I can't," he told her. "But if it plays true, I can do it every time."[113]

Critics were not kind to *Gentleman's Fate*, blaming the story and author, Ursula Parrott. *Variety* wrote: "Miss Parrott seems capable of writing for women, like Norma Shearer and that style of stuff, but she's a flop for men, if this is Miss Parrott's best. With the story of *Gentleman's Fate* reeling off the sheet as though Miss Parrott had no idea of what she was doing from the silly start to the bad finish. While the base of the story is so ridiculously worked out the players in the film must have wondered at its dumbness."[114]

MGM premiered the film at Warner's Strand instead of their own Capitol Theater, eight months after it opened in the rest of the country.

In earlier films, Gilbert's voice had soprano qualities at which "fans giggled." However, critics agreed that *Gentleman's Fate* proved that Gilbert's voice was adequate. "The talker brings out that Gilbert is all right on the audible screen if the story is right," one critic wrote, but went on to say that the film was "little good otherwise."[115]

Unfortunately, or fortunately, critics ignored Anita. *Variety*'s only note was "Other performances okay. Leila Hyams and Anita Page provide plenty of looks for one picture."[116]

## Reviews

"This is a picture for adults who like action melodramas and gangster stories. Not for children up to 20. The ending may have a depressing effect, but generally it marks a step in Gilbert's march back to popularity. Not suitable for Sunday nights in small towns."—*Harrison's Reports*, March 14, 1931.

"We do not hear much of John Gilbert these days, but if he can act well as he does in this picture it is a great pity."—*The Picturegoer Weekly*, October 10, 1931 [UK].

# *Sidewalks of New York*

Metro-Goldwyn-Mayer Corp. (Loew's, Inc.)
A Buster Keaton Production
1931
Tagline: "Nothing but laughs!"

## Statistics

Sound (Western Electric Sound System) / Black & White / 35mm / Comedy-Drama. Runtime: 8 reels, 70–71 min. © Metro-Goldwyn-Mayer Distributing Corp., 21 Sep 1931, LP2490. Production date: mid–May to mid–June 1931. New York opening, Loew's Eighty-Third and 175th Street Theaters, November 11, 1931. Release date: September 26, 1931.

## Prologue

Los Angeles: Los Angeles Theater. Performers included the Hubbard Sisters, Traver and Gary, Decker and Van Epps, and the Royal Cascoynes. Babe Egan's Orchestra supplied the music.

## Credits

Directed by Jules White and Zion Myers; assistant director Bob Barnes (uncredited); story by George Landry and Paul Gerard Smith; dialogue by Robert E. Hopkins, Eric Hatch and Willard Mack (uncredited); cinematography by Leonard Smith; art direction by Cedric Gibbons; edited by Charles Hochberg and Basil Wrangell (uncredited); recording director, Douglas Shearer.

**Anita tries to free Buster Keaton while Cliff Edwards (holding Keaton's arm) and Syd Saylor look on in *The Sidewalks of New York* (MGM, 1931).**

## Cast

Buster Keaton (Harmon), Anita Page (Margie), Cliff Edwards (Poggle), Frank Rowan (Butch), Norman Phillips, Jr. (Clipper), Frank LaRue (Sergeant), Oscar Apfel (Judge), Syd Saylor (Mulvaney), Clark Marshall (Lefty), Ann Brody (Tenement Mother), Bobby Burns (Attorney), Monte Collins (James—Harmon's Chauffeur), Drew Demorest (Dresser), Harry Strang (Cop), Jerry Tucker (Little Boy Sitting on Curb), Dorothy Vernon (Tenement Woman in Window), Harry Wilson (One of Butch's Henchmen), Robert Winkler (Little Boy), Clifton Young (Street Gang Member).

## Plot

A philanthropist millionaire named Harmon opens a gym for the poor boys of New York's east side. With the support of Margie, one boy's big sister, he tries to help the boys stay out of trouble. A petty criminal persuades the boy to steal and murder Harmon, but after he loses his nerve and refuses, the boy makes good and Harmon confesses his love for Margie.

## Behind the Scenes

The studio reportedly forced Buster Keaton to make *Sidewalks of New York* under protest. "I knew before the camera was put up for the first scene that it was practically impossible to get a good motion picture," Keaton said. However, it was his most commercially successful film.[117]

Anita was not privy to the backstage monkeyshines between Keaton and the studio, but enjoyed collaborating with comedians, particularly Buster Keaton. "One can always learn so much in comedy," she said. "In the first place, comedy is so scientifically timed or spaced in every detail that one can pick up hundreds of little ideas in timing that are invaluable in straight roles. Mr. Keaton is specially [sic] good at this—and to watch him work is a revelation."[118]

MGM had an elaborate street set built on the back lot specifically for *The Sidewalks of New York* using film and still photographs of New York tenements, and close-ups of sections of walls, to perfectly reproduce the structures.

To promote the film, the publicity department had Anita posing with assorted items to then tie to local businesses to promote not only the film but also the exhibitors' own products, using the photos in window displays, from Sunkist oranges, to radios, watches, and clothing, among other goods.

Anita considered Keaton an immense talent: "In order to be as great a comedian as Keaton was, I think you have to be born with something like that in you. I don't think it's something you just acquire. He was just so funny! We don't have anyone today quite like my dear Buster. He was one of a kind, a real comic genius."[119]

Instead of premiering the film at MGM's flagship Capitol Theater as was usual, it quietly opened at Washington Heights Loew's 175th Street theater. The film was a financial success even though some critics, such as *Variety*, called it a "routine comedy" that was "so outdated, so elementary, that prospects for money are anything but bright." *Variety* was wrong.[120]

## Reviews

"A laugh a moment and just the right number of moments with 'dead pan' Buster Keaton, Cliff Edwards and Anita Page."—*Photoplay*, November 1931.

"*Sidewalks of New York* is packed with typical Keaton humor, usually uproarious, sometimes sly, sometimes sharply satirical."—*Los Angeles Times*, October 10, 1931.

"Buster Keaton fans will find this offering considerably below standard. There aren't many new gags in the story and the old ones just managed to get by."—*The Film Daily*, November 15, 1931.

# *Under Eighteen*

Warner Bros. Pictures, Inc.
The Vitaphone Corp.
1932

Tagline: "Too young to know better!"

## Statistics

Alternate title: *Poor Little Ritz Girl*. Sound / Black & White / 35mm / Melodrama. Runtime: 9 reels, 79–81 min. © Warner Bros. Pictures, Inc., 18 Dec 1931, LP2704. Production date: September 1931. Release date: January 2, 1932.

## Prologue

Los Angeles: Warner Bros. Hollywood Theater. Jess Stafford and his Brunswick Recording Orchestra, White & Stanley and other personalities.

## Credits

Directed by Archie Mayo; screenplay by Charles Kenyon and Maude Fulton (uncredited), based on the short story "Sky Life" by Frank Mitchell Dazey and Agnes Christine Johnston in *Everybody's Magazine* [October 1929]; dialogue by Charles Kenyon; cinematography by Barney McGill; art direction by Esdras Hartley; edited by George Marks; gowns by Earl Luick; Vitaphone Orchestra conductor, Leo F. Forbstein.

## Cast

Marian Marsh (Marge Evans), Anita Page (Sophie), Regis Toomey (Jimmie), Warren William (Raymond Harding), Emma Dunn (Mrs. Evans), Norman Foster (Alf), Joyce Compton (Sybil), J. Farrell MacDonald (Pop Evans), Claire Dodd (Babsy), Paul Porcasi (Francois), Maude Eburne (Mrs. Ged), Judith Vosselli (Miss Gray), Dorothy Appleby (Elsie), Lillian Bond (Penthouse Party Guest), Wade Boteler (Cop), Mary Doran (Lucille), Murray Kinnell (Walters), Walter McGrail (Gregg), Claude King (Doctor), Edward LeSaint (Minister at Wedding), Claire McDowell (Seamstress), Ben Taggart (Detective French), Edward Van Sloan (Assistant to Francois), Kathrin Clare Ward (Mrs. Howe), Renee Whitney (Model), Clarence Wilson (A.J. Dietrich).

Anita nags her lazy husband Norman Foster to get a job in *Under Eighteen* (Warner Bros., 1931).

## Plot

Seamstress Marge Evans is in love with truck driver Jimmie but worried their relationship will end up like her sister Sophie's disintegrating marriage. Sophie and her unemployed husband Alf move in with Marge and constantly fight. Marge envies the clear easy and glamorous lifestyle of the girls who model at work. One day Marge must model and though hesitant she soon meets playboy Raymond Harding. After Alf becomes physically abusive, Sophie seeks a divorce but cannot afford the legal fees. Marge swears off marriage for love, but Jimmie overhears and is crushed. Unsuccessful in her quest to raise the money for Sophie's divorce, Marge visits Raymond at his New York penthouse to seek financial help. Raymond offers his help and tries to seduce Marge, though he soon realizes Marge's plea is an honest one. A confrontation ensues when Jimmie arrives just in time to save Marge. Raymond still wishes to help but soon there is no need, as Sophie and Alf reconcile after he wins top prize in a pool tournament. Jimmie and Marge reunite and plan to marry.

## Behind the Scenes

In 1931, Warner Bros. borrowed Anita to play the sister of Marian

Marsh, a new star they were promoting. In the routine picture *Under Eighteen*, Anita's character, trapped in an unhappy marriage, screams hysterics at her lazy husband who will not look for a job. While the plot is predictable, Anita had her funny moments.

Norman Foster, who played her husband, was married to actress Claudette Colbert and asked Anita to join him at his apartment to share some lamb chops. "Thank you very much," she told Foster, "but I don't go up to young men's apartments for lamb chops or anything else."

"Why not?" Foster asked.

"Because you're married, that's why."

"Oh, that's an open marriage," he explained. Open marriage or not, Anita refused his request and went home.[121]

Warner Bros. released *Under Eighteen* without fanfare. At the time, Anita was again fighting a weight problem, which was noticed by *Variety*'s critic: "None of the cast looks any too well, from Marian Marsh, whose name is over the title in the press matter, but beneath on the lead screen caption, to the borrowed Anita Page, who is growing quite chubby."[122]

### Reviews

"The sexiness of the theme in this picture is overstressed and moreover, it is all rather pointless. On the other hand, the cast is a strong one and the presentation lavish and sensational in effect…. Anita Page, as the sister married to a worthless husband, is very good."—*Picturegoer Weekly*, May 28, 1932 [UK].

"Marian Marsh enlists some sympathy as the mainstay of her family but fails to rise to the occasion when action demands some display of dramatic force. Regis Toomey is the best of the cast as the long-suffering fiancé, while Warren William has little opportunity of showing his undoubted ability. Norman Foster is splendid as the husband, and Anita Page does her best as the unhappy wife."—*The Bioscope*, January 13, 1932 [UK].

"Anita Page, the financially-harassed sister, makes the most of her part…"—*Photoplay*, February 1932.

## *Are You Listening?*

### Metro-Goldwyn-Mayer Corp. (Loew's, Inc.)
### 1932

Tagline: "Don't touch that dial!"

## Are You Listening? 155

### Statistics
Sound (Western Electric Sound System) / Black & White / 35mm / Melodrama. Runtime: 8 reels, 73 or 76 min. © Metro-Goldwyn-Mayer Distributing Corp., 23 May 1932, LP3046. Production date: January 1932. Release date: March 21, 1932.

### Credits
Directed by Harry Beaumont; assistant director, Harold S. Bucquet (uncredited); adaptation by Dwight Taylor, based on the novel *Are You Listening?* by J.P. McEvoy (Boston, 1932); cinematography by Harold Rosson; art direction by Cedric Gibbons; edited by Frank Sullivan; recording director, Douglas Shearer.

### Cast
William Haines (Bill Grimes), Madge Evans (Laura O'Neil), Anita Page (Sally O'Neil), Karen Morley (Alice Grimes), Neil Hamilton (Jack Clayton), Wallace Ford (Larry Barnes), Jean Hersholt (George Wagner), Joan Marsh (Honey O'Neil), John Miljan (Ted Russell), Murray Kinnell (Carson), Ethel Griffies (Mrs. Peters), Donald Novis (Singer), Jack Baxley (Speakeasy Doorman), Herman Bing (Radio Actor), Wade Boteler (Gas Station Attendant), Truman Bradley (Radio Announcer), Louise Carter (Mrs. O'Neil), Charles Coleman (Butler), Frank Darien (Desk Clerk), Jesse De Vorska (Mr. Chutzpah), James Donlan (Butch), Charley Grapewin (Pierce), Ben Hall (Yokel with Ukulele), Lucien Littlefield (Fred), Jerry Mandy (Tony), Hank Mann (Hank), Hattie McDaniel (Aunt Fatima), Sam McDaniel (Prisoner at Train Station), Gene Morgan (Orchestra Leader), William H. O'Brien (Mike), Herbert Prior (Sponsor), Virginia Sale (Marjorie), Rolfe Sedan (Hotel Manager), Frank Whitbeck (Radio Announcer).

### Plot
Trapped in a loveless marriage, radio sketch writer Bill falls for radio presenter Laura but his nagging wife Alice denies him a divorce. Laura lives with sister Sally, a receptionist at the radio station, who spends her evenings dating rich older men, and younger sister Honey, who lands a role as a reporter. On Christmas Eve, Bill accidentally kills his estranged wife when she demands money. Wanted for murder, Bill goes on the run with Laura but is captured and sentenced to jail for manslaughter. After three years pass, Bill and Laura are free to marry.

### Behind the Scenes
Anita began 1932, her final year at MGM, working on *Are You Listening?*, the last film she made with William Haines and director Harry

**Anita in her last film with William Haines, *Are You Listening?* (MGM, 1932).**

Beaumont. Robert Montgomery was originally slated to play the lead, but Haines replaced him at the last minute. Haines was feeling pressure from Mayer to dump his companion, Jimmy Shields, and find a wife. In fact, it was during the making of *Are You Listening?* that Haines reportedly proposed marriage to Anita, a proposal which she turned down.[123]

Haines was slipping at the box office and he was no longer profitable; Mayer could drop him at any time. *Are You Listening?* was an attempt to rescue Haines' career, but it ended up being his last film at MGM.

The role of Haines' nagging wife, a role without sympathy, was shunned by most actresses on the lot. However, Karen Morley, who had small roles in *Mata Hari* and *Scarface*, begged for the part, saying, "I don't want sympathy. I want parts."[124]

Although *Are You Listening?* turned a small profit, the critics claimed that it screamed of a bad script, unimportant story, and spotty direction. It was unique only because it was the first of a series of films about the broadcast business, but critics declared it mediocre. *Variety* called Anita a "highly decorative eyeful," and proclaimed the picture overall as "one of those disagreeable messes."[125]

For Anita, the highlight was the performance of Hattie McDaniel, who had a small part as a singer. McDaniel later skyrocketed to fame as Mammy in *Gone with the Wind* and would be the first black performer to receive an Academy Award. "Hattie was wonderful," Anita recalled. "She was so fascinating to watch."[126]

## Reviews

"Madge Evans, Karen Morley and Anita Page were well chosen aside from their photographic contrast and gave excellent performances."—*Hollywood Filmograph*, February 27, 1932.

"Anita Page and Joan Marsh as Madge's [Evans] sisters are splendid."—*Photoplay*, May 1932.

"The picture on the whole is one of those disagreeable messes. Everybody is out to do dirt by each other."—*Variety*, April 26, 1932.

# *Night Court*

Metro-Goldwyn-Mayer Corp. (Loew's, Inc.)
1932

Tagline: "This is the Picture You Heard So Much About! This is the Picture You Want to See—"

## Statistics

Sound (Western Electric Sound System) / Black & White / 35mm / Melodrama. Runtime: 9 reels, 89 or 95 min. © Metro-Goldwyn-Mayer Distributing Corp., 22 Sep 1932, LP3262. Production date: mid–February to early March 1932. Release date: June 4, 1932.

## Prologues

Los Angeles: Loew's State. Fanchon and Marco's presentation of "Gus Edwards Radio Stars." Violinist Jan Rubini was guest conductor. Also showing was a Hal Roach comedy short, *Strictly Unreliable*, starring Thelma Todd and ZaSu Pitts.

New York: Capitol Theatre. The stage show "Hells' Belles" with Walter (Dare) Wahl, Cardini, Russell Hicks, the Chester Hale Dancers, and others.

## Credits

Directed by W.S. Van Dyke; assistant director, Jay Marchant (uncredited); screenplay by Bayard Veiller and Lenore Coffee, based on the unproduced play

*Night Court* by Mark Hellinger and Charles Beahan; cinematography by Norbert Brodine; art direction by Cedric Gibbons; edited by Ben Lewis; recording director, Douglas Shearer; sound by Ralph Shugart (uncredited).

## *Cast*

Phillips Holmes (Mike Thomas), Walter Huston (Judge Moffett), Anita Page (Mary Thomas), Lewis Stone (Judge William Osgood), Mary Carlisle (Elizabeth Osgood), John Miljan (Crawford), Jean Hersholt (Herman), Tully Marshall (Grogan), Noel Francis (Lil Baker), Rafaela Ottiano (Woman on Steps), Reginald Barlow (District Attorney Grant), Clarence Burton (Detective Madigan), Frederick Burton (Judge Oscar "Jim" Erskine), Eddy Chandler (Thug Beating Up Mike), George Cooper (Safecracking Thug), Henry Hall (Committee Man), DeWitt Jennings (Court Policeman), Lew Kelly (Mr. Davis), George Magrill (Strong Arm Man), Eily Malyon (Hungry Woman in Court), Eva McKenzie (Apartment House Tenant), Philip Morris (Court Policeman), Edmund Mortimer (Assistant District Attorney), Field Norton (Courtroom Observer), Warner Richmond (Ed), Dick Rush (Detective), Frank Sheridan (Thomas H. "Sam" Haskins), Charles Sullivan (Court Bailiff), Harry Wilson (Acquitted Truck Driver).

## *Plot*

Housewife Mary is framed and arrested for prostitution by Judge Moffett when he wrongly believes she is involved in Judge Osgood's team to clean up the city and convict him of corruption. Mary is sent to the county workhouse. Arriving home from work, Mary's husband Mike finds their baby alone. Mike learns of his wife's fate and pleads with Judge Moffett for Mary's release but instead their baby is taken into care. Visiting his wife in jail, Mike realizes Mary was framed. Soon after, Mike is set upon by Moffett's gang and forced on a ship bound for South America but escapes and swims to shore. Moffett's gang murders Judge Osgood. Wanted for murder, Mike captures Moffett and takes him to court. Moffett denies killing Osgood but confesses to Mary being innocent. The young couple are set free and reunited with their baby.

## *Behind the Scenes*

Just before her last confrontation with Mayer, the studio assigned her to a film which could arguably be the best performance of her career. *Night Court* included other top-rate talent such as director W.S. Van Dyke and actors Phillips Holmes and Walter Huston. She enjoyed working with Huston, whom she considered a "great actor." She believed that, when collaborating with gifted actors, "you get something very nice out of it. You admire the other person's talent."[127]

Framed housewife Anita is sentenced by Walter Huston in *Night Court* (MGM, 1932).

*Night Court* was based on an unproduced play by Mark Hellinger and Charles Beahan. Originally, Clark Gable was to play Anita's husband, but he was replaced by Phillips Holmes; similarly Huston substituted for Lionel Barrymore.

*Night Court* was historic in its expression of corrupt American legal practices but suffered from labored emotionalism and a sense of artificiality. The acting was good and the characters well drawn. Producer Paul Bern was touched by Anita's performance and told another executive, "When I saw this poor girl go to jail, I cried with the pity of it."[128]

## Reviews

"The characters are far more than mere puppets on a directorial string; they are portrayed with sufficient force to make them real people, who incur wholehearted hate or sympathy, as the case may be.... Anita Page is extremely moving and sympathetic as the victimized wife who is cruelly parted from her baby and thrown into prison."—*Film Weekly*, August 12, 1932 [UK].

Stars of the MGM film *Freaks*, Siamese twins Daisy and Violet Hilton visit the set of *Night Court* (MGM, 1932). (From left) Anita, Jean Hersholt, director W.S. Van Dyke, Daisy and Violet Hilton, Phillips Holmes, and Noel Francis.

"Anita Page is said to have given one of the finest portrayals of the season in the role of the wife."—*Los Angeles Herald and Express*, June 5, 1932.

# *Skyscraper Souls*

Metro-Goldwyn-Mayer Corp. (Loew's, Inc.)
A Cosmopolitan Production
1932
Tagline: "A Drama That Soars Halfway to Heaven and Reaches Half Way to Hell!"

## Statistics

Alternate title: *Skyscraper*. Sound (Western Electric Sound System) / Black & White / 35mm / Melodrama. Runtime: 10 reels, 80 or 90 min. © Metro-Goldwyn-Mayer Distributing Corp., 13 Oct 1932, LP3324. Production date: June 1932. Release date: July 16, 1932.

## Prologues

Los Angeles: Loew's State. Ben Turpin, Walter Hiers, and Snub Pollard performed in *Hollywood Slapstick Revue*. Music from *Irene* and two newsreels were on the program along with special Olympic-star introductions.

New York: Capitol Theatre. Ben Bernie, Morton Downey, Lillian Shade, Veloz & Yolanda, Gordon, Reed & King, and Milton Berle.

## Credits

Directed by Edgar Selwyn; assistant director, Cullen Tate (uncredited); dialogue continuity by Elmer Harris; adaptation by C. Gardner Sullivan, based on the novel *Skyscraper* by Faith Baldwin (New York, 1931); cinematography by William Daniels; art direction by Cedric Gibbons; edited by Tom Held; recording director, Douglas Shearer; sound by Fred R. Morgan (uncredited).

*Song*: "Metropolitan March" by Emil Frey.

## Cast

Warren William (David Dwight), Maureen O'Sullivan (Lynn Harding), Gregory Ratoff (Vinmont), Anita Page (Jenny LeGrande), Verree Teasdale (Sarah Dennis), Norman Foster (Tom), George Barbier (Charlie

Norton), Jean Hersholt (Jake Sorenson), Wallace Ford (Slim), Hedda Hopper (Ella Dwight), Helen Coburn (Myra), John Marston (Bill), Oscar Apfel (Brewster's Associate), Edward Brophy (Man in Elevator), Billy Gilbert (Second Ticket Agent), Boris Karloff (Man Approaching Ticket Counter), Tom Kennedy (Masseur), William Morris (Hamilton), Dennis O'Keefe (Stock Brokerage Clerk), Purnell Pratt (Harrington Brewster), John Ince (Elevator operator).

## *Plot*

A young secretary named Lynn falls for bank clerk Tom, but she is seduced at a penthouse party by David Dwight, the owner of the skyscraper. Dwight is having an extramarital affair with Sarah, the head of the building office, who is also Lynn's boss. Jenny is a model and prostitute working for a fashion house and is pursued by Jake, a diamond merchant. Myra is in a loveless marriage and relies on Jenny and radio presenter Slim for financial help. Dwight secures a financial deal to pay off a loan and own the building outright, but he double crosses the new partner. When Tom is given a tip off about the merger, he buys stocks in the bank as do many others in the building. When the stock market crashes, there are disastrous results for many of the skyscraper's workers. Sarah confronts Dwight about Lynn, and in doing so, shoots him. With Dwight dead, Sarah jumps to her death from the skyscraper. Jenny has lost her job and savings due to the crash and accepts a marriage proposal from Jake. Slim and Myra visit Jake and try to steal from his safe, but Slim gets locked in and suffocates. Myra meets her estranged husband by chance and leaves with him. Sometime later, Lynn returns to Tom and they reconcile.

## *Behind the Scenes*

*Skyscraper Souls* was based on the bestselling novel *Skyscraper* by Faith Baldwin. It is the story of the Dwight Building, the star of this first-rate production. *Variety* described it as a sort of "Grand Hotel in an office building."[129]

Eight months earlier, an entirely different cast was set to film *Skyscraper Souls*. Robert Young, Una Merkel and Madge Evans were assigned with Harry Beaumont as director, but when production began in June 1932, it had a new director, cast, and writers.

*Frankenstein* actor Boris Karloff was originally to make a cameo, but he was cut. He can, however, be seen briefly around the film's 20-minute mark as Norman Foster is leaving. One-time director in silent films John Ince (brother of Thomas Ince) has a bit part as the elevator operator.

(From left) Gregory Ratoff, Maureen O'Sullivan and Anita in *Skyscraper Souls* (MGM, 1932).

Although the role was routine, Anita put everything into it. The *New York Telegraph* said that Page "incidentally plays the floozy and steals those few scenes allotted to her."[130]

## Reviews

"Melodrama that sets out to probe the lives of the people in a skyscraper in much the same way as Grand Hotel reveals the life of a great hotel. The idea has not been fully developed, and the side issues are confusing, but there is good, all-around entertainment in this unusual picture. There are good performances in a minor key from Maureen O'Sullivan, Jean Hersholt and Anita Page."—*Film Weekly*, January 20, 1933 [UK].

"And of all things, Anita Page appears as a sort of model who capers around in sheer black undies and refers to her profession as 'the oldest in the world!' But since her speech doesn't sound quite convincing, as she says it, it is as if she is not sure of what it means, so it's all right."—*Picture Play Magazine*, October 1932.

# *Prosperity*

Metro-Goldwyn-Mayer Corp. (Loew's, Inc.)
A Sam Wood Production
1932

Tagline: "All the world's been waiting for *Prosperity*!"

### Statistics

Sound (Western Electric Sound System) / Black & White / 35mm / Comedy-Drama. Runtime: 9 reels, 76 or 87 min. © Metro-Goldwyn-Mayer Distributing Corp., 14 Nov 1932, LP3414. Production date: March 1932. Release date: November 18, 1932.

### Prologues

Los Angeles: Loew's State. A novelty film titled *Chill and Chills*, a travel talk about Russia, and a newsreel.

New York: Capitol Theatre. A comic who had a trick piano and adagio dancers in luminous costumes against a black background were featured. Abe Lyman and his musicians contributed along with Herb Williams, the Yacht Club Boys, Sheila Barrett, Gaston Palmer, and Starnes and Kover.

### Credits

Produced and directed by Sam Wood; screenplay by Zelda Sears and Eve Greene; story by Sylvia Thalberg and Frank Butler; contributing writers: Frances Goodrich, Leo McCarey (uncredited) and Ralph Spense (uncredited); continuity by Willard Mack (uncredited) and Zelda Sears (uncredited); cinematography by Leonard Smith; art direction by Cedric Gibbons; edited by William LeVanway; music by William Axt (uncredited); recording director, Douglas Shearer; sound by Fred R. Morgan (uncredited); casting by Benjamin Thau.

### Cast

Marie Dressler (Maggie Warren), Polly Moran (Lizzie Praskins), Anita Page (Helen Praskins Warren), Norman Foster (John Warren), John Miljan (Holland), Jacquie Lyn Dufton (Cissy), Jerry Tucker (Buster), Charles Giblyn (Mayor), Frank Darien (Ezra Higgins), Henry Armetta (Barber), John Roche (Knapp), Edward Brophy (Ice cream salesman), Billy Gilbert (Driver). Additional cast: Jack Baxley, Harry C. Bradley, James Bush, Claire

(From left) Polly Moran, Wallace Ford, Marie Dressler, and Anita in *Prosperity* (MGM 1932). *Prosperity* was reshot with Norman Foster replacing Wallace Ford in the completed version (courtesy Joseph Yranski).

Du Brey, Henry Hall, Edward LeSaint, Jack "Tiny" Lipson, James T. Mack, Jerry Mandy, Lee Phelps, Herbert Prior, Tiny Sanford, Nick Stewart, Carl Stockdale, Gertrude Sutton, Walter Walker.

## Plot

Maggie Warren is owner of the local bank. Her son John marries Helen, daughter of Lizzie Praskins. The two mothers fight and try to control their children's lives. After a row, Lizzie withdraws her savings from the bank, creating panic among the customers. Soon the entire town has withdrawn their savings, forcing Maggie to close. Maggie vows to reopen but learns that John has invested her money in a corrupt construction deal. Maggie sells and moves in with Lizzie and the newlyweds, but the young couple soon separate due to their mothers fighting. Maggie plans to commit suicide, but John finds the rogues and recovers the money. The bank is saved, John and Helen reconcile, and both families make peace.

## Behind the Scenes

Anita's last film made on the MGM lot was *Prosperity*, which was another Marie Dressler and Polly Moran vehicle that used Anita as window dressing. By now, Marie Dressler was getting older and would have less than two years to live. "While we were making one of these, Marie told me she had cancer," Anita said, "and in another, she was beginning to get sick. She was so brave; she was such a trooper."[131]

Dressler was forgetting her lines but was more concerned about her costars. "I'm so sorry," she would say, "I thought maybe Polly was trying to get that line." Through it all, Anita had nothing but admiration for Dressler. "Marie set the standard for older women who hoped they could make it in the movies," Anita said. "She inspired a lot of older women to think, well, Marie Dressler could do it, maybe I can too."[132]

The studio assigned Leo McCarey to direct *Prosperity* in March 1932. When the film wrapped, Mayer and Thalberg did not like portions of the film and ordered retakes. When that did not work out, they scrapped the entire film and reshot the picture with Sam Wood as the director (Norman Foster also replaced Wallace Ford).

This was the final joint appearance of Marie Dressler and Polly Moran. Ironically, Sam Wood directed Anita's first film at the studio, *Telling the World*, and would direct *Prosperity*, her last film produced on the MGM lot.

### Reviews

"Anita Page does quite well as Helen…"—Mordaunt Hall, *New York Times*, November 26, 1932.

"Especially gratifying is the return of Anita Page to sylph-like contours with a proportionate increase of facial beauty, the only fault in her performance being an overabundance of pulchritude unlooked for in a troubled wife, but she plays her role pleasantly and well with a marked improvement in voice and enunciation."—Norbert Lusk, *Los Angeles Times*, December 4, 1932.

## *Jungle Bride*

### Monogram Pictures Corporation
### 1933

Tagline: "On a Desolate African Coast! Could Social Ethics Last in Primitive Surrounding—See this picture!"

## Statistics

Sound / Black & White / 35mm / Drama. Runtime: 7 reels, 5,632 ft., 63 min. © Monogram Pictures Corp., 6 Apr 1933, LP3781. Release date: February 15, 1933.

## Credits

Produced by Trem Carr, I.E. Chadwick (uncredited); associate producer, Arthur F. Beck (uncredited); directed by Harry O. Hoyt and Albert Kelley; assistant director, William L. Nolte; story by Leah Baird; cinematography by André Barlatier and Harry Jackson; art direction by Ernest R. Hickson; edited by Arthur Huffsmith; sound recordist, Homer Ellmaker.

*Song(s):* "That's the Call of the Jungle" and other songs and music by Marcy Klauber and Harry Stoddard.

## Cast

Anita Page (Doris Evans) [Courtesy of MGM], Charles Starrett (Gordon Wayne) [Courtesy of Paramount], Kenneth Thomson (John Franklin), Eddie Borden (Eddie Stevens), Gertrude Simpson (Laura), Clarence Geldert (Captain Andersen), Jay Emmett (Jimmy), Alfred Cross (Passenger on Deck).

## Plot

Doris Evans and her news reporter fiancé coerce Gordon Wayne back to the United States to stand trial for murdering a police officer. Doris' brother is in jail for the crime, but she believes Gordon did it. On an ocean liner which sinks, romance blossoms between Doris and Gordon after he saves her from a lion on a desert island. Soon after the ship's captain marries them. A passing ship comes to the rescue and Doris receives news that her brother confessed to the killing on his deathbed. The newlyweds take the opportunity to honeymoon on the island before the boat returns 10 days later to collect them.

## Behind the Scenes

After *Prosperity*, Mayer loaned Anita to Monogram Pictures. It was then she saw the handwriting on the wall. "Monogram was the last gas station on the way to the desert," Anita said. When a studio like MGM loaned you to a low rated studio such as Monogram, it meant they no longer had any use for you. Since Anita was still under contract, she had no say in the matter and had to report to Monogram for filming. However, decades later she noticed a newspaper ad for *Jungle Bride* and proudly noted, "My name is above the title. I was the star."[133]

The film, *Jungle Bride*, was a run-of-the-mill programmer costarring

**Anita as Doris Evans shipwrecked on a desert island in *Jungle Bride* (Monogram, 1933).**

Charles Starrett, appearing through the courtesy of Paramount. Starrett later gained fame as a cowboy star. Anita remembered Starrett as a man who loved his wife and loved to talk about her.[134]

*Jungle Bride* gave Anita star billing with her name above the title; however, the critics were not kind to her or the picture. One scene has Starrett in a hand-to-hand struggle with a lion that acts like a playful kitten. The audience at the Seventh Street Roxy greeted the scene with well-bred laughter. *Variety* wrote: "[the film] has an unconvincing plot inexpertly filmed. Action may impel laughs when not intended. Miss Page exaggerates the dramatics of her role, and her makeup is faulty."[135]

The *New York Times*, in their review, reflected Anita's feelings about where her career was going. "The scene of *Jungle Bride* is that well-traveled veldt somewhere in darkest Hollywood where all bad little melodramas are born and where lions are put out to graze when they become too old and feeble for active service."[136]

### Reviews

"Miss Page a dream of blond loveliness with a coiffure and complexion undisturbed by her harrowing experiences."—*New York Times*, May 13, 1933.

"But the treatment is old fashioned, the direction weak, and the acting of Anita Page and Charles Starrett no more than adequate."—*Film Weekly*, September 1, 1933 [UK].

"The story is well put together, acting and direction are satisfactory, and it should prove adequate entertainment for the theatres in which it will be shown."—*Motion Picture Herald*, February 25, 1933.

# *The Big Cage*

Universal Pictures Corp.
1933

Tagline: "A Man Alone—unarmed—tames 40 lions and tigers by sheer will power!"

### Statistics

Sound (Western Electric Noiseless Recording) / Black & White / 35mm / Drama. Runtime: 8 reels, 71 or 75–77 min. © Universal Pictures Corp., 8 Mar 1933, LP4267. New York opening: May 8, 1933, Mayfair Theater. Release date: March 3, 1933, Warners' Western and Beverly Hills Theaters.

### Prologue

Los Angeles: Warners' Western Theater. Assorted short subjects including Morton Downey in *Broadcast Train*.

### Credits

Carl Laemmle, President; produced by Carl Laemmle, Jr.; directed by Kurt Neumann; screenplay by Edward Anthony and Ferdinand Reyher, based on the book *The Big Cage* by Clyde Beatty with Edward Anthony (New York, 1933); adaptation by Dale Van Every (uncredited); additional dialogue by Clarence Marks; cinematography by George Robinson; edited by Philip Cahn; Animals courtesy of the Hagenbach—Wallace Circus.

### Cast

Clyde Beatty (Clyde Beatty), Anita Page (Lilian Langley), Andy Devine (Scoops), Vince Barnett (Soupmeat), Mickey Rooney (Jimmy O'Hara), Wallace Ford (Russ Penny), Raymond Hatton (Timothy O'Hara), Reginald Barlow (John Whipple), Edward Peil, Sr. (Glenn Stoner), Robert McWade (Henry Cameron), Wilfred Lucas (Bob Mills), James Durkin (Silas Warner), Louise Beavers (Mandy), Walter Brennan (Ticket-Taker), Tom London (Ship Captain).

### Plot

Animal tamer Clyde Beatty puts on a circus show to train lions and tigers together for the first time in history. Acrobatic star Lilian and her animal trainer boyfriend Russ join the show. A thunderstorm destroys the marquee and wild cats escape, leaving Russ to rescue Lilian while Clyde bravely captures the lions and tigers.

### Behind the Scenes

Anita's next loan on her MGM contract was to Universal, who borrowed her again for *The Big Cage*, famous wild animal trainer Clyde Beatty's first feature film based on his book of the same name. Beatty was renowned as the greatest in the world.[137]

Initial filming on *The Big Cage* started several weeks before Anita became a late addition to the film; she signed her contract the day before Christmas 1932, the same day she found a horseshoe. "This isn't only good luck," she said of the horseshoe, "it's valuable. I'm going to save it up as a museum piece."[138]

Filmed on Universal's old *Phantom of the Opera* stage, *The Big Cage* was the first time that lions and tigers were together on film. Beatty had been mauled more than a hundred times in front of an audience, which caused the Hays Office to express concern about the cast's safety. In a letter

Anita as acrobatic star Lilian Langley in *The Big Cage* (Universal, 1933).

to Universal they warned that "it could turn out disastrously if not done with much care. Mr. Beatty himself says he has never fought a lion and a tiger in a single battle … but he expects to put it over without it costing his life."[139]

"Clyde was a very brave man," Anita recalled.

One of Anita's costars was 12-year-old Mickey Rooney. Besides being "cute," he impressed Anita with his acting ability. "He was a natural," she said.[140]

The main asset of *The Big Cage* was Beatty, who showed his "forty man-eating lions and tigers"; however, in presenting him, filmmakers forgot that a relevant story was also a necessity. The cast was strong and was worthy of better material. Those who enjoyed the circus and the goings-on behind the canvas were the main fans of *The Big Cage*. But to others, it moved slowly at times and was full of repetitions. As for Anita's performance, *Film Weekly* called it a "love story which occasions the graceful but meaningless presence of Anita Page at odd moments."[141]

## Reviews

"Wallace Ford and Anita Page were seen briefly in what there was of romance."—*Hollywood Filmograph*, March 18, 1933.

"Anita Page, who can wear tights, does a Lietzel, with Ford her animal training sweetheart, who loses his nerve after being badly mangled in action."—*Variety*, May 16, 1933.

## *Soldiers of the Storm*

Columbia Pictures Corp.
1933

Tagline: "Sky High Thrills! Daring, Dangerous, Exciting Romance."

### Statistics

Sound / Black & White / 35mm / Drama. Runtime: 7 reels, 67–68 min. © Columbia Pictures Corp., 22 Mar 1933, LP3736. Production dates: February 16–February 27, 1933. Release date: April 4, 1933.

### Credits

Directed by D. Ross Lederman; assistant director, Wilbur McGaugh; screenplay by Charles R. Condon; story by Thomson Burtis; dialogue by Horace McCoy; cinematography by Ted Tetzlaff; edited by Maurice Wright; sound engineer, George Cooper.

### Cast

Regis Toomey (Brad Allerton), Anita Page (Natalie Adams), Barbara Weeks (Spanish waitress), Robert Ellis (John Moran), Wheeler Oakman (George), Barbara Barondess (Sonia), Dewey Robinson (Chuck Bailey), George Cooper (Red Gurney), Arthur Wanzer (J. T. Adams), Henry Wadsworth (Dodie Harmon).

### Plot

Brad Allerton is a border patrol pilot sent to capture a gang of crooks smuggling liquor over the Mexican border. He receives the license card of an imprisoned criminal pilot to get close to the gang. Brad meets the mayor's daughter Natalie and they fall in love, unaware the Mayor is involved in the gang's activity. Brad breaks many engagements with Natalie, and she soon believes he does not love her. Natalie becomes involved with the gang leader, and the mayor is murdered when he refuses to help further. The

(From left) Regis Toomey, Barbara Barondess, Anita, and Robert Ellis in *Soldiers of the Storm* (Columbia, 1933).

gang leader tries to escape but Brad chases him in his plane and shoots the car, which plummets from a cliff edge. Brad reunites with Natalie.

### Behind the Scenes

Filming of *Soldiers of the Storm* began at Columbia Studios on February 16, 1933, starring Anita, Regis Toomey, Barbara Barondess, and D. Ross Lederman directing under the supervision of Louis Sarecky. This was the last of three loan-outs filmed under Anita's MGM contract which would expire the end of February 1933.

There were thrills in the excellently done air sequences and plenty of punch in the simple dramatic situations. The cast did splendid work keeping up the pace of the picture. The mixture of bootlegging, flying, fighting and romance, which made up the backbone of the story, caused the picture to be acceptable to the youngsters as well as to the adults.

Not surprisingly, Anita remembered little or nothing about the making of *Soldiers of the Storm*, except that her costar Regis Toomey was "very nice; a wonderful actor."[142]

And finally, after four years of trying, Benito Mussolini received an autographed photo of Anita when Columbia's Harry Cohn gave in to the Italian dictator's many requests.

### Reviews

"Regis Toomey does quite well as the indefatigable Allerton and Anita Page appears as Natalie. Miss Page's acting is acceptable."—Mordaunt Hall, *New York Times*, May 17, 1933.

"Not much above an ordinary Western in style or treatment. Toomey is adequate in the stereotyped leading role, and Anita Page is a good heroine."—*Film Weekly*, September 1, 1933 [UK].

"A straightforward but entertaining melodrama with plenty of action. Regis Toomey is a virile and pleasant hero, and Anita Page ... is a decorative heroine."—*Picturegoer*, September 2, 1933 [UK].

# *I Have Lived*

## Chesterfield Motion Pictures Corp.
## 1933

Tagline: "She Taught Men Life, Love and Laughter. A daring theme, daringly dramatized behind the glamor of Broadway's Night Life."

### Statistics

Alternate titles: *Love Life*, *After Midnight*. Sound Mono (RCA Victor Systems) / Black & White / 35mm / Drama. Runtime: 7 reels, 65 min. © Chesterfield Motion Picture Corp., 23 Jun 1933, LP3958. Distributed by First Division Exchanges (New York) and States Rights (elsewhere). Production date: May 1933. Release date: June 15, 1933.

### Credits

Produced by George R. Batcheller; directed by Richard Thorpe; assistant director, Melville Shyer; story by Lou Heifetz; screenplay and dialogue by Winifred Dunn; edited by Roland D. Reed; cinematography by M.A. Anderson; sound engineer, Pete Clark.

### Cast

Alan Dinehart (Thomas Langley), Anita Page (Jean St. Clair), Allen Vincent (Warren White), Gertrude Astor (Harriet Naisson), Maude Truax (Mrs. Genevieve Reynolds), Matthew Betz (Blackie), Eddie Boland (Sidney Cook), Dell Henderson (J. W.), Florence Dudley (First Actress), Gladys

# I Have Lived

With Allen Vincent in *I Have Lived* (Chesterfield, 1933).

Blake (Second Actress), Harry C. Bradley (Small Town Man), Edward Keane (Leading man), Lafe McKee (Stage Manager).

## Plot

Thomas Langley, a producer and playwright, cannot find the right girl for his latest play. Langley is tipped off by his secretary that a nightclub is about to be raided and suggests that the experience will be good atmosphere for the raid scene in his new play. While at the club, Langley is attracted to the hostess, Jean St. Clair, who is perfect for the female lead. Langley rescues Jean from the nightclub scene and gives her a new name for the stage—Esther Rivers. Through Langley, Esther meets a gentleman named Warren. They fall in love and become engaged. The nightclub owner recognizes Esther on a theater billboard and blackmails her for five thousand dollars. Meanwhile, Warren learns of Esther's shady past and breaks off their engagement. Langley threatens the blackmailer with arrest, but during the altercation, Esther is shot. While she recovers in a hospital, Warren visits Esther and the two lovers are reunited.

## Behind the Scenes

In the early part of 1933, Anita had ended her MGM contract and accepted an offer from Chesterfield, another Poverty Row studio.

Filming of *I Have Lived* began the second week of May 1933 at the old Mack Sennett Studios in Silver Lake. The cast included Alan Dinehart, Anita, and Allen Vincent, with Richard Thorpe directing. This film would be the first of the 18 scheduled by Chesterfield and their co-producer, Invincible, for the 1933–1934 schedule.[143]

The acerbic Mordaunt Hall of the *New York Times* actually took time to review the film but was far from being an admirer; among other things he called *I Have Lived* a "banal backstage" story—"inept" and "offensive." The film played for one week only at New York's Mayfair Theatre beginning on September 5, 1933.[144]

### Reviews

"Life is made exciting for Anita Page by Alan Dinehart and Allen Vincent. Of course, she pays for her fun."—*Silver Screen*, November 1933.

"Crass, crude and clumsy attempt to make frailty 'noble.'"—*The Educational Screen*, October 1934.

"Anita Page gains sympathy from the start and she displays some gorgeous gowns as the film progressed."—*The Film Daily*, July 19, 1933.

# *Hitch Hike to Heaven*

Chesterfield Motion Pictures Corp.
Invincible Pictures Corp.
1936

Tag line: "See the movie-makers at work and play ... let *Hitch Hike to Heaven* take you stargazing."

### Statistics

Alternate title: *Footlights and Shadows*. Sound (RCA Victor High Fidelity Recording System) / Black & White / 35mm / Drama. Runtime: 7 reels, 63 min. © Invincible Pictures Corp., 22 Nov 1935, LP5945. Production date: October 1935. Release date: March 12, 1936.

### Prologue

Los Angeles: Orpheum Theatre. Herbert Rawlinson (who also starred in the film) opened his one-week stage engagement.

## Credits

Produced by Maury M. Cohen and Lon Young; directed by Frank R. Strayer; assistant director, Melville Shyer; story and screenplay by Robert Ellis and Helen Logan; cinematography by M.A. Anderson; art direction by Edward C. Jewell; edited by Roland D. Reed; recording engineer, Richard Tyler; production manager, Lon Young.

## Cast

Henrietta Crosman (Deborah Delaney), Herbert Rawlinson (Melville Delaney), Russell Gleason (Daniel Delaney), Polly Ann Young (Geraldine "Jerry" Daley), Al Shean (Herman Blatz), Anita Page (Claudia Revelle), Syd Saylor (Spud), Harry Harvey (Gabby), Harry Holman (Philmore Tubbs), Ethel Sykes (Kitty O'Brien), Lela Bliss (Nadia De La Ney), Crauford Kent (Edgar), John Dilson (Charlie Reed).

## Plot

A young actress named Jerry Daley is innocently discovered alone with middle-aged matinee idol Melville Delaney, who loses his film contract on a morality clause during a scandal caused by his wife's divorce suit. Mel believes Jerry was paid to frame him, and the innocent actress runs away and joins a travelling theater troupe. The troupe is headed by Deborah Delaney, Mel's mother. Also in the group is Mel's son Daniel. Due to Deborah's sudden illness, Jerry becomes the lead of the troupe. Jerry is to play Camille opposite Daniel on the Los Angeles stage. A sudden change in cast puts Mel on the stage opposite Jerry and he publicly condemns her for ruining his career. Jerry flees but Daniel brings her back to straighten out the truth. Mel gives his blessing for Daniel and Jerry's marriage and Deborah manages to regain Mel's film contract.

## Behind the Scenes

According to Anita, she felt most of the film studios had blackballed her, so when she was offered the opportunity to appear in *Hitch Hike to Heaven*, even though it was for another Poverty Row studio, she took it. "At the time, I realized what was going on, but there was nothing I could do about it," she recalled. "I just did the best I could." In fact, she would apologize when someone asked about her independent films. However, several decades later she watched some of them again and thought she "did a darn good job in them."[145]

All that Anita remembered about *Hitch Hike to Heaven* was that she had bought new make-up and took the role to see how it looked on film. When she saw it, she liked it and kept the make-up for years.[146]

*Hitch Hike to Heaven* had mixed reviews with critics calling it a pleasing yarn of movie and stage life, well-acted by good troupers, and predicting it should do well in the family theaters. Giving fans a bit of insight into the backstage operations of Hollywood, and performed by a cast that contained plenty of good acting talent, this story of show life was entertaining despite that it was neither radically new or particularly punchy.

## Review

"While the cast members perform capably under assignments that give them none of the edge of it, there are no names for the mazdalamps."—*Variety*, March 18, 1936.

"Here is as nice a back-stage comedy as you're likely to find in all the reels that have come out of Hollywood. This picture doesn't only take you backstage, it also provides an exciting and informative trip to a studio lot where you are privileged to watch a movie in the making."—*Madera Tribune*, June 5, 1936.

# The Runaway

Arpix Productions
Ostrow & Company
1961

## Statistics

Working title: *Saint Mike*. Sound (Mono) / Black & White / 35mm / Drama. Runtime: 85 min. © Not confirmed. Broadcast print bears a © 1964. Release date: Not released to theaters. Television broadcast premiere, November 30, 2008, Turner Classic Movies (TCM).

## Credits

Produced by Arthur N. Rupe; coproduced by Page Ostrow; directed by Claudio Guzman; assistant director, Richard Evans; written by Samuel Roeca; story editor, Carl Gabler; cinematography by Ray Foster, Wayne Mitchell, Haskell Wexler; gaffer, Lloyd Garnell; composer, Michael Anderson; makeup artist, John G. Holden; edited by George Boemler and Harold V. McKenzie; sound, Ben Winkler; sound effects editor, Rich Harrison; production manager, George Moskov; animal trainer, Rill Mitchell.

## Cast

Cesar Romero (Father Dugan), Roger Mobley (Felipe Roberto), Anita Page (Nun), Lewis Martin (Captain Dawn), Chick Chandler (Joe Sullivan), Nacho Galindo (Max Fernandez), Alex Montoya (Salazar), Ray Boyle (uncredited), Dudley Manlove (Minor Role), Brian O'Hara (Minor Role), Frank Wolff (Vagrant).

## Plot

Felipe, a delinquent boy living on the streets of a small Mexican border town, steals a greyhound dog and hides on Father Dugan's truck. After they cross the border, the dog falls from the truck and injures his leg. Local surgeons mend the dog's injury using a silver staff from a statue of St. Michael. Once healed, Father Dugan trains the greyhound, which he names St. Mike, to race. After winning a significant race, the man from whom Felipe stole the dog is suspicious. Now, the boy must decide whether to run away or admit what he has done and return St. Mike to his owner.

## Behind the Scenes

In the early 1960s, Anita made a cameo appearance as a salty Mother Superior in *The Runaway*, starring Cesar Romero. During filming, a terrible storm came up and everyone got soaking wet, including Anita. Instead of changing, she stayed in her wet habit for several hours. The next day, she developed laryngitis and could not talk, delaying filming.[147]

Thirty years later, on Anita's 83rd birthday, Cesar Romero was a guest at her party held on the Sunset Strip. He recalled that Anita's legs were "just as beautiful today as when she was a top MGM star!"[148]

In August 1962, *Boxoffice* magazine reported that a new film distribution firm, Summit Releasing Organization (SRO), announced that *The Runaway* would be its first of a slate of eight films and would go into national release in November. However, the amount of money that producer Arthur Rupe needed from SRO and other distribution companies did not meet his expectations.[149]

Rupe tried to distribute the film himself, but that effort failed, even after he created a promotional comic book version of the film. The film languished in storage until its airing on Turner Classic Movies on Sunday evening, November 30, 2008.

"*The Runaway* is an unfortunate victim of distribution problems that have kept it from the public eye for decades," said Charles Tabesh, senior vice president of programming for TCM. "This is a charming family adventure, beautifully filmed by Haskell Wexler and featuring enjoyable performances by a good cast."[150]

### Review

"While *The Runaway* might not be a masterpiece, it is a refreshing change of pace from the usual cliché-ridden 'boy and his dog' stories churned out by Hollywood."—Jeff Stafford, *Turner Classic Movies*, October 8, 2008.

# *Sunset After Dark*
## Wildcat Entertainment Productions
## 1996

### Statistics

Sound / Color / Drama. Runtime: 87 min. © Wildcat Entertainment. MPAA: Rated R for nudity and strong sexuality, and for violence and language. Release date: Opened in wide release in 1996. VHS release date: June 19, 1996.

### Credits

Executive produced by Albert J. Gordon; associate producers, Steve Harpst and Margaret O'Brien; produced and directed by Mark J. Gordon; first assistant director, Robert Sidis; second assistant director, Mimi Douglas; screenplay by Frank Spotnitz; cinematography by David Hallinger; first assistant camera, Kurt Fry; art direction by Robert Joseph; assistant art director, Scott Duthie; set decoration by Darla Hitchcock; film edited by Craig Kitson; costume design by Katzoff; music by Fernando Cavazos; sound by Marty Kasparian; set design by Darla Hitchcock; make-up and hair by James Robert Mackinnon

### Cast

Tony Maggio (John Harbor), Monique Parent (Gina), Anita Page (Anita Bronson), Margaret O'Brien (Betty Corman), Randal Malone (Gaylord Van Slyke), Corbin Timbrook (Peter D'Angelo), George Kuchar (George Kilman), April Breneman (Michelle Martin), J. Lyle Randolph (Case), Miranda Gibson (Arlette), Jeffrey Markle (Detective Flynn), Paul Brewster (Haskell), Steve Harpst (Bennett), Scott Forrest (Todd), Andrea Riave (Stripper), Rick Bennett (Second Detective), Mio Miyake (Geisha Girl), Paolo Nona (Pool man), Dale Vandegriff (Cameraman).

(From left) Anita, Randal Malone and Margaret O'Brien in *Sunset After Dark* (1996).

## Plot

To find inspiration, a struggling screenwriter rents a room in an eerie old mansion on Sunset Boulevard. He becomes involved with the wife of a missing man and the plot of an unsolved murder. Mix in the disappointments of a fading silent screen star and the bitterness of a former child actress and you have a plot of intrigue and suspense.

## Behind the Scenes

The idea for *Sunset After Dark* came about when producer Mark J. Gordon was interviewing Anita Page. Anita's manager and friend, actor Randal Malone, arranged the interview. The idea was about a great silent movie star; Gordon hoped that Anita would play that role.

Several months later Mark Gordon presented a completed script, written by Frank Spotnitz, to Anita. Spotnitz would gain fame for his work on the highly successful television show *The X-Files*. The script had a part for a former child star and Malone suggested his friend Margaret O'Brien. "That would be great. Do you think she would do it?" Gordon asked. O'Brien agreed to come out of retirement and do it as a favor for Malone.[151]

The film was shot in an old house once owned by banker Harry Crocker in the Sugar Hill district of Los Angeles. Crocker had dated Anita in the 1920s and escorted her to the Academy Awards in 1929. The neighborhood, where actress Hattie McDaniel also owned a house, was at one time a grand showplace for the rich and elite but was now somewhat run down.

During a dinner scene, O'Brien has a line where she calls Anita's character a "tramp". "It's one of my favorite scenes in the film," recalled Mark Gordon. "We wanted to show the jealousy and rivalry that exists between fallen stars and they play along with that beautifully." However, Anita opposed the term "tramp," so Gordon and screenwriter Frank Spotnitz explained that they had tried other variations and "tramp" seemed to work the best. "I don't like tramp. I think tramp is terrible and I don't want you to use it," Anita insisted.

"Well, Anita," Malone asked, "what about slut? Do you think that sounds better?"

When Anita agreed that "slut is fine. I can live with that," everyone on the set broke into laughter. In Anita's day, calling someone a "tramp" was scandalous, but "slut" hardly was used, so it meant little to her.[152]

For Margaret O'Brien, working with Anita was an interesting experience. Anita's character was much like herself. "Anita really was a silent film star," O'Brien recalled. "She had a very fascinating look about her and a real flair for the dramatic which she still has."[153]

On another occasion, during a scene with Tony Maggio, O'Brien asked if she could adjust her lines, which Frank Spotnitz approved. Of course, Anita overheard O'Brien's request.

In Anita's day, the studio was in control; actors had little to say unless it was Garbo or a similar high-profile star. They would come to the studio, say their lines and leave. So Anita associated O'Brien's request for script changes with great stardom. In a loud voice, Anita asked Malone, "Don't you think that's bold, changing the lines like that?"

"Apparently it's for the better or they wouldn't let her do it," he whispered to her.

"I think she's doing that because she thinks she's the star of this picture," Anita cheekily replied.

The set was quiet. Smiling, O'Brien glanced at Malone and continued with the scene; she let it go. Even though Anita acknowledged O'Brien's status as a "remarkable child actress," she felt that she was manipulating Malone's time on the set. "I was a big star too," Anita insisted, "and I was not about to play second fiddle to anyone."[154]

Yet, even though they had never worked together at MGM, Anita was aware of O'Brien's ability. "I have always admired her work," Anita acknowledged, "and she still has a very natural appeal. It was a thrill to actually work with her."[155]

O'Brien understood Anita's reaction: "Anita has the temperament of the twenties, from when the stars were very grand, and they would sweep in and out. We actually were in awe of her."[156]

*Sunset After Dark* was in limited release in the United States, but in Europe and South America it had a popular and successful run.

## Review

"Fine acting on the part of Randal Malone, Margaret O'Brien and of course Miss Anita Page. Amazing to see that the old gal still has it!"— *Southern California Motion Picture Council*, 1996.

# Theater

## Crazy Quilt of 1933

Billy Rose
1933–1934

"Billy Rose's All New 1933 Edition of the Million Dollar Musical Extravaganza Presenting a Dazzling Array of Delectable Girlhood."

### Statistics

Musical revue; post Broadway tour produced by Billy Rose. Premiered on July 28, 1933.

### Credits

Produced and directed by Billy Rose and John Murray Anderson; scenery created by Clark Robinson (chief lieutenant of Roxy Theatre); staging of girl ensembles conceived by Chester Hale (dance director of Capitol Theater); effects by Colden Weld (theatrical costume designer).

*Song(s)*: "I Want to be Kissed," "Wedding of the Painted Doll," "You Were Meant for Me," "It's Only a Paper Moon" (originally titled "If You Believed in Me").

*Skits*: "The Last National Bank," "The Doctor's Office," by Smith and Dale.

*Dance*: "Wiggle of the World," by Wilma Novak.

### Cast

Anita Page (Glamorous Screen Star), Charles King (Popular Stage and Screen Star), Joe Smith and Charlie Dale (That Classic Comedy Team), Eleanor Powell (America's Foremost Tap Dancer), Cardini (The Suave

Deceiver—English Mystifier of cards and lighted cigarettes), Avon Comedy Four, Ann Pennington, Wilma Novak.

## *Plot*

*Crazy Quilt* was not a condensed version of the original musical hit but rather a new musical revue devised expressly for presentation in the larger deluxe film theaters of the country by a group of individual producing technicians who ranked at the head of their respective professions in New York theatrical circles.

## *Behind the Scenes*

When Anita agreed to do *Crazy Quilt of 1933*, it helped her decision to leave MGM. Once, Anita had asked Robert Montgomery how he achieved his manner of acting and his line delivery. "Stage work," he told her. "Learning basic acting is essential, but real technique must come from working before a live audience. You learn how to time comic line-delivery, as well as develop your acting skills."

"Do you play people like yourself?" she asked.

"No, no. We got costumes that were entirely different," Montgomery explained. "That was one way that helped get rid of stage fright. It helped keep you anonymous with the audience—so if you forgot your lines, they wouldn't recognize you when you became another character. You were less nervous."

"I never forgot Bob's tip that day on the set, so when the door was open for me to do a live performance, I jumped on it!"[1]

Anita (right) with Ann Pennington in Billy Rose's *Crazy Quilt*. Portrait by White Studio (New York, 1933).

She knew that working before a live audience would develop her craft and learn timing. Soon she was on her way to New York and rehearsals for *Crazy Quilt*. Her costar was Charlie King, her friend and costar from *The Broadway Melody*. "I enjoyed working with Charlie King," she recalled. "He sang and danced in several of my numbers and it was nice having an old friend around during all of this."

The rest of the cast included comedians Smith & Dale, Ann Pennington, and dancer Eleanor Powell, who had been on Broadway for five years and had not yet made a film. Watching her perform, Anita told the young dancer: "Eleanor, I don't like tap dancing as a rule. Why is it I love to watch you?"

"Well, Anita, maybe it's because I took ballet when I was a kid," Powell explained.

"I loved to watch her dance," Anita recalled. "She was so graceful. The ballet is what taught her the grace. She did a tremendous job besides being the greatest tap dancer in the world. What a trouper!"

In *Crazy Quilt*, Anita performed in 16 different numbers, which meant 16 costumes changes per show, five shows per day, seven days a week. "I honestly don't know how I did it without collapsing," she said.

The cast of Billy Rose's *Crazy Quilt*: (from left) Ann Pennington, *The Broadway Melody* costar Charles King, Joe Smith, Charles Dale, and Anita. Portrait by White Studio (New York, 1933).

During one extravagant number, Anita and King entered at the top of a flight of long winding stairs, lined with chorus girls. While waiting for their entrance, they stood on a narrow strip of wood about 20 feet above the stage floor. Anita warned Billy Rose that it was too narrow, and she was afraid of falling. Sure enough, one night just as she and King were about to enter, she felt her foot slipping. She tried to put the other one back to catch her—but there was nowhere to place it. King sensed that she was in trouble and reached over and grabbed her until she found her balance, and the show could continue. The crew fixed the board before the next performance.

King continued to act on Broadway and in occasional films. During World War II, he went overseas and entertained the troops where one evening he caught a cold during a performance. It turned to pneumonia and he died not long afterward. "He was just as much a hero as anyone who fought in the war," Anita declared.

At the time, Billy Rose was a top Broadway producer and was married to comedienne Fanny Brice. Fanny was friendly to Anita, helping her with her hair and wardrobe stage bits that she was not sure about. Anita signed with Rose for six months, which included a 24-week vaudeville tour and then a New York run on Broadway. "I didn't realize what I was getting myself into," Anita said. "Sleeping on trains and playing nearly every city across the country was not my idea of learning my craft! I thought to myself, I've been a film star for five years, so why am I doing this to myself? Is it really worth it?"

It was almost worth it when the show played in Washington, D.C., in December 1933. President Franklin Roosevelt had recently introduced the March of Dimes and read that Anita was in town with *Crazy Quilt*. He asked Anita to sit in his box at a festivity to begin the charity. Anita was an admirer of Roosevelt's, but Rose would not allow her to do it since she was in every scene of the show and could not be spared. Instead, he sent Eleanor Powell in her place. "I was very upset about that," Anita said.

On another occasion, she was furious with Rose when he cancelled her Christmas vacation to Louisiana to be with friends. He originally approved it, but a week before leaving, he changed his mind. If he allowed her to go, the show would have to close and put the chorus members out of work. "Could you let these poor girls go without pay?" Rose told her, playing on her guilt.

When *Crazy Quilt* arrived on Broadway at Loew's Metropolitan, Anita wanted to change her hair. On the road, she fixed it herself, but in New York she went to Bloomingdale's for a light perm. However, the hairdresser was busy with other customers and left the solution on too long which made her hair look like steel wool. Furious, Anita returned to the theater. "What happened to your hair?" someone asked. That was the last straw. Anita ranted and raved until a chorus member covered Anita's hair with styling gel, which straightened it out, but she had to wear her hair like that for the rest of the show. It took three months for her hair to return to normal.

## Review

"Fast-paced, cleverly routine, adequality mounted and with a musical background that is pleasing to the ear, *Crazy Quilt* rates with the best of the season's revues."—*Syracuse Herald*, January 20, 1934.

# Foreign Language Films

*Estrellados* [trans. *Starry*] (1930). Metro-Goldwyn-Mayer Corp. Spanish version of *Free and Easy*. Runtime: 95 min. Release dates: Havana, Cuba, July 14, 1930; Barcelona, Spain, and New York, October 17, 1930.

*Credits:* Directed by Edward Sedgwick; assistant director, Salvador de Alberich (uncredited), supervisor, George E. Kann; Spanish adaptation by Salvador de Alberich; recording engineer, Antonio Samaniego.

*Song(s):* "La reina de mi corazón" and "Estrellados," music by Fred E. Ahlert, Spanish lyrics by Salvador de Alberich.

*Partial Cast:* Buster Keaton (Canuto Cuadratin), Raquel Torres (Elvira [de Rosas]), Maria Calvo (La mama), Juan de Homs (Un director), Carlos Villarias (Jack Colier [Master of ceremonies]), Don Alvarado, Anita Page (Herself).[1]

*Note:* This was filmed simultaneously as *Free and Easy*.

*Wir schalten um auf Hollywood* [trans. *We Switch to Hollywood*] (1931). Metro-Goldwyn-Mayer Corp. Runtime: 82 min. Release date: June 10, 1931.

*Credits:* Directed by Frank Reicher; screenplay by Paul Morgan; cinematography by Ray Binger; set designer, Cedric Gibbons; edited by Adrienne Fazan; costumes by David Cox; recording director, Douglas Shearer.

*Cast:* [partial listing] Paul Morgan (Ein Erfinder und Reporter), Buster Keaton, Ramón Novarro, Adolphe Menjou, Heinrich George, John Gilbert, Wallace Beery, Joan Crawford, Hoot Gibson, Anita Page, Norma Shearer.

*Plot:* A German reporter (Paul Morgan) comes to Hollywood to visit MGM, not speaking English, and meet a German nobleman who works as an extra. Morgan rehearses a scene in German with Adolphe Menjou. He speaks to several actors, mainly Buster Keaton, John Gilbert and Joan Crawford, who speaks a few sentences in German. The final scene shows celebrities arriving at a film premiere, including Jean Harlow, Norma Shearer and Anita Page.

*Note:* MGM produced *Wir schalten um auf Hollywood* specifically for the German market and used scenes from *The Hollywood Revue of 1929* and fragments of the unfinished *The March of Time*.[2]

*Review*: "Heinrich George appears as a walking monument of anti-prohibition. And Joan Crawford finally gets Morgan to hear that he is 'a beautiful German man.' This is all very charming."—*Filmkurier*, June 11, 1931.

# Shorts

*The Voice of Hollywood No. 3* (1930) / I. Short. Louis Lewyn Productions. Release date: January 1930. *Cast*: Reginald Denny, Julian Eltinge, Anita Page, Mack Sennett.

*The Voice of Hollywood No. 3* (1930) / II. Short. Louis Lewyn Productions. Release date: January 5, 1930. *Cast*: Richard Dix, Julian Eltinge, Anita Page, Mack Sennett.

*Fox Movietone News* (5–246). Filmed on February 8, 1930. Sound. Short. Runtime: 12 min. Abe Lyman and his Orchestra performing at the forecourt of Grauman's Chinese Theater. Shots of Lyman directing his band. Anita Page "conducts" the band. Scenes of African cannibals brought to MGM to be in the film *Trader Horn* (1931), standing with Page, Lyman, and his orchestra.

*Screen Snapshots Series 9, No. 20* (1930). Short. Columbia Pictures. Directed by Ralph Staub. Runtime: 9 min. Release date: June 1930. *Cast*: Billy Bevan, Nils Asther, Billie Burke, Karl Dane, Bebe Daniels, Al Jolson, Ruby Keeler, Anita Page.

*Fox Movietone News* (6–622). Filmed on June 10, 1930. Sound. Short. Runtime: 6:41 min. Botany expert Robert Armacost explaining flowers to actress Anita Page.

*Fashion News* (1930). Documentary, Short. Fashion Features. Produced by George W. Gibson. Runtime: 5 min. Release date: October 1930. The style reel *Fashion News*, which was in Technicolor, had Catherine Dale Owen, Myrna Loy, Sue Carol and Anita Page and other top female stars as models displaying the latest fall creations from Paris in hats, gowns and furs, vocally described by the fashion expert Marguerite Swope.

*Jackie Cooper's Birthday Party* (1931). Documentary, Short. Metro-Goldwyn-Mayer. Directed by Charles Reisner. Release date: September 25, 1931. *Cast*: Jackie Cooper, Lionel Barrymore, Wallace Beery, Marion

Davies, Marie Dressler, Clark Gable, Ramón Novarro, Anita Page, Norma Shearer.

*The Voice of Hollywood No. 7* (Second Series) (1931). Short. Tiffany Productions. Release date: January 1931. Runtime: 10 min. *Cast*: Roscoe Ates, Robert Montgomery, Anita Page, Jean Hersholt.

*The Christmas Party* (1931). Short. Metro-Goldwyn-Mayer. Directed by Charles Reisner. Release date: December 17, 1931. Runtime: 9 min. *Cast*: Jackie Cooper, Lionel Barrymore, Marion Davies, Marie Dressler, Clark Gable, Anita Page, Ramón Novarro. Norma Shearer.

*Going Hollywood* (1994). Short, Comedy. Kuchar Brothers. Directed by George Kuchar. Release date: Video 1994. Runtime: 13 min. *Cast*: Mark J. Gordon, Tony Maggio, Randal Malone, Anita Page, Linda Sterne.

*A Silent Star* (2008). Short. Directed by Vera Iwerebor. Release date: October 9, 2008 (Netherlands). Runtime: 24 minutes. *Cast*: Randal Malone, Rose Marie, Margaret O'Brien, Anita Page.

# Documentaries and Television

*The Big Parade of Comedy* (1964). Comedy / Documentary. Metro-Goldwyn-Mayer. Release date: September 3, 1964. Runtime: 90 min. Robert Youngson (director). Anita Page appears as Vivian Truffle in a scene from *Reducing* (1931) [archive footage].

*Skip E. Lowe Looks at Hollywood* (1993). TV / Cable interview. Release date: December 31, 1993. *Cast*: Skip E. Lowe (Host), Anita Page (Interviewee).

*Hollywood Blvd.* (1996). Swiss Television. Directed by Leonardo Colla. Edited by Grant Smith. *Cast*: Holly Woodlawn, Anita Page, Randal Malone, Michael Schwibs.

*E! Mysteries & Scandals: Jean Harlow* (1998). TV Series / Documentary. E! Entertainment Television. Release date: May 11, 1998. *Cast*: A.J. Benza (Host), Jean Harlow (archive footage), Anita Page, David Stenn, Marc Wanamaker.

*E! Mysteries & Scandals: Clara Bow* (1998). TV Series / Documentary. E! Entertainment Television. Release date: August 31, 1998. *Cast*: A.J. Benza (Host), Clara Bow (archive footage), David Stenn, Rudy Behlmer, Budd Schulberg, Anita Page, A.C. Lyles, Rex Bell, Jr.

*I Used to Be in Pictures* (2000). Documentary. Astoria Productions Ltd. Release date: Apparently unreleased and unavailable. Peter Turner (director). Austin Mutti-Mewse, Howard Mutti-Mewse (writers). *Cast*: Joan Marsh, Marion Shilling, Gloria Stuart, Frances Drake, Sybil Jason, Anita Page, Rose Hobart, Lupita Tovar.

*Joan Crawford: The Ultimate Movie Star* (2002). Documentary. Fitzfilm. Release date: August 1, 2002. Directed by Peter Fitzgerald. Runtime: 87 min. *Cast*: Angelica Huston, Christina Crawford, Douglas Fairbanks, Jr., Anna Lee, Margaret O'Brien, Anita Page.

*Broadway: The American Musical—Syncopated City: 1919–1933* (2004). TV mini-series / Documentary. British Broadcasting Corp (BBC). Release date: October 19, 2004. Runtime: 360 min. Anita Page appeared as Queenie Mahony in a scene from *The Broadway Melody* (1929) [archive footage].

*The Dawn of Sound: How Movies Learned to Talk* (2007). Documentary. Warner Bros. Entertainment. Release date: September 2, 2007. Runtime: 85 min. Anita Page appeared in archive footage.

*Hollywood Singing and Dancing: A Musical History—The 1920s: The Dawn of the Hollywood Musical* (2008). Documentary / Musical. Great Musical Treasures. Release date: January 10, 2008. Runtime: 60 min. Directed by Phillip Dye. *Cast*: Robert S. Birchard, Leslie Caron, Shirley MacLaine, Anita Page.

# Video Films

When Anita completed *Sunset After Dark*, she hoped to be able to work with Randal Malone again and the opportunity came with *Hollywood Mortuary*. Director Ron Ford had worked with Malone in several films and decided to find a starring vehicle for the *Singled-Out* star. As it happened, Malone had an idea for a project that he had been mulling around for a while, an idea which played into Ford's love of old horror films and his sense of camp. What resulted was *Hollywood Mortuary*, a spoof of the rivalry between Bela Lugosi and Boris Karloff, two of the biggest names in horror films.

Ford thought that Malone would be perfect for the lead, Pierce Jackson Dawn, an arrogant monster make-up king. Anita agreed, saying, "If all my leading men would have been like Randy, I could have just relaxed."[1]

Anita consented to play herself in a documentary-style part of the film.

The plot dealt with the murder of a fictional horror movie star. Unfortunately, because of Anita's health, she was past the point of memorizing lines. To achieve realism from Anita's performance, as the cameras ran, Malone asked her to talk about her former costar, Ramón Novarro, and his 1968 murder by male prostitutes. Speaking of the brutality of Novarro's murder, Anita emoted with a true sense of horror; that "interview" was used in the film as if she was referring to the script's slain horror star. She gave an enthusiastic performance from the heart, but her words were unscripted.

While audiences were not aware of the technique used, those who did thought it was cheating. Still, Anita could mimic, and many agreed that she gave a marvelous performance.

After *Hollywood Mortuary*, Anita made cameo appearances in four independent low budget films.

*Hollywood Mortuary* (1998). Brimstone Productions. Comedy/Horror. Runtime 70 min. Produced and directed by Ron Ford. *Cast:* Randal Malone,

(From left) Anita, Margaret O'Brien, and Randal Malone in *Hollywood Mortuary* (1998).

Tim Sullivan, Margaret O'Brien, Anita Page, Conrad Brooks. Re-released: October 7, 2008.

*Witchcraft XI: Sisters in Blood* (2000). Horror. Runtime: 90 min. Produced by Jerry Feifer. Directed by Ron Ford. *Cast*: Miranda Odell, Lauren Ian Richards, Wendy Blair, Anita Page. Released: May 9, 2000.

*The Crawling Brain* (2002). Combs Pictures International. Horror / Sci-Fi. Produced by William Combs. Directed by Ron Ford. *Cast*: Athena Demos, Randal Malone, Anita Page, Amy Hudson. Released: April 22, 2016 (Monsterpalooza).

*Bob's Night Out* (2004). American Mutoscope & Biograph. Comedy. Runtime: 120 min. Produced and directed by Thomas R. Bond II. *Cast*: Tommy Bond, Conrad Brooks, Lois Hamilton, Randal Malone, Anita Page. Released: 2004.

*Frankenstein Rising* (2010). Sterling Entertainment. Horror. Runtime: 95 min. Produced by David S. Sterling. Directed by Eric Swelstad. *Cast*: Randal Malone, Gary Jazon, Margaret O'Brien, Anita Page, Jerry Maren. Released: April 8, 2010.

# Chapter Notes

## Preface

1. Hanna, *A Portrait of a Star*, p. 74.
2. Anita Page to Allan Ellenberger, August 20, 1993.
3. Hugh Hefner to Allan Ellenberger, August 4, 1993.
4. Betty Garrett to Allan Ellenberger, August 4, 1993.
5. Sandra House to Allan Ellenberger, August 4, 1993.
6. Robert Murdoch Paton, December 19, 2019.
7. Margaret O'Brien to Allan Ellenberger, August 4, 1993.01

## Anita Page

1. Anita Page to Allan Ellenberger, July 31, 1994. Note: Anita's eyes were blue.
2. "Their First Fans," *New Movie Magazine*, February 1930. At the time of Anita's birth, the Pomares were living with Maude's sister, Rosetta, at 560 West 160th Street.
3. Anita Page to Allan Ellenberger, July 31, 1994.
4. Manuel Muñoz obit, *New York Times*, February 24, 1906. Ancestry.com.
5. Marino Pomares was born in Brooklyn, New York, on May 22, 1887, to Marino Pomares and Ana Muñoz. Maude Mullane was born in New York, New York, on July 5, 1893, to James Mullane and Katherine Potts. They were married in Manhattan on October 5, 1909. Anita Page to Allan Ellenberger, July 31, 1994.
6. "Their First Fans," *The New Movie Magazine*, February 1930. The Pomares were living in an apartment at 822 Amsterdam Avenue.
7. *Ibid*. Anita attended Richmond Hill High School in Queens.
8. Richmond Hill High School is at 89-30 114 Street, Richmond Hill, Queens. Anita Page to Allan Ellenberger, July 31, 1994. Washington Irving High School was founded as an all-girls school in 1913 and is at 40 Irving Place in Manhattan, New York. Other notable alumni include comedians Joy Behar and Whoopi Goldberg, cohosts of *The View*; actresses Gertrude Berg, Claudette Colbert and Patricia Morrison; and writer Bella Spewack.
9. Anita Page to Allan Ellenberger, July 31, 1994.
10. *Ibid*.
11. Anita Page to Allan Ellenberger, July 31, 1994. Thanks to Bronson's recommendation, Pomares bought a house on the next block at 21-63 28th Street, Astoria.
12. Anita Page to Allan Ellenberger, July 31, 1994. There was one more Bronson child at home, Frank, 15. Arthur Bronson, Anita's first boyfriend, tried acting and appeared in bits parts in two films: *Delicious* (1931) and *Thrill of a Lifetime* (1937). Bronson died from a heart attack on June 9, 1960. He was 51 years old.
13. Anita Page to Allan Ellenberger, July 31, 1994.
14. In Martha Graham's class, Anita reenacted a scene from *The Volga Boatman*. John Murray Anderson's School for the Dramatic Arts was located at 128-30 East 58th Street. Two of the alumni of the school were Lucille Ball and Bette Davis. Anita Page to Allan Ellenberger, July 31, 1994.
15. "Up from Smiling Ads," *Picture Play*, January 1934.
16. New York newspapers published fictional narratives in their pages, illustrating

models with emotional expressions; this was Anita's specialty. In one advertisement, she dressed as "Little Bo Peep" for a story about the nursery rhyme character.

17. "They Had Beauty, But—," *Picture-Play magazine*, December 1926. "Manhattan Medley," *Picture-Play magazine*, February 1927.

18. "Up from Smiling Ads," *Picture Play*, January 1934. There is no confirmation that she appeared in "all the pictures."

19. "World's Softest 'Angel' is Harry K. Thaw," *Variety*, July 18, 1928.

20. The Cosmopolitan Theater was located at 5 Columbus Circle and was owned by William Randolph Hearst and later by Florenz Ziegfeld. The theater was razed in 1954 to build the New York Coliseum. In 2000, the Time Warner Center was erected.

21. Anita Page to Allan Ellenberger, July 31, 1994.

22. *Ibid.* Ana Pomares died on February 25, 1928, a little more than two months after Anita arrived in Hollywood.

23. Anita Page to Allan Ellenberger, July 31, 1994.

24. Nesbit had testified on behalf of Thaw and he supported her financially for years. In 1912, Nesbit had a son in Germany, but Thaw denied that it was his. The pair were divorced in 1916.

25. Madison Square Garden was located at 51 Madison Avenue and was designed by Stanford White. It was razed in 1925 to build the New York Life Insurance Company building.

26. Pathé Studios located at Park Avenue and 134th Street.

27. "Thaw Slapped by a Woman," *New York Times*, June 16, 1927.

28. This statement was not true. There was never a deal with United Artists.

29. "Thaw and Company Here," *Los Angeles Examiner*, December 7, 1927.

30. Anita Page to Allan Ellenberger, July 31, 1994.

31. *Ibid.*

32. "Thaw and Company Here," *Los Angeles Examiner*, December 7, 1927.

33. "Thaw Genial on Arrival," *Los Angeles Times*, December 7, 1927.

34. "Anita Rivers Becomes Anita Page," *Photoplay*, May 1928.

35. Reportedly, the negatives for the three films that Kenilworth made, including *Beach Nuts* with Anita, were taken to Paris by Thaw and stored in a vault. Perhaps they are still there waiting to be found.

36. "Anita Rivers Becomes Anita Page," *Photoplay*, May 1928.

37. Anita Page to Allan Ellenberger, July 31, 1994.

38. Paul R. Baker, *Stanny: The Gilded Life of Stanford White* (New York: Free Press, 1989), 397.

39. Harvey Pugh's tasks at Paramount included dealing with the gatecrashers trying to break in at the studio's iconic entrance. While gatecrashing was an art, to Pugh, it was "easy to spot one."

40. Anita Page to Allan Ellenberger, July 31, 1994.

41. *Ibid.*

42. Eve Golden, *Golden Images: 41 Essays on Silent Film Stars* (Jefferson, NC: McFarland, 2001), 131. Anita Page to Allan Ellenberger, July 31, 1994.

43. Anita Page to Allan Ellenberger, July 31, 1994.

44. *Ibid.*

45. "Fate Kind to Anita Page," *Los Angeles Times*, October 6, 1929.

46. Anita Page to Allan Ellenberger, August 7, 1994.

47. *Ibid.*

48. "MGM Signs Girl," *Los Angeles Times*, undated.

49. "From Anne to Anita," *Variety*, March 28, 1928.

50. Anita Page to Allan Ellenberger, August 7, 1994.

51. *Ibid.*

52. Katherine Albert Eunson (1902–1970) was a magazine editor, novelist, and playwright. In later years, she collaborated with her husband, Dale Eunson, on television scripts. She had a daughter, Joan, named after her friend actress Joan Crawford.

53. "The Unknown Hollywood I Know," *Photoplay*, March 1932.

54. "Anita Rivers Becomes Anita Page," *Photoplay*, May 1928.

55. "Up from Smiling Ads," *Picture Play Magazine*," January 1934.

56. William J. Mann, *Wisecracker: The Life and Times of William Haines, Hollywood's First Openly Gay Star* (New York: Viking, 1998), 138.

57. Haines' partner and longtime companion, Jimmy Shields, sometimes visited the set. For whatever reasons, Anita did

not care for Shields and believed he was the cause of Haines' problems at MGM.
58. Anita Page to Allan Ellenberger, August 7, 1994.
59. Mann, *Wisecracker*, 202.
60. Anita Page to Allan Ellenberger, August 7, 1994.
61. *Ibid.*
62. Mann, *Wisecracker*, 138–139. Michael G. Ankerich, *The Sound of Silence: Conversations with 16 Film and Stage Personalities Who Bridged the Gap Between Silents and Talkies* (Jefferson, NC: McFarland, 2011), 186.
63. Ankerich, *The Sound of Silence*, 186. Randal Malone to Allan Ellenberger, October 4, 2019. Stories have circulated that what Mrs. Pomares saw in Crawford's bathroom were sex toys or aids, but nothing has ever been confirmed.
64. Ankerich. *The Sound of Silence*, p. 179.
65. Anita Page to Allan Ellenberger, August 14, 1994.
66. Anita Page to Allan Ellenberger, August 20, 1993.
67. Anita Page to Allan Ellenberger, August 20, 1993. "Anita Page: Star of the Silent Screen," *The Independent*, September 7, 2008.
68. Anita Page to Allan Ellenberger, August 20, 1993.
69. Anita Page to Allan Ellenberger, August 14, 1994.
70. "Dating Anita," *Photoplay*, February 1930.
71. Anita Page to Allan Ellenberger, August 14, 1994.
72. *Ibid.*
73. "Home Rules for Hollywood Flappers," *Photoplay*, June 1929.
74. "Anita Page Interviews Anita Page," *Talking Screen*, August 1930.
75. Anita Page to Allan Ellenberger, August 14, 1994.
76. *Ibid.*
77. Louella Parsons column, *Los Angeles Examiner*, May 7, 1929.
78. Unsourced and undated article.
79. "Oh Honey, His Letters were so Gooey, so Touching...," *The Guardian*, November 2, 2000.
80. "Society of Cinemaland," *Los Angeles Times*, August 9, 1931.
81. "The 'No-Date' Girl," *Screenland*, December 1931.

82. "Hollywood High Lights," *Picture Play Magazine*, February 1932.
83. Anita Page to Allan Ellenberger, August 21, 1994.
84. *Ibid.*
85. Anita Page to Allan Ellenberger, August 7, 1994.
86. Anita Page to Allan Ellenberger, August 14, 1994.
87. A fan letter from Cecil Jackson-Craig of Barkingside, England, June 4, 1932.
88. "Oh Honey, His Letters were so Gooey, so Touching...," *The Guardian*, November 2, 2000.
89. Anita Page to Allan Ellenberger, August 14, 1994.
90. *Ibid. Los Angeles Times*, November 28, 1932.
91. Anita Page to Allan Ellenberger, August 7, 1994.
92. Kylo-Patrick R. Hart, *Film and Television Stardom* (Newcastle upon Tyne: Cambridge Scholars, 2008), 16.
93. Anita Page Fan Club Newsletter, undated.
94. "Anita Page: Star of Silent Screen," *The Independent*, September 7, 2008.
95. "Baby Star's Job Clinched," *Los Angeles Times*, February 9, 1929.
96. Unfortunately, the home where Anita lived in Manhattan Beach with her parents is no longer standing. Anita Page to Allan Ellenberger, August 21, 1994.
97. Henry Joseph "Harry" Crocker (1893–1958) was a columnist for the *Los Angeles Examiner*, a Hearst paper. He joined that paper in 1928 at Heart's invitation serving as his assistant until the publisher's death in 1951. Ironically, Anita's 1996 comeback film, *Sunset After Dark*, was filmed in Crocker's old mansion on Sugar Hill.
98. Anita Page to Allan Ellenberger, August 7, 1994.
99. Many have insisted that Pickford won because she had invited five members of the Academy's Central Board of Judges to Pickfair for tea, launching the first campaign to receive an Academy Award.
100. Robert Ames (1889–1931) acted on the stage and in films including *The Trespasser*, *Holiday*, and *Rich People*. Ames, an alcoholic, died only one year after the release of *War Nurse* in his room at New York's Hotel Delmonico from delirium tremens, most likely brought on by a sudden abstinence from alcohol.

101. Anita's make-up box was a battered and worn leather kit that had so many mirrors broken and replaced that she stopped keeping count.
102. Anita Page to Allan Ellenberger, August 21, 1994.
103. The list of WAMPAS Baby Stars of 1929 included Mona Rico, Josephine Dunn, Caryl Lincoln, Helen Twelvetrees, Loretta Young, Betty Boyd, Jean Arthur, Doris Dawson, Anita Page, Doris Hill, Helen Foster, Ethlyne Clair and Sally Blane.
104. Anita Page to Allan Ellenberger, August 21, 1994.
105. Ibid.
106. Ankerich, *The Sound of Silence*, 190. Anita Page to Allan Ellenberger, August 21, 1994.
107. Anita Page to Allan Ellenberger, August 21, 1994. Marino Bello was married to Harlow's mother.
108. Anita Page to Allan Ellenberger, August 21, 1994.
109. Ibid.
110. Ibid.
111. Randal Malone to Allan Ellenberger, August 21, 1994.
112. Anita Page to Allan Ellenberger, August 21, 1994.
113. Ibid.
114. Anita Page to Allan Ellenberger, August 21, 1994.
115. Ibid.
116. Ibid.
117. Anita Page to Allan Ellenberger, September 11, 1994.
118. Marion Davies' white marble mausoleum at Hollywood Forever Cemetery is engraved with the family name Douras. It was built in 1928, after Davies' mother died, and those interred in it are her parents, her two sisters, her niece Pepi Lederer, her daughter Patricia and her husband Arthur Lake, and Davies' husband Horace Brown. Anita Page to Allan Ellenberger, September 11, 1994.
119. Unsourced and undated article.
120. Anita Page to Allan Ellenberger, September 11, 1994.
121. Mark A. Vieira, *George Hurrell's Hollywood: Glamour Portraits 1925–1922* (Philadelphia: Running Press, 2013), 55.
122. Golden, *Golden Images*, 131.
123. "What's the Matter with Anita Page," *Movie Mirror*, 1932. Photographer Elmer Fryer also took photos of Anita looking like Barbara La Marr while on loan out at Warner Bros. for *Under Eighteen* (1931).
124. Ibid.
125. "The Girl That Hollywood Can't Figure Out," *Movie Classic*, September 1932.
126. Anita Page to Allan Ellenberger, September 11, 1994.
127. Ibid.
128. Ibid.
129. Ibid.
130. Ibid.
131. Anita Page to Allan Ellenberger, August 14, 1994.
132. Ibid.
133. Anita Page to Allan Ellenberger, August 21, 1994.
134. Ibid.
135. "Anita Page Married to Composer," *Los Angeles Times*, July 28, 1934.
136. Anita Page to Allan Ellenberger, August 21, 1994.
137. Anita Page to Allan Ellenberger, September 11, 1994.
138. Anita Page to Allan Ellenberger, August 21, 1994.
139. "Wanted—Lillian Russell Portrayer," *Los Angeles Times*, April 1, 1935.
140. Produced as *We're in the Legion Now* (1936) with Esther Ralston in the female lead role.
141. Herschel Austin House was born on May 31, 1907, in Clay, Indiana. He had three sisters, Vera, Grace, and Ruth.
142. Anita Page to Allan Ellenberger, September 11, 1994.
143. "Anita Page's Love Story is Still Going On," *Abilene Reporter News*, May 5, 1973.
144. Anita Page to Allan Ellenberger, September 11, 1994.
145. "Secret Marriage of Anita Page and Naval Officer Told," *Los Angeles Times*, March 5, 1937. *Los Angeles Times*, March 18, 1937.
146. "Anita Page Weds at Beach," *Los Angeles Times*, March 22, 1937. Anita Page to Allan Ellenberger, September 11, 1994.
147. Owsley died one month after his father's sudden death. "Death Calls Actor Owsley," *Los Angeles Times*, June 9, 1937.
148. Anita Page to Allan Ellenberger, September 11, 1994.
149. Ibid.
150. "Rescue Ship Brings 1,342 From Orient," *New York Times*, December 9, 1940.

151. *Nevada State Journal*, May 25, 1943. Maude Evelyn Pomares died at 3120 Ocean Drive, Manhattan Beach, from breast cancer which spread to her liver. She was buried at Holy Cross Cemetery in Culver City, only three miles from the former MGM Studios.
152. Linda House was born on May 29, 1950.
153. Marino Pomares was living with his second wife Jewell at 2812 Strand Street, Manhattan Beach. Pomares died at Torrance Memorial Hospital from a heart attack on February 23, 1951. At the time of his death, Marino Jr. was married to Marjorie Vienna. He died on March 28, 1960.
154. "Anita Page's Love Story Is Still Going On," *Abilene Reporter News*, May 19, 1973.
155. "Anita Page: Star of the Silent Screen," *The Independent*, September 7, 2008.
156. *Vancouver Sun*, April 16, 1988.
157. Herschel A. House died in San Diego. He was buried at San Diego's Holy Cross Cemetery. Anita Page to Allan Ellenberger, September 11, 1994.
158. Anita Page to Allan Ellenberger, September 11, 1994.
159. Anita Page to Allan Ellenberger, August 20, 1995.
160. Randal Malone to Allan Ellenberger, October 4, 2019.
161. Ankerich, *The Sound of Silence*, 198.
162. Sandra House Young Bhardwaj was buried at Forest Lawn-Hollywood Hills (God's Acre, Lot 741, Space 1). Her daughter Elizabeth is buried next to her.
163. Randal Malone to Allan Ellenberger, October 4, 2019.
164. Holy Cross Cemetery, San Diego, CA. Plot: St. Jude, Lot 141, Grave 1.
165. "Clooney Pays Tribute to Page," contactmusic.net, September 10, 2008.
166. Anita Page to Allan Ellenberger, August 21, 1994.

# The Films

## A Kiss for Cinderella

1. The set for the royal ball scene was reportedly the largest erected under a studio roof at that time.
2. Anita Page to Allan Ellenberger, July 31, 1994.
3. Ibid.
4. Ibid.
5. *Exhibitor's Herald*, December 26, 1925. The film was first shown in Chicago at a private showing for 800 orphans on December 26, 1925 (*Chicago Tribune*, December 27, 1925).

## Love 'Em and Leave 'Em

6. Anita Page to Allan Ellenberger, July 31, 1994.

## Beach Nuts

7. Anita Page to Allan Ellenberger, July 31, 1994.
8. "World's Softest 'Angel' is Harry K. Thaw," *Variety*, July 18, 1928.
9. "Anita Rivers Becomes Anita Page," *Photoplay*, May 1928.

## Telling the World

10. "The Newest Picture Girl," *Screenland*, June 1928.
11. "Anita Goes to School," *Screenland*, April 1930.
12. "The Newest Picture Girl," *Screenland*, June 1928.
13. Anita Page to Allan Ellenberger, August 7, 1994.
14. Ibid.
15. "The Newest Picture Girl, Anita Page, Our Debutante," *Screenland*, June 1928.
16. Anita Page to Allan Ellenberger, August 7, 1994.
17. "Paramount Has Sound Picture," *Los Angeles Times*, July 22, 1928.
18. "Hers is Breathless Tale," *Los Angeles Times*, July 8, 1928. As a result of *Telling the World*, Anita's fan mail rose to 1,000 letters a week.

## While the City Sleeps

19. Anita's friend, Betty Bronson, replaced her in *The Bellamy Trial*.
20. Anita Page to Allan Ellenberger, August 14, 1994.
21. *Broadway and Hollywood Movies*, July 14, 1930.
22. Anita Page to Allan Ellenberger, August 14, 1994.
23. "Anita Page Goes to School," *Screenland*, April 1930.

24. Anita Page to Allan Ellenberger, August 14, 1994.
25. *Exhibitor's Daily Review*, October 27, 1928. To promote the film, MGM suggested to theater managers that they capitalize on Anita's charm and beauty by holding an "Anita Page Resemblance Contest" as was successfully done for *Telling the World*. Even though exhibitors had used it before, Anita's "captivating youthfulness and charm" would inject a fresh note of appeal to build up feminine interest in the film.

## Our Dancing Daughters

26. Anita Page to Allan Ellenberger, August 7, 1994.
27. MGM Files, USC.
28. Anita Page to Allan Ellenberger, August 7, 1994.
29. *Photoplay*, July 1928.
30. Anita Page to Allan Ellenberger, August 7, 1994.
31. "Anita Page Goes to School," *Screenland*, April 1930.
32. Anita Page to Allan Ellenberger, August 7, 1994.
33. *Ibid*.
34. "Hers is Breathless Tale, *Los Angeles Times*, July 8, 1928.
35. Ankerich, *The Sound of Silence*, p. 187.
36. Anita Page to Allan Ellenberger, August 7, 1994.
37. Kevin Brownlow, *The Parade's Gone By...* (New York: Dutton, 1981), 305.
38. *New York Times*, October 8, 1928.
39. Ankerich, *The Sound of Silence*, 179.
40. *Variety*, October 10, 1928.

## The Flying Fleet

41. Anita Page to Allan Ellenberger, August 7, 1994.
42. Anita Page to Allan Ellenberger, August 20, 1993.
43. *Ibid*.
44. *Ibid*.
45. "Anita Page Goes to School," *Screenland*, April 1930.
46. The San Diego Pantages Theatre was located at Fifth Avenue and B Street (demolished in 1964).
47. Anita Page to Allan Ellenberger, August 20, 1993.
48. "Anita Page Goes to School," *Screenland*, April 1930.

## The Broadway Melody

49. Unsourced and undated article.
50. Peter Hay, *Movie Anecdotes* (Oxford: Oxford University Press, 1991), 6.
51. *Ibid*.
52. "Anita Page Goes to School," *Screenland*, April 1930.
53. Hart, *Film and Television Stardom*, 14.
54. Anita Page to Allan Ellenberger, August 7, 1994.
55. *Ibid*.
56. *The Broadway Melody* was first in several categories. Besides being the first film musical in the sound era, it was also the first musical, and the first sound film to win the Academy Award, and the first MGM production to win Best Picture.
57. Anita Page to Allan Ellenberger, August 7, 1994.
58. Kobal, A History of Movie Musicals, p. 31.
59. Anita Page to Allan Ellenberger, August 7, 1994.
60. *Ibid*.
61. Unsourced and undated article.
62. Anita Page to Allan Ellenberger, August 7, 1994.
63. Letter from Milton Berle to Randal Malone, Los Angeles, undated.
64. "M-G-M Film Smashing Hit," *Los Angele Times*, February 17, 1929.

## Speedway

65. Anita Page to Allan Ellenberger, August 14, 1994.
66. *Ibid*.
67. *Exhibitor's Herald-World*, February 1, 1930.

## Our Modern Maidens

68. Anita Page to Allan Ellenberger, August 14, 1994. Filming continued without incident except for an automobile accident that Fairbanks had one morning on the way to the studio. Fortunately, he was unhurt, and filming continued.
69. Mark A. Vieira, *Irving Thalberg: Boy Wonder to Producer Prince* (Berkeley: University of California Press, 2009), 97.
70. >"Fate Kind to Anita Page, *Los Angeles Times*, October 6, 1929.
71. *Ibid*.

## The Hollywood Revue of 1929

72. Affidavits were obtained as a response to public complaints that the performers' voices were often dubbed.
73. *New York Daily News*, August 9, 1929.

## Navy Blues

74. *Motion Picture News*, March 30, 1929.
75. *Hollywood Filmograph*, July 6, 1929.
76. Anita Page to Allan Ellenberger, August 14, 1994.
77. *Variety*, January 15, 1930; *Film Daily*, January 12, 1930.

## Free and Easy

78. Anita Page to Allan Ellenberger, August 14, 1994.
79. *The Educational Screen*, June 1930; *New York American*, March 18, 1930.
80. Beth Day Romulo, *This Was Hollywood: An Affectionate History of Filmland's Golden Years* (New York: Doubleday, 1960), 44.
81. *Ibid*. Matthew Kennedy, *Marie Dressler: A Biography, with a Listing of Major Stage Performances, a Filmography, and a Discography* (Jefferson, NC: McFarland, 2006), 160. *Detroit Times*, May 31, 1930.
82. "Dressler at Home in Rags of 'Shadow Women,'" *Los Angeles Times*, September 14, 1930.

## Our Blushing Brides

83. "Anita Page: Star of the Silent Screen," *The Independent*, September 7, 2008.
84. *Film Daily*, Our Blushing Brides, August 3, 1930.

## The Little Accident

85. Anita Page to Allan Ellenberger, August 14, 1994.
86. *Ibid*.
87. *Ibid*.
88. *Film Weekly*, December 27, 1930. The film was remade by RKO in 1944 under the title *Casanova Brown*, directed by Sam Wood and starring Gary Cooper and Teresa Wright.

## War Nurse

89. Loretta Young's footage was discarded and re-shot with Anita. However, Young can be seen briefly in a long shot.
90. *Variety*, October 29, 1930.
91. *The Herald Tribune*, October 25, 1930.
92. "Versatility Anita's Lot," *Los Angeles Times*, December 7, 1930.

## Reducing

93. The easiest job offered extra players came to a group of 200 who were ordered to "come just as you are," without special make-up. *Sheboygan Press*, March 16, 1931.
94. Marie Dressler had to crawl on all fours one day from 9 a.m. to 5p.m., inclusive with time out for lunch and camera changes only.
95. Kennedy, *Marie Dressler*, 160.
96. "Actress Creates Illusion," *Los Angeles Times*, December 14, 1930.
97. *New York Times*, January 17, 1931. At the film's release, author and dramatist, Ivan Abramson, filed suit in federal court for $250,000 damages against MGM and *Reducing* screenwriter William Mack for alleged plagiarism. He charged that the defendants took the plot, main characters, episode, story and underlying idea of *Enlighten Thy Daughter*, a film plot written by him in 1917.

## The Easiest Way

98. MPAA/PCA Collection, AMPAS, Margaret Herrick Library, September 30, 1927.
99. MPAA/PCA Collection, AMPAS, Margaret Herrick Library, October 28, 1928.
100. MPAA/PCA Collection, AMPAS, Margaret Herrick Library, November 1930.
101. *Ibid*.
102. Anita Page to Allan Ellenberger, August 21, 1994.
103. *Ibid*.
104. Barbas, *Movie Crazy*, 152.
105. Anita Page to Allan Ellenberger, August 21, 1994.
106. Golden, *Golden Images*, 134.
107. Anita Page to Allan Ellenberger, August 21, 1994.
108. *Ibid*.

109. *Ibid.*
110. *Variety*, March 4, 1931.
111. MPAA/PCA Collection, AMPAS, Margaret Herrick Library, February 1931.
112. MPAA/PCA Collection, AMPAS, Margaret Herrick Library, undated.

### Gentleman's Fate

113. Anita Page to Allan Ellenberger, August 21, 1994. In author Eve Golden's biography of John Gilbert, she notes that "actually it was Page who cried in this scene, and very nicely, too." Eve Golden, *John Gilbert: The Last of the Silent Film Stars* (Lexington: University Press of Kentucky, 2013), 224.
114. *Variety*, June 30, 1931.
115. "Voice Lowering Modern Vogue," *Los Angeles Times*, March 8, 1931.
116. *Variety*, June 30, 1931.

### Sidewalks of New York

117. AFI Catalogue. The film grossed $885,000 with a net profit of $200,000.
118. MGM Pressbook.
119. Anita Page to Allan Ellenberger, August 14, 1994.
120. *Variety*, November 31, 1931.

### Under Eighteen

121. Anita Page to Allan Ellenberger, August 14, 1994.
122. *Variety*, December 29, 1931.

### Are You Listening?

123. By this time Jimmy Shields was no longer hanging around the set.
124. *Photoplay*, April 1932.
125. *Variety*, April 26, 1932.
126. Anita Page to Allan Ellenberger, August 14, 1994.

### Night Court

127. Anita Page to Allan Ellenberger, August 21, 1994.
128. *Ibid.*

### Skyscraper Souls

129. *Variety*, August 9, 1932.
130. *New York Telegraph*, August 5, 1932.

### Prosperity

131. Ankerich, *The Sound of Silence*, 192.
132. Anita Page to Allan Ellenberger, August 21, 1994.

### Jungle Bride

133. Anita Page to Allan Ellenberger, August 21, 1994. Ankerich, *The Sound of Silence*, 195.
134. Charles Starrett (1903–1986), an All-American football star, he graduated from college with honors and then went on the stage, joining Stuart Walker's stock company for three years. With the development of his training in acting, Starrett was placed under contract by Paramount as a feature player. Anita Page to Allan Ellenberger, August 21, 1994.
135. *Variety*, February 10, 1933.
136. *New York Times*, May 13, 1933.

### The Big Cage

137. More than 800 pounds of beef was the daily ration of the 43 lions and tigers during production. On one day of each week the animals went without meat and were fed great quantities of milk and eggs to keep their fur glossy.
138. "Hobnobbing in Hollywood with Grace Kingsley," *Los Angeles Times*, December 21, 1932.
139. MPAA/PCA Collection, AMPAS, Margaret Herrick Library, November 22, 1932.
140. Anita Page to Allan Ellenberger, August 21, 1994.
141. In 1944 Universal incorporated scenes from *The Big Cage* in *Jungle Woman* starring Evelyn Ankers. Film Weekly, April 28, 1933.

### Soldiers of the Storm

142. Anita Page to Allan Ellenberger, August 21, 1994.
I Have Lived
143. Additional filming was done at Universal Studios.
144. Mordaunt Hall, *New York Times*, September 6, 1933.

### Hitch Hike to Heaven

145. Ankerich, *The Sound of Silence*, 195.

146. Anita Page to Allan Ellenberger, August 21, 1994.

*The Runaway*

147. Anita Page to Allan Ellenberger, August 21, 1994.
148. Caesar Romero to Allan Ellenberger, August 4, 1993.
149. *Boxoffice*, August 27, 1962.
150. "Turner Classic Movies' Ongoing Lost & Found Series Presents World Television Premiere of *The Runaway*," *Turner Classic Movies*, October 7, 2008.

*Sunset After Dark*

151. Allan Ellenberger, *Margaret O'Brien: A Career Chronicle and Biography* (Jefferson, NC: McFarland, 2000), 183.
152. Ellenberger, *Margaret O'Brien*, 185.
153. *Ibid.*
154. Anita Page to Allan Ellenberger, July 20, 1999.
155. Anita Page to Allan Ellenberger, August 20, 1995.
156. Ellenberger, *Margaret O'Brien*, 186.

## Theater

*Crazy Quilt of 1933*

1. All quotes by Anita Page are from an interview with Allan Ellenberger on September 11, 1994.

## Foreign Language Films

1. Only Spanish cast and crew are listed. For plot and those that worked on both pictures, see credits for *Free and Easy*.
2. The Oberprüfstelle Berlin, Germany's film censor, cut some scenes because during previews it was determined that certain scenes violated the religious beliefs of the audience.

## Video Films

1. Anita Page to Allan Ellenberger, July 20, 1999.

# Bibliography

Ankerich, Michael G. *Broken Silence: Conversations with 23 Silent Film Stars.* Jefferson, NC: McFarland, 1993.
Ankerich, Michael G. *The Sound of Silence: Conversations with 16 Film and Stage Personalities Who Bridged the Gap Between Silents and Talkies.* Jefferson, NC: McFarland, 2011.
Baker, Paul R. *Stanny: The Gilded Life of Stanford White.* New York: Free Press, 1989.
Barbas, Samantha. *Movie Crazy: Stars, Fans, and the Cult of Celebrity.* New York: St. Martin's Press, 2002.
Barris, Alex. *Hollywood According to Hollywood.* Cranbury, NJ: A.S. Barnes, 1978.
Baxter, John. *The Hollywood Exiles.* New York: Taplinger, 1976.
Blake, Michael F. *Lon Chaney: The Man Behind the Thousand Faces.* Vestal, NY: The Vestal Press, 1993.
Brownlow, Kevin. *The Parade's Gone By...* New York: Dutton, 1981.
Carey, Gary. *All the Stars in Heaven: Louis B. Mayer's MGM.* New York: Dutton, 1981.
Crowther, Bosley. *Hollywood Rajah: The Life and Times of Louis B. Mayer.* New York: Henry Holt, 1960.
Crowther, Bosley. *The Lion's Share: The Story of an Entertainment Empire.* New York: Dutton, 1957.
Eames, John Douglas. *The MGM Story: The Complete History of Fifty Roaring Years.* New York: Crown, 1975.
Edmonds, I. G. *Hollywood, R.I.P.* Evanston, IL: Regency Books, 1963.
Ellenberger, Allan R. *Margaret O'Brien: A Career Chronicle and Biography.* Jefferson, NC: McFarland, 2000.
Ellenberger, Allan R. *Ramón Novarro: A Biography of the Silent Film Idol, 1899–1968; With a Filmography.* Jefferson, NC. McFarland, 1999.
Fernett, Gene. *American Film Studios: An Historical Encyclopedia.* Jefferson, NC: McFarland, 1988.
Finch, Christopher, and Linda Rosenkrantz. *Gone Hollywood: The Movie Colony in the Golden Age.* Garden City, NY: Doubleday, 1979.
Franklin, Joe. *Classics of the Silent Screen.* Secaucus, NY: Citadel Press, 1959.
Golden, Eve. *Golden Images: 41 Essays on Silent Film Stars.* Jefferson, NC: McFarland, 2001.
Golden, Eve. *John Gilbert: The Last of the Silent Film Stars.* Lexington: University Press of Kentucky, 2013.
Goodman, Ezra. *The Fifty-Year Decline and Fall of Hollywood.* New York: McFadden Books, 1961.
Green, Stanley. *Hollywood Musicals Year by Year.* Milwaukee: Hal Leonard, 1990.
Guiles, Fred Lawrence. *Marion Davies.* New York: McGraw-Hill, 1972.
Hanna, David. *Ava: A Portrait of a Star.* New York: Putnam, 1960.

Hart, Kylo-Patrick R. *Film and Television Stardom*. Newcastle upon Tyne: Cambridge Scholars, 2008.
Hay, Peter. *Movie Anecdotes*. Oxford: Oxford University Press, 1991.
Heisner, Beverly. *Hollywood Art: Art Direction in the Days of the Great Studios*. Jefferson, NC: McFarland, 1990.
Katchmer, George A. *Eighty Silent Film Stars: Biographies and Filmographies of the Obscure to the Well Known*. Jefferson, NC: McFarland, 1991.
Kennedy, Matthew. *Marie Dressler: A Biography, with a Listing of Major Stage Performances, a Filmography, and a Discography*. Jefferson, NC: McFarland, 2006.
Kobal, John. *A History of Movie Musicals*. Blackpool: Outlet, 1990.
Kobal, John. *People Will Talk*. New York: Alfred A. Knopf, 1985.
Lamparski, Richard. *Whatever Became of...? The New Fifth Series*. New York: Bantam Books, 1974.
Mann, William J. *Wisecracker: The Life and Times of William Haines, Hollywood's First Openly Gay Star*. New York: Viking, 1998.
Marx, Samuel. *Mayer and Thalberg: The Make-Believe Saints*. New York: Random House, 1975.
Mordden, Ethan. *The Hollywood Musical*. New York: St. Martin's Press, 1981.
Parish, James Robert, and Gregory Mank. *The Best of M-G-M: The Golden Years: 1928–1959*. Westport, CT: Arlington House, 1981.
Romulo, Beth Day. *This Was Hollywood: An Affectionate History of Filmland's Golden Years*. New York: Doubleday, 1960.
Slide, Anthony. *Silent Portraits: Stars of the Silent Screen in Historic Photographs*. Vestal, NY: The Vestal Press, 1989.
Soares, André. *Beyond Paradise: The Life of Ramón Novarro*. New York: St. Martin's Press, 2002.
Thomas, Bob. *Thalberg: Life and Legend*. New York: Doubleday, 1969.
Vermilye, Jerry. *The Films of the Twenties*. Secaucus, NJ: Citadel Press, 1985.
Vieira, Mark A. *George Hurrell's Hollywood: Glamour Portraits 1925–1922*. Philadelphia: Running Press, 2013.
Vieira, Mark A. *Irving Thalberg: Boy Wonder to Producer Prince*. Berkeley: University of California Press, 2009.
Vogel, Frederick G. *Hollywood Musicals Nominated for Best Picture*. Jefferson, NC: McFarland, 2003.
Zierold, Norman. *The Moguls*. New York: Cowan McCann, 1969.

# Index

Numbers in **bold *italics*** indicate pages with illustrations

Academy of Motion Picture Arts and Sciences 21, 42–43, 65, 181
*Across to Singapore* (1928) 94
Adelman, Angela 67–68
Adorée, Renée 105
Adrian 105
Albert, Katherine 22
Alex Theater (Glendale) 143
*Alien Force* (1996) 65
Ambassador Hotel (Los Angeles) 15, 42, 55, 77
Ames, Robert 44, 135
Anderson, John Murray 10
Anita Page Fan Club 38
Ankerich, Michael 25
*Anna Christie* (1930) 127
*Are You Listening?* (1932) 24, 154–157
Arnold, Edward 58
Arnold, John 103
Arthur, Jean 45
Asher, E.M "Eph" 16
Asther, Nils 90
Astor Theater (New York) 105
Austin and Moore 8, 10

Bakewell, William 140
Baldwin, Faith 162
Banky, Vilma 113
Barnes, Binnie 58
Barnes, George 93
Barondess, Barbara 173
Barrie, Sir James 9
Barrymore, John 148
Barrymore, Lionel 123, 159
*Beach Nuts* (1927) 11, 12, 13, 76–77
Beahan, Charles 159
Beatty, Clyde 170–171
Beaumont, Harry 42, 43, 52, 88–90, 91, 103, 104, 106, 108, 155–156, 162
Beerbohm, Herbert, Sir 10
Beery, Wallace 126
*The Bellamy Trial* (1929) 85
Bello, Marino 46

Bennett, Constance 10, 109, 143, 144–145
Benny, Jack 117
Berkeley, Busby 35, 50, 51, 60
Berle, Milton 4, 105
Bern, Paul 19, 45, 159
*The Big Cage* (1933) 54, 169–172
*The Big Parade* (1925) 136
Biltmore Hotel (Los Angeles) 30
*The Birth of a Nation* (1915) 100
Blane, Sally 45
*Blondie* 50
*La Bohème* 112
Booth, Margaret 91
Bow, Clara 37, 76, 101
Brenon, Herbert 74
Brent, Evelyn 17, 38
Brice, Fanny 188
*Bringing Up Father* (1928) 126
*The Broadway Melody* (1929) 35, 36, 40, 41, 42, 43, 51, 52, 53, 54, 56, 64, 98–106, 113, 120, 187
Bronson, Arthur 9
Bronson, Betty 9, 17, 18, 74
Bronson, Eleanor 9
Bronson, Nellie Smith 9, 10, 17, 73–74
Brooks, Louise 76
Brown, Clarence 24, 120,
Brown, Johnny Mack 26, 88, 90
Brown, Nacio Herb (husband) 4, 35, 50, 54–56, 101, 116–117
Brown, Willie 11, 77
Brown Derby (Los Angeles) 31, 49
*Brown of Harvard* (1926) 19, 82
Bruce, Virginia 148
Bucquet, Harry 89
Burton, David 120
Busby, Marquis 29–30

California Aircraft Operators Association 112
*The Callahans and the Murphys* (1927) 126
"Can't Help Lovin' That Man of Man" 91
Cantor, Eddie 126
Capitol Theater (New York) 105, 148, 151

211

# Index

Carlisle, Mary 48
Carol, Sue 105
Carroll, Nancy 35
*Caught Short* (1930) 124–127, 138
Central Airport (Burbank) 108
Chaney, Lon 1, 65, 83–86
Chaplin, Charlie 47, 49, 123, 124, 131
*Chasing Rainbows* (1930) 126
Chesterfield Pictures 175–176
Chevalier, Maurice 35–36
Cinecon Film Festival 133
*City Lights* (1931) 47
Clooney, George 68
Close, Glenn 4, **5**
Coconut Grove (Los Angeles) 30, 37, 42
Cody, Lew 17, 20
*The Cohens and Kelleys* (1926) 16
Cohn, Harry 145, 173
Colbert, Claudette 48, 154
*College* (1927) 123
Collier, Buster 35, 140
Columbia Studios 37, 54, 143, 145, 173
Conroy, Peter, Father 60
Conway, Jack 112, 145
Coogan, Jackie 123
Coolidge, Calvin 117
Cooper, Edna May 41
*Coquette* (1929) 43
Coronado City Planning Commission 64
Coronado Community Theater 64
Coronet Arts Ball 64
Cosmopolitan Productions 126
Cosmopolitan Theater (New York) 12
Costello, Dolores 148
Crane, Ivy 53
Crawford, Christina 27
Crawford, Joan 4, 25–27, 36, 38, 54, 86–92, 94, 105, 112, 113, 117, 130, 133
*Crazy Quilt of 1933* 54, 58, 185–189
Crocker, Harry 43, 181
Cryer, George 37

Damita, Lili 32, 33
Dane, Karl 108
Daniels, William 81
Davies, Marion 28, 43, 47–50, 80, 101, 105, 117
Davis, Bette 39, 55
DeMille, Cecil B. 105, 123
de Mille, William 142
*Diamond Jim* (1935) 58
DiCicco, Pat 57
Dietrich, Marlene 48
Dinehart, Alan 176
*The Divine Lady* (1928) 43
Dove, Billie 105
Drake Hotel (Chicago) 12
Dressler, Marie 126–127, 138–140, 166
Dunn, Josephine 4, 45, 94, 105
Durante, Jimmy 37

*The Easiest Way* (1931) 140–145
Edwards, Cliff 151
Eilers, Sally 140
Ellenberger, Allan R. 3–4, 6
Embassy Club (Hollywood) 31
Evans, Madge 157, 162

Fairbanks, Douglas, Jr. 59, 112, 113, 132–133
Farnham, Joe 82
Farrell, Charles 35
Fetchit, Stepin 32
Fields, W.C. 37
Fink, David 142
First National 142
*The Flying Fleet* (1929) 3, 27, 59, 60, 93–97, 105
Flynn, Errol 60–61
Ford, Martha 56
Ford, Ron 197
Ford, Wallace 56, 166, 171, 172
Forshay, Harold 11, 12, 14, 77
Foster, Norman 154, 162, 166
Fox-Movietone Follies 116
Fox Studios 143
Fox-Wilshire Theater (Westwood) 91
Francis, Noel **160**
*Frankenstein* (1931) 162
*Free and Easy* (1930) 121–124
Freed, Arthur 55, 101, 116

Gable, Clark 1, 3, 28, 33, 143–144, 145, 159
Garbo, Greta 36, 47, 51, 53, 68, 117, 148
Gardner, Ava 3,
Garrett, Betty 4, 5
Gaynor, Janet 58
*Gentleman's Fate* (1931) 146–149
*Gentlemen Prefer Blondes* (Broadway) 136
Gibbons, Cedric 117
Gibson, Charles Dana 13
Gilbert, John 47, 105, 117, 148–149
Gish, Lillian 112
Gleason, James 101
*The Gob* 119, 120
*Gone with the Wind* (1939) 157
Good Samaritan Hospital (Los Angeles) 49, 65
Gordon, Mark 65, 181–182
"Gotta Feelin' for You" 117
Gould Memorial Library 13
Goulding, Edmund 101
Graham, Martha 10
Grant, Ulysses S. 8
Grauman's Chinese Theater (Hollywood) 105
Grauman's Metropolitan Theater (Los Angeles) 82
Graves, Ralph 27, 97
*The Greenwich Village Follies* 10
Griffith, Corinne 105
Griffith, D.W. 100

# Index

Haines, Ann 33
Haines, William 19, 20, 21, 23–25, 33, 78–82, 108–109, 119–120, 155–156
Hall, Mordaunt 82, 92, 106, 114, 127, 137, 166, 174, 176
Harlow, Jean 5, 33, 44–47, 60
Hays Office 133, 142–143, 145, 148, 170–171
Hearst, William Randolph 43, 49–50, 126
Hearst Castle 43, 45–50, 58
Hefner, Hugh 4
Hellinger, Mark 117, 159
*Hell's Angels* (1930) 45
Hersholt, Jean **160**, 163
Hesser, Edwin Bower 16, **17**
Hill, George 27
Hilton, Daisy **160**
Hilton, Violet **160**
*Hit the Deck* 100
*Hitch Hike to Heaven* (1936) 58–59, 176–178
Hitler, Adolf 36
Hollywood Forever Cemetery 50
*Hollywood Mortuary* (1998) 1, 197
*The Hollywood Revue of 1929* (1929) 43, 114–117, 126
Holmes, Phillips 158, 159
Holy Cross Cemetery (Culver City) 64
Holy Cross Cemetery (San Diego) 68
Hopper, Hedda 136
Hotel del Coronado (San Diego) 59, 60, 95–96
House, Herschel (husband) 1, 3, 36, 47, 59–60, 62, 64, 65, **66**
House, James 59
House, Linda (daughter) 1, 63, 65, **66**
House, Rebecca 59
House, Sandra (daughter) 1, 5–6, 63, 65, **66**–67
Houston, Norman 101
Hughes, Howard 45, 47
Hughes, Susan 11, 12, 14–**15**, 16, 77
Hurrell, George 51–52
Huston, Walter 158–**159**
Hyams, Leila 148
Hyman, Bernard 21, 80, 94

*I Have Lived* (1933) 174–176
Ince, John 162
Indianapolis Speedway 108
Invincible Pictures 176

*The Jazz Singer* (1927) 101
Jones, Lorenz 34
Jordan, Dorothy 54
Joy, Jason S. 142
Joy, Leatrice 85
*Jungle Bride* (1933) 166–169

Karloff, Boris 35, 162, 197
Käsebier, Gertrude 13
Keaton, Buster 1, 123–124, 149–151

Keetch, Arthur 39–**40**
Kelly, Grace 3, 144
Kenilworth Productions 11–12, 16, 22, 77
Kennedy, Matthew 139
King, Charles 100, 101, 105, 117, 187–188
Kirkland, David 21
*A Kiss for Cinderella* (1925) 1, 10, 73–75

Laemmle, Carl 35
Laemmle, Carl, Jr. 33, 35, 132
Lake, Arthur 50
La Marr, Barbara 52
Lancaster, John 19–20
La Rocque, Rod 112, 113
Lasky, Jesse 19
Lathan, Maude 33
Lederer, Pepi 49
Lederman, D. Ross 173
LeRoy, Mervyn 148
Levee, Michael 53
*Limelight* (1952) 124
*The Little Accident* (1930) 42, 130–133
Lloyd, Frank 43
Loew's Metropolitan Theater (New York) 188
Loew's 175th Street Theater (Washington Heights) 151
Loew's State Theatre (Los Angeles) 126
Lombard, Carole 49
Love, Bessie 42, 43, 100, 103, 105, 106
*Love 'Em and Leave 'Em* (1926) 1, 10, 75–76
Lovett, Josephine 93
Lowe, Edmund 35
Lugosi, Bela 35, 197
Lusk, Norman 82, 92, 97, 105, 166
Lux Soap 37–38
Lytell, Bert 11, 77
Lytell, Wilfred 11, 77

Mack Sennett Studios 176
Maddox, Ben 34
Madison Square Garden 13
Maggio, Tony 182
Malone, Randal 1, 3, 6, 50, 65, 67–68, 181–183, 197
*Mamzelle Champagne* 13
March, Fredric 60
March of Dimes 188
Marsh, Joan 157
Marsh, Marian 153–154
Marx, Groucho 37
Marx, Harpo 37
Marx Brothers 116
Mason, Sarah 101
*Mata Hari* (1931) 156
Mayer, Jerry 33
Mayer, Louis B. 21–22, 24, 27, 32, 38–39, **41**, 44, 53–54, 58, 80, 88, 90, 100, 131–132, 147, 156, 158, 166, 167
Mayfair Theatre (New York) 176

# 214  Index

McCarey, Leo 166
McDaniel, Hattie 156–157, 182
Menjou, Adolphe 105
Merkel, Una 162
Metro-Goldwyn-Mayer (MGM) 1, 3, 18–20, 36, 39, 49, 51, 58, 64, 123, 126, 138, 143, 145, 148, 151, 155, 156, 165, 167, 170, 173, 175, 182, 186
Miljan, John 108
Milton, Robert 10
*Min and Bill* (1930) 126
*Mr. Cinderella* (1936) 59
Mocambo (Hollywood) 50, 54
*Mommie Dearest* (1981) 27
Monogram Pictures 167
Monroe, Marilyn 5
Montgomery, Robert 130, 135, 156, 186
Montmartre 31
Moran, Polly 120, 126–127, 138–140, 166
Morley, Karen 156, 157
Moulin Rouge (Paris) 36
Muñoz, Enrique M. (great uncle) 8
Muñoz y Castro, Manuel (paternal grandmother's father) 7
Mussolini, Benito 3, 36–37, 51, 105, 173
*My Sister Eileen* (1955) 5

Nagel, Conrad 117
*Navy Blues* (1929) 24, 118–120
Negri, Pola 54–55
Nesbit, Evelyn 12, 16
*New Moon* (1930) 136
Newcom, Vivian 101
*Night Court* (1932) 157–161
*A Noisy Noise* (1927) 11, 77
Novarro, Ramón 1, 3, 24, 27–28, 59, 80, 93–97, 105, 117, 197

O'Brien, George 36
O'Brien, Margaret 4, 6, 181–183
*On the Town* (1949) 5
O'Sullivan, Maureen 163
*Our Blushing Brides* (1930) 127–130
*Our Dancing Daughters* (1928) 4, 25, 26, 31, 43, 51, 52, 65, 85, 86–93, 112
*Our Dizzy Divorcees* 130
*Our Galloping Grandmothers* 130
*Our Modern Maidens* (1929) 38, 39, 109–114, 119
Owsley, Monroe 59, 60

"Pagan Love Song" 54
Page, Anita: ancestry 7–8; arrival in Hollywood 14–15; artistic talents 8; beauty contest 9; birth 7; burial 68; childhood and youth 8–9; contract negotiations 20, 39–40, 54, 132, 173, 175; dating 34–36; death 67–69; divorce 56; fame and popularity 36–38; feud with Joan Crawford 25–27; friendship with Marion Davies 47–50; Harry K. Thaw and 12–16, 21–23; marriage proposals 24, 28, 59; marriages 55–56, 60; name change 21; residences 16, 42; salary 39; sexual assault 43–44; wanting a family 32
Page, Ann 21
Page, Anne 21
*Paging Anita Page* 38
Palos Verde Country Club (San Diego) 59
Pantages Theatre (San Diego) 97
"Paradise" 54
*Paramount on Parade* (1930) 116
Paramount Studios 17–18, 19, 20, 45, 101
Paramount's Famous Players (Astoria) 10–11, 74,
Parr, Jack 3
Parrott, Ursala 148
Parsons, Harriet 52
Parsons, Louella 32,
Pathé Studios 11, 13,
Paton, Robert Murdoch 6
Pennington, Ann 187
*Peter Pan* (1924) 9, 75
*Phantom of the Opera* (1925) 170
Pickford, Mary 8, 11, 18, 35, 43
Pitts, ZaSu 135, 137
Plaza Hotel (New York) 74
Pomares, Ana Muñoz (grandmother) 8, 12
Pomares, Anita (aunt and godmother) 12
Pomares, Marino (father) 8, 10, 12, 22, 28–30, **29**, 32, 34–35, 38–39, 52, 55, 58, 63–64, 95–96, 117
Pomares, Marino (paternal grandfather) 7
Pomares, Marino, Jr. (brother) 9, 18, **29**, 31, 64
Pomares, Maude (mother) 7, 8, 12–13, 14, 16, 17, 18, 22, 26, **29**, 30, 32, 36, 44, 49, 52, 53, 62, 63, 73–74, 77, 95–96, 109, 143–144
Powell, Eleanor 187, 188
Powell, William 33, 45–48
Powers, John Robert 1, 10–11, 23, 77
Praiswater Mortuary (Van Nuys) 68
Press Club Ruckus 40
Prevost, Marie 148
Prince Louis Ferdinand 3, 31–32
*Prosperity* (1932) 164–166, 167
Prouty, Jed 105
Pugh, Harvey 17–18, 20, 38–40, 53

Ralston, Esther 18
USS *Ranger* 59
Rapf, Harry 88, 116
Rasch, Albertina 130
*Red-Headed Woman* (1932) 45
*Reducing* (1931) 35, 137–140
Reisner, Charles 138
*The Rest Cure* (1936) 59
Rico, Mona 36
Risso, John 37
Rivers, Anita (stage name) 18, 77
Robinson, Edward G. 61–62

# Index

Rogers, Charles "Buddy" 35
Rolph, James, Jr. (California governor) 37, 40–42, *41*, 105
*Romeo and Juliet* 117
Romero, Cesar 4, 179
Rooney, Mickey 171
Roosevelt, Franklin D. 188
Roosevelt Hotel (Hollywood) 31, 32–33, 34, 42, 133
Rose, Billy 54, 101, 188
Rosson, Harold 45
*The Runaway* (1961) 178–180
Rupe, Arthur 179
Russell, Lillian 58

*Sadie Thompson* (1928) 142
St. Clair, Malcom 17–18, 19
St. Francis Hotel (San Francisco) 55
St. James Hotel (Sunset Strip) 4
St. Paul the Apostle Church (New York) 13
Samaniego, Carmen 34
Santa Fe Chief 12
Sarecky, Louis 173
*The Saturday Night Kid* (1929) 45
*Scarface* (1932) 156
Schallert, Edwin 106, 130
Schenck, Joseph 142
Scheuer, Philip K. 114
Schwibs, Michael 4, 50, 67
Screen Actors Guild 66
Sebastian, Dorothy 59, 90, 130
Sedgwick, Edward 24, 119, 120
Selwyn, Edgar 136
Selznick, David O. 142
Seventh Street Roxy (New York) 169
Shearer, Douglas 104–105
Shearer, Norma 80, 102, 117, 148
Shields, Jimmy 156
Shilling, Marion 32–33, 36
*Show Boat* (1929) 32
Shubert Theatre (Century City) 4
*The Sidewalks of New York* (1931) 123, 149–151
"Singin' in the Rain" 54
*Singled Out* 65, 197
*Skyscraper Souls* (1932) 161–163
Sleeper, Martha 37
Smith & Dale 187
*Soldiers of the Storm* (1933) 54, 172–174
*Speedway* (1929) 106–109
*The Spirit World* (1927) 11–12, 77
Spotnitz, Frank 181, 182
Stanwyck, Barbara 10
Starrett, Charles 168–169
*Steamboat Bill, Jr.* (1928) 123
Strickling, Howard 28
Stromberg, Hunt 88, 143
Summit Releasing Organization 179
*Sunset After Dark* (1996) 1, 65, 180–183, 197
*Sunset Boulevard* (musical) 4

Sunset Tower Hotel 4
Swanson, Gloria 18, 48, 105

Tabesh, Charles 179
Talmadge, Natalie 123
Talmadge, Norma 8
*Telling the World* (1928) 21, 23, 25, 28, 78–82, 88, 94, 119, 166
Thalberg, Irving 21–22, 45, 101, 104, 112, 116, 126, 143, 166
Thau, Benny 100
Thaw, Harry K. 12–16, 18, 21–23, 77, 88
Thorpe, Richard 176
Tibbett, Lawrence 136
Todd, Thelma 56–58
Toomey, Regis 154, 173, 174
Tormé, Mel 4
Torrence, Ernest 108, 109
Torres, Raquel 105
*The Trial of Mary Dugan* (1929) 102
Trout, Bobbie 41
Truman, Harry S. 60
Turner Classic Movies 179
Twentieth Century-Fox 58

*Unashamed* (1932) 59
*Under Eighteen* (1932) 152–154
United Artists 77
Universal Studios 35, 42, 54, 58, 132, 170–171
University of San Diego 64
University of Southern California 101–102

Valentino, Rudolph 68
Van Cleve, Patricia 50
Van Dyke, W.S. 158
Vignola, Robert 33
Vincent, Allen 176
Voight, Hubert 101

Walker, Helen 22
Walker, June 136
Walt Disney Studios 66
Walter, Eugene 142
WAMPAS Baby Stars 38, 44–45
*War Nurse* (1930) 44, 52, 134–137
Warner Bros. 39, 148, 153, 154
Warner's Strand Theater (New York) 148
Washington Irving High School 8, 9, 74
Washington Square (New York) 13
Webber, Andrew Lloyd 4
"The Wedding of the Painted Doll" 104
Weintgarten, Lawrence 101
Wexler, Haskell 179
*While the City Sleeps* (1928) 65, 83–86
Whitbeck, Fred 126
White, Stanford 13, 16
William, Warren 154
Wilson, Lois 105
Wolheim, Louis 148

*A Woman Commands* (1932) 54
Wood, Sam  19, 21, 25, 52, 80–81, 94, 120, 166
Wright, Cyril  34
Wyntoon  48

*The X-Files*  181

Yankawer, Alfred  34
"You Were Meant for Me"  54, 56, 105, 117
Young, Elizabeth (granddaughter)  67
Young, Loretta  45, 135
Young, Robert  32–33, 162

Zanuck, Daryl F.  58

www.ingramcontent.com/pod-product-compliance
Lightning Source LLC
Chambersburg PA
CBHW032041300426
44117CB00009B/1147